OF Whom THE WORLD WAS NOT WORTHY

Marie Chapian

marshalls

Guide to Pronunciation

At the northeast corner of Jugoslavia is the small republic of Slovenia where this story takes place. To be true to the language and people, the spellings of the Slovene words in this book are Slovene.

There is no "y" in the Jugoslav languages (there are three). "J" is always pronounced as the English "Y." Therefore, the name of the country is spelled Jugoslavija (although for our purposes we spell it Jugoslavia).

As example of the "J" being the "Y" sound, Jozeca is pronounced Yo-sheetsa, Jakob is Yah-kob; Josip is Yo-sip; Julijanne is Yuli-yanna, and Janez is pronounced Yah-nez.

Marshalls Paperbacks
Marshall Morgan & Scott
3 Beggarwood Lane, Basingstoke, Hants, RG23 7LP, UK

Copyright © 1978 Marie Chapian

First published by Bethany Fellowship, Inc. Minneapolis, U.S.A.
First published in the UK by Marshall Morgan & Scott 1984

ISBN 0 551 01099 1

Printed and bound in Great Britain by
Richard Clay (The Chaucer Press) Ltd, Bungay, Suffolk.

Acknowledgements

I dedicate this book to *moja ljubim*, my beloved ones in Jugoslavia, who loved me as one of their own, sharing their homes, tears, joys and lives with me and who will always remain a part of me. I thank also the many friends in Europe who gave unselfishly of themselves as I travelled, interviewed and gathered material for this book. The prayers and love of friends and family all over the world sustained and held me up. And I must thank my dear spiritual mother, Myra Gebhard, as well as prayer partners Gladys Dunbar, Jim and Lorraine Lamonaco, Doris Whitesell, Judy Bozman, Jan Persons; my own beautiful mother, Dorothy Svenvold; and lastly, my two most faithful cohorts, my daughters, Christa and Liza.

I give deepest thanks to my typists, secretaries and proofreaders who worked far into the wee hours many nights alongside me as we readied this manuscript for publication; namely, Dorothy Svenvold, Bette Carlson, Corrine Jordan, Penny Pelletter, Eleanore Spraungel, Barbara Maxwell and Sue Slee.

Thanks also to my friends and editors, Carol and Gary Johnson, and to Lee and Anne Salisbury whose vision it first was that I write this book.

I also thank the University of Minnesota Immigrant Archives Curator, Mr. Joseph D. Dwyer; the librarians of the University of Minnesota Libraries, the St. Paul and Minneapolis Public Library Systems; Ms. Betty Burch who gave the valuable research advice; and to Dr. William Backus for assistance and information on cerebral seizures, Lupus and nervous disorders.

Preface

Heroes of the past as well as now are people like you and me—not extraordinary supermen and superwomen, but people, as the Bible puts it, who "are made strong in weakness." This strength has given the power to fight so valiantly that enemies have fled in terror.

The heroes of the faith throughout the ages have been men and women who, because of their faith in God, subdued kingdoms, brought about righteousness, received promises, and even stopped mouths of lions. They quenched the violence of fire, escaped the edge of the sword, but they also suffered.

Thousands of men and women have suffered. They have suffered in the past; many are suffering today, and many will suffer in the future.

The Bible talks about such people in the book of Hebrews in the New Testament. It says that they are people "of whom the world was not worthy."

This book is about such people.

Introduction

This is a true story. The Jakob Kovac family is real, although their names have been changed in order to protect their safety. The places and events in this book are all true. Exact names and dates have, in some cases, been altered for the protection of those involved.

It is a book about faith and love. The little-known nation of Jugoslavia, no bigger than the state of Pennsylvania, is one of the most complex countries in Europe. In order to research this country one is faced with a country with two alphabets (Cyrillic and Latin), three languages (Slovenian, Serbo-Croatian, and Macedonian), three religions (Orthodox, Catholic and Moslem), five nationalities (Serbian, Croatian, Slovenian, Macedonian and Montenegrin) and six republics. It also possesses one of the bloodiest histories of Europe.

The story developed out of the heartbeat and cries of the Balkan people and their insistent belief that God is a good God who answers prayers. I interviewed workers and peasants in Slovenia, Croatia, Bosnia, Serbia, Macedonia and Montenegro. After living with the Kovac family, travelling the land where the story takes place and careful research, this book took shape.

And out of the struggles, wars, invasions, poverty and destitution there came a family who chose to pray and cling to God. Believing and trusting in Him, they have changed the destiny of thousands of lives. Perhaps they can even touch our lives.

This is my prayer and theirs.

Marie Chapian

Chapter One

All around, silent linden trees were buried in snow. Jakob stood in the snow and saw a small stone farmhouse snuggled in the corner of the hills, shaded by the surrounding mountains. Smoke belched from the stone chimney and he heard the clucking of chickens and geese in the yard. A dog barked.

Slowly he descended the hill toward the house, making deep furrows with each step in the snow. His clothing was wet and he was tired. He had been walking since daybreak.

Smells of wet hay, manure and wood smoke bit his nostrils as he walked across the yard. The dog yapped at his feet and chickens scattered. He rapped on the wooden door and a tiny woman with a black kerchief knotted beneath her chin opened the door. Her eyes widened at the sight of him.

"*Zdravo!* Hello! I am Jakob, the evangelist," he announced. "I have come from Lasko this day."

"*Zdravo.* Come, enter," said the woman.

Jakob stepped through the door and entered the big room. Sitting on the large ceramic stove inside was a pretty round-faced daughter and in the corner by the window sat the father on a wooden bench. He was carving a piece of wood. Jakob took a deep breath and announced in a clear, clarion voice, "Today Jesus Christ has entered this house!"

The family seemed startled, as did Jakob. The sound of his own voice surprised him, yet he was confident in his message. He pushed his hand out to the wide-eyed father on the wooden bench. "*Dober dan!* Good day, I am Jakob Kovac, evangelist."

"*Dober dan.*" The head of the house nodded to the teenage daughter perched on the stove and she hurried to fetch Jakob a pair of slippers and help him off with his boots.

Staring incredulously, the mother had not moved from her position in the doorway. "Please, woman, something to eat for our guest!"

Still staring over her shoulder, she slipped into the kitchen at the other side of the small stone entryway. From the big room you could hear her moving about on the stone floor, opening and closing cupboards and dipping water from the wooden bucket by the door.

"You have come far?" asked the father, surveying Jakob's wet clothes.

"I have come from Lasko and before that, Trbovlje."

"Ah, Lasko . . . Trbovlje. Here, a glass of *slivovica*," and he pulled a bottle of plum brandy from behind the bench. Jakob began to protest, but at that moment the teenage daughter had yanked one of his boots off with a great heave and then, losing her balance, went sprawling to the floor.

"You are Slovene?" asked the father, ignoring his daughter's ill fortune.

"I am," answered the evangelist. He reached an arm out to help the girl.

"Ah, then vermouth it will be!"

"Thank you very much, but I do not drink liquor."

The young girl, an array of petticoats and displayed woolen knees, stared at the stranger with sudden interest. Her father narrowed his eyes, examining Jakob suspiciously. They had never had a guest who refused a glass of brandy.

"Ah, the devil," he said, shrugging his shoulders, "I will have to drink alone."

Jakob noticed by the unsteady hand with which he poured the wine that he had already consumed several glasses.

His wet coat and boots were placed by the stove to dry, and before the food was brought into the room, the old man invited Jakob to wash, if he cared to. He accepted gratefully.

Jakob prayed silently as he dried his hands on a damp piece of gray homespun which hung from a peg on the wall. He felt there was something special about this house.

"Podgornk is the name," the man said with a broad smile. "I am Lojze, my wife, Nezka, and this is my stepdaughter, Jozeca."

They all shook hands and the stepdaughter courtsied and also shook his hand.

The woman, Nezka, still wearing the kerchief on her head, served him a large plate of *polenta*[1] and chunks of hard, crusty bread which she had baked in the oven in the stone wall. There was steaming mulberry tea to wash it down with.

The sun shone through the small windows, brightening the room which was lined with high beds piled with pillows, quilts and carpets. There were large heavy cupboards along the walls, and lining the walls and floor were heavy tapestries and carpets to keep out the cold.

Jakob's face shone in the light of the sun as it streaked across the table. His eyes, though tired, were bright and clear. His long tanned face with its firm jaw, prominent nose and high broad cheek-

---

1. Hominy.

bones and high forehead had never been ordinary, but now it held a strength as never before—perhaps it was his eyes, shining, intense. He was fifty-one years old.

They talked until late in the afternoon. Lojze, who had been listening to Jakob with interest, said, "You are a strange man. We are Catholic in this house and we go to church like most Slovene people. Besides, I have many troubles which are too many to burden you with. I do not wish to burden God with them either." He was now quite drunk.

It was the young girl, Jozeca, who sat enraptured at the evangelist's message. Cheeks flushed, hands trembling, she listened to every word as though she were receiving a rare treasure.

She asked questions breathlessly and the evangelist answered her as best he could. He was, to her thinking, the kindest man she had ever seen and this message the finest she had ever heard.

"It is wonderful that God gave us His only Son," Jozeca murmured, " . . . Jesus Christ. . . . " She savoured the name, rolling it over her tongue and whispering it softly.

When his clothes were dry and his stomach full, Jakob prepared to continue his journey. But before leaving, he helped the woman and her daughter milk the cows and the goat. Lojze, drunk and snoring, was slumped against the wall by the stove.

"You have blessed our house this day," said Nezka, smoothing her apron tied around her heavy sweaters and woolen skirt. "My daughter and I would like to hear more about this new life in Christ you talk about."

"Oh, yes!" inserted the daughter. "We would like to hear more!"

"It would be an honor to visit you again," answered Jakob. He gave them a Bible from his rucksack.

They watched him leave, watched until his form disappeared into the horizon beyond the snow-covered slopes beneath the mountains.

"He was a good man," said the mother, "even though a Protestant."

Jozeca blushed, "Oh, *ja! ja!*"

The villagers and peasants called Jakob "the Bible Man." For twenty years he had been walking from village to village, farm house to farm house in the Slovenian mountains. Carrying his Bibles on his back, he preached the Gospel in every house he entered and collected a few dinars selling the Bibles. Although many thought that the Protestant doctrine which he had learned in Germany was a strange one, the peasants liked him enormously.

Jozeca Podgornik had just turned sixteen. She was born the same year as the fateful assassination of Archduke Franz Ferdinand at

Sarajevo which plunged Europe into World War I. She was born a year after the first and second Balkan wars when the Turks were finally expelled from Serbia after 500 years of invasion and dominion.

She was a Slovene, and although at the time of her birth her country was occupied by the Austrians and Italians, she would never learn either language. She was Slovene and the Slovenes had their own language, something no tyranny had been able to take from them.

She would come to know and understand the agonies of war, of futile toil, of destruction and terror, and also of prejudices. A slogan that year in a Berlin church said, "God save us from war, plague and the Jugoslavs." The rolling hills nestled between towering mountains in her tiny part of the world would see the assassinations of a king and a duke and duchess, the ravages of two world wars, the topple of a monarchy and its governing classes, and the takeover and rebuilding of a nation under Communism. Jozeca would never see the sun rise beyond her shores, yet she would deeply affect the lives of thousands of people in all parts of the world. She was a Slovene peasant and she was sixteen.

"What shall I do with you, my noisy one?"

"O Mama, it is wonderful! Wonderful!"

"It will not be wonderful when your father awakes and throws his plate at you for this disturbance."

"But, Mother, listen to me. Mama, I prayed. I prayed on my knees in the stinging nettles. I prayed for God to help us in our troubles. I prayed for Him to send us a sign that He heard my prayers. O *Mamica*, God has sent us a sign! He has heard my prayers and He will help us!"

The mother tossed a hand in the air. Her name was Nezka, meaning a thorny flower. She had the appearance of an old woman with her tanned, lined face, dark gaps where teeth once were, and stooped body, but she was still not yet forty.

"Do not be foolish, daughter. What can God do for us? Can He give us back our farm which my first husband, your father, willed to me? Can He stop your stepfather from drinking away all we have? We have lost everything, everything. If your father, God rest his soul, knew that the farm he worked so hard on was lost due to a man's drinking, he would turn over in his grave!"

"God will help us, Mama. He sent the evangelist. It is a good sign. I will pray some more!"

"Ah, Jozeca, pray for yourself. Pray that God will give you a man such as your real father, God rest his soul."

"I will be a nun, Mama."

"Ah!" Nezka whistled through her teeth. "And while you are becoming a nun, reading and writing in all those fine books, what is to become of your mother, I ask you? Without a penny to be added to the house and debts coming in all directions, how are we to eat, eh?"

"But, Mama! It is my deepest desire!"

The older woman pressed her eyes shut and slumped into a chair. She looked small and defenseless. It was true. If Jozeca went to the convent, her mother would be left alone and without hope. Lojze exhausted all she had.

Slowly she knelt by her mother's side. "If it is your wish, Mama, I will not go to the convent school."

"You will take the job in Zagreb?"

"I will, Mama."

"It is best. When Lojze has not money to drink, he is without senses. He sells anything he can. Go, Jozeca, earn money and send some to your mother."

Zagreb is the capital city of Croatia, one of the republics of Jugoslavia, and is built on two hills above the Pannanian Plain down through which flows the river Sava. A gray mist hung over the city that day. Jozeca held the small parcel containing her few belongings and stared around her at the crowd passing by in the large train depot, their faces grim, their steps firm and deliberate, their voices quiet.

The trip had been tense and eight hours seemed endlessly long. There had been talk on the train of Serbian trains being blown up by the Ustase.[2] Out in the country you didn't feel the political pressures as you did in the cities. Here in Zagreb, under King Alexander's military dictatorship, thousands of people were in prisons and the city swarmed with secret agents. Newspapers, books, and periodicals were strictly censored. All meetings except those organized by the dictatorial regime were forbidden.

She had been naïve about these things as she travelled on the train and had voiced openly the message she had heard by Jakob Kovac, the itinerant evangelist. She had stood on the platform at Zidani Most and repeated almost word for word what she had heard in the big room of her farmhouse that Sunday afternoon. She shouted and pointed her finger heavenward and insisted the people come

2. A resistance movement in Croatia led by Dr. Ante Pavelic who, during World War II, sided with the Nazis in the hopes of making Croatia an independent nation. Pavelic formed a dictatorship on Fascist, or Nazi, lines with himself as the Poglavnik or Führer, and the Ustase as his Praetorian guards. His accession to power was followed by a reign of terror unprecedented even in the Balkans, being responsible for widespread terrors and atrocities.—Maclean, Fitzroy: *Escape to Adventure*.

to Jesus before it was too late. It went unreported, perhaps because she was thought a little mad.

Her new employer was Samuel Marosavic, a Jewish school teacher. His wife was a tall, pale woman of intense literary energies who devoted days and nights to translating books and writing journals. The three daughters, still in elementary school, were like their father, sad-faced and shaped like egg cups.

They were a pleasant family and *Gospod* Marosavic was kind to his new Slovene servant. *Gospa* Marosavic taught her the Serbo-Croatian language as well as how to cook and clean in a city apartment. There was no hay on the floor in the Marosavic flat and no chickens in the kitchen like in the villages at home. There was running water and most exotic of all, down the hall and shared by four other families, a toilet.

Every day there were demonstrations in the city followed by arrests. Unemployment, slashed wages and rising prices were said to be the causes of strikes and civil riots. Nine out of ten industrial workers were reported unemployed. Jozeca found all this confusing and frightening and so she stayed indoors except when she went to the market for bread each morning and when she went to church on Sunday.

Only three years before, the Tsar had abdicated, forced out by a Menshevik revolution. And in Petrograd, Socialism had come to power for the first time on earth. But the Bolsheviks overthrew the regime and the Communist party took power. Now the Bolsheviks were firmly in control of most parts of Russia.

A few months before Jozeca arrived in Zagreb, the Police Minister, Milorad Draskovic, closed Communist party headquarters in Belgrade, seized the party newspaper and ordered an end to Red propaganda. The following year one of the first acts of Parliament was to outlaw the Communist party. But Draskovic was assassinated.

The illegal and now underground Communist party promised freedom and better wages for the workers. A promising leader named Josip Broz, later known as "Tito," denounced the Croat party leaders and forced election of a militant new Central Committee for the Zagreb area. He was made the new Secretary of the party.

In 1929 King Alexander, in his alarm at the growing demonstrations against him, suspended the Jugoslav Parliament and denied Croats any voice in government. Suspected Communists were shot down on the streets in cold blood.

Fiery protests and demonstrations continued, and on the streets of Zagreb bloody clashes with the police led to mass arrests. Jozeca, wearing her white fringed shawl over her head and clutching her prayer book, slipped down the streets on her way to church, hearing the angry shouts of protestors: "Long live the Communist party! Long live the world revolution!"

the angry shouts of protestors: "Long live the Communist party! Long live the world revolution!"

She turned her face in horror at the sound of the police approaching. The sentences for such demonstrations were death or long imprisonments.

One bright sunny morning when she went out to buy bread, Jozeca walked along the peaceful Jelacic Square among the city people, peasants and fluttering pigeons. Suddenly she heard the shouts of a crowd. She saw moving toward her a teeming mass of men, women and children demonstrating against unemployment and hunger. They were dressed in rags and their shouts rang across the square: "Work and bread! Work and bread!"

Windows opened along the thoroughfare of Ilica and the people on the sidewalks cheered the marchers, hundreds of them marching four abreast. Traffic was stopped and more joined the bulging barrage of bodies.

"Work and bread! Work and bread!"

Then without warning forty or fifty uniformed and helmeted men charged the marchers. Swinging their rifles by the barrels over the crowd, they pelted people on the shoulders, heads and necks. The mob scattered, screaming, into the doorways and side streets, leaving several lying across the tramway tracks. Jozeca huddled in a doorway watching police drag the bodies off like sacks of potatoes. Then in only a matter of minutes traffic was resumed and the street looked as though nothing unusual happened at all.

When Jozeca returned to the Marosavic home with the loaf of bread tucked under her arm, she was trembling and could barely speak. Struggling for words, she told *Gospa* Marosavic what she had witnessed on the street. The woman reacted with a pained flicker of her eye.

"Things will only get worse, my dear," she said solemnly. "A man named Adolph Hitler is forging into power in Germany. The terror there is a hundred times worse than what is going on in our Jugoslavia."

That evening Jozeca heard *Gospod* say, "Hitler puts the clock farther back for all of us. Nothing worse could have happened to the world than that man's rise to power."

In the spring of 1932 when women in the factories were earning twenty-two dinars a day (29¢) for working ten hours a day, Jozeca felt fortunate to receive board and room and forty-three dinars (about 52¢) a week. She knew that women who worked in the Croatian uplands textile mills earned no more than she for 164 hours of labor. But her work was not easy. Often her feet became numb from standing on them all day as she ironed clothes. Her hands were dried and cracked from washing the clothes by hand. She worked seven days a week. She did not mind the work but she missed her own republic and her own people.

In the early spring when the Slovenian mountainsides were ablaze with fresh, sweet smelling green and the fields purple with violets, she looked at the brown and gray city of Zagreb with increased anxiety. There was nothing warm and natural about a city, she thought. She longed for her forests and fields. Here the *neboticnik*, the tall buildings, crowded out the vast Jugoslavian sky and the smells of petrol burned the nose. Zagreb could have its coiffed and perfumed ladies and lawyers in their black suits and tight shoes. It was the country she longed for, the smell of fresh-mown hay and the sound of the grindstone crushing wheat into flour. And adding to her homesickness, her letters to her mother were seldom answered.

There were bright moments to break the bleak and dark days, however. One Sunday afternoon she was invited to attend a secret prayer meeting in one of the believer's apartments near the park. She entered the small room with the curtains drawn and the people crowded inside on chairs, against the walls and crouched on the floor, and she saw a face she recognized.

"*Gospod* Evangelist!"

The graying man with rough tanned skin turned quickly and recognized her.

"Ah *ja*," he said softly. "The young girl from Brice. *Zdravo!*"

The color rose in her cheeks and she felt her knees weaken. People were agitated by her outburst and motioned for her to be quiet. "*Gospod*, sir," she half whispered and half cried, forcing her voice to a quieter pitch, "you are in Zagreb! Can it be?"

He looked at the young girl beaming before him. Her round face was framed by thick brown braids which hung to her shoulders. Her bright eyes twinkled and her tiny heart-shaped mouth smiled, showing two even rows of small white teeth. She was overjoyed at seeing someone she knew from home even though he was practically a stranger since they had met just once and briefly.

The meeting began and it was Jakob Kovac, the evangelist, who brought the message. Jozeca was lifted to dizzying heights as she absorbed his words. Never had she heard such wonderful words. He spoke of the love of God for the people of the world and he told how God would give strength to endure for those who asked. He quoted scripture verses and Jozeca drank them in like sweet wine. When he finished speaking, she discovered she had been crouching forward on her knees, so eager to grasp every word, every syllable spoken in his Slovenian accent, that her legs and feet were numb.

They talked together later and Jozeca discovered that things were bad at home. Her mother had been forced to sell the farm to help pay her husband's debts. It was almost impossible to get sugar and salt. There was talk of revolution among the Slovene peasants, too.

Jozeca listened to his words with dismay. "What is to become of our Jugoslavia? I was four years old when Jugoslavia was born, when we were freed from Austro-Hungarian rule. In my life I have no recollection of a time without war and troubles."

"You are yet young, Jozeca."

"If there is another war, will you fight, *Gospod*?"

"I was an officer in the Austro-Hungarian army, but during World War I I preached the Gospel in the coal mines. I will not kill a man. The God I serve tells me to love my enemies."

Others joined to listen as they talked, following their natural inclination and love for conversation.

"I believe God tells us to love all men, no matter who they are," Jakob continued.

A broad-faced man said, "*Gospod* Evangelist, I remember many years ago, in 1910 before the wars against the Turks, the first time you came to our village and preached the Gospel in our house."

"Ah, *ja*, Jernej, was it so long ago?"

"And you preached the Gospel to everyone in the village. Then you went to Ljublijana, then to the next village, walking on foot. You had no horse, no mule. We called you the 'Man of God,' the 'Sent One.'"

Jakob lowered his eyes.

The man's wife, a buxom woman with two gold teeth gleaming at the fore of her smile, said, "Do you remember, *Gospod*, in those days, how you brought us this new message? Was it not in Germany where you first heard it? You told us we could belong to God and have confidence that we are His people. You told us about eternal life and you said God dearly loves all people."

An old woman dressed in black, wearing a babushka knotted at her chin, added, "We never had heard such words! I remember the first time you came to our village also. 'The just shall live by faith,' you said. You were the first to preach such a message in Slovenia, I believe."

Heads moved up and down in agreement.

Then an unfamiliar voice was heard from the back of the group. It was a soft, quiet voice with the lilt of an accent.

"There was a young Serb," the stranger began, "and he hated the Slovenes because they had fought against Serbia on the side of Austria in 1906. He had the misfortune to meet up with you, *Gospod* Evangelist, you being a Slovene."

The group made room for the speaker, a small man with sallow cheeks, a thick black mustache and wearing spectacles.

"This Serb wanted to kill our Brother Kovac. They met quite by accident—or destiny, I should say, at the *kavana* in Zagreb. The Serb was drinking *slivovica*, and sitting alone at the table. Kovac asked if he could join him. The Serb agreed. They began to exchange thoughts across the table, but when the Serb discovered Kovac was a Slovene, he went for his knife to slice his throat."

The group leaned forward, listening to the little man who spoke in a soft, barely audible voice.

"I tell you, this Serb was out of his senses. Then Kovac began to tell him about the love of Jesus Christ. Imagine! Telling a Moslem Serb who was ready to run him through with the blade of his knife that a Slovene God loves him!"

"Ahh, Oh!"

"But something kept the Serb's hand from coming down on his neck. Maybe it was the kindness in the evangelist's face, maybe the truth of the words which he spoke—only the heavens know. But the Serb sat down on his chair and listened to him speak. Many hours later when he left the *kavana*, he had his arm around his Slovene brother and he was a believer in Jesus Christ."

A tear glistened at the edge of his eye. "That was twenty years ago. The man went back to his Serbia and told all that had happened, and because of such a great change in him, many believed in Jesus Christ. Today there are many who love the Lord Jesus and who are free from all hatred toward any person!"

Jakob suddenly released a loud unrestrained sob. "Damjan! My brother!" The two men fell into each others' arms, embracing and kissing first one cheek, then the other.

The small man removed his spectacles and wiped his eyes with his large white handkerchief. "The Serb I have told you of in this story—I am that Serb."

The people took turns embracing and kissing Damjan's cheeks. In better times food would have been served and there would have been music. There was much reminiscing. Jozeca watched it all with her eyes sparkling and her heart beating rapidly. It was wonderful, too wonderful. And Jakob Kovac was truly God's Sent Man.

Jakob told the group how he had been working in the coal mines in Germany when an old man from Poland told him about the love of God through His Son, Jesus Christ. He had been so impressed that he decided to be a follower of Jesus and become a Christian. His life had been one of carousing and conniving but God changed his ways.

"It is men like Damjan and like me whom God touches to prove that nothing is impossible to Him!"

"And you have been walking the mountains and hills of Jugoslavia preaching the Gospel ever since!"

"This is true. I believe God wants to give people life, not take it away from them." Then turning to Jozeca he said, "You see, that is why I cannot fight in a war and kill any person."

"But *Gospod* Evangelist, supposing the enemy were to attack your home and threaten to butcher your wife and children, would you not fight?"

The evangelist sucked in a deep breath. "Your questions are from a heart which searches for truth. Jozeca, the enemy will not attack my family, for I am not married. And if I were married and such a thing were to happen, I would still not kill."

"Ah."

Later Jozeca asked him, "*Gospod* Kovac, if it is not too personal, I would like to present you with a question."

"Please?"

"Why are you not married? You are well past the marrying age."

Again the older man sucked in a deep breath. "It is true that I am past marrying age. I am fifty-two years old. God has not directed me to marry. I believe I am called to be alone."

"And I also."

"Ah!"

"I have seen the troubles my mother has suffered and I do not wish the same."

Then with a sudden flush of emotion, she said, "O *Gospod* Kovac, I desire to be as you! I want to help people in their troubles as you do. I want to be as you and tell many of the higher life with our God who loves all people."

He smiled at her, his tanned, handsome face hidden in the shadows of the darkening street. He reached a large rough hand to hers and shook it vigorously.

"*Na svidenje*, Good-bye," he said. "God be with you."

"*Na svidenje!*" she answered.

Chapter Two

The months passed and Jozeca dedicated her little free time to prayer and to study of the Scriptures. She had always been a good student. She remembered the nuns who told her mother she should be in the convent. It had been her dream to be a nun. But now all that had changed. Since she had met Jakob Kovac she saw in her dreams a life of spreading the Gospel to all people. She no longer wanted to be closed within the walls of a convent. She wanted to be out among the people telling them that there was a wonderful God who loved them and sent His son, Jesus Christ, to die for them.

She prayed as she worked in the Marosavic home, imagining the Lord in the room with her. She thought of the hands of the Lord in the soapy water as she scrubbed floors, she imagined His breath on her face as she polished silver, dusted, or carried coal for the stove. In the Bible she was told that every hair on her head was counted, so surely every action was important to the Lord, too, and He was there with her in everything she did.

On Sunday mornings, smitten with evangelistic fervor, she donned her long black woolen Sunday dress with the large white collar, her white shawl and her shiny black shoes laced up to her ankles. Holding her Bible in the air she marched back and forth in front of the church and called out to startled passers-by, "Come in! Come to church! Now is the time to come to church!"

When the priests discovered her out there waving her arms and calling to the people, they promptly bustled her inside the church with an admonition to devote herself to penance and prayer.

One day the job at the Marosavic home came to an end. She was told simply that another family would be moving in with them, a family from Germany, and she was no longer needed. Jozeca found herself alone in Zagreb without money or a place to go. Her mother wrote her that she would arrange for her to marry a factory worker in one of the villages near Brice. Jozeca wept in alarm.

"Dear God! Save me! I will never do it! I will die first! O Jesus! O God! Help me!"

Mr. Marosavic, whose home throbbed with nervous and fearful whisperings, and who was in constant danger of losing his job, helped Jozeca to get another job. She went to work in a ceramic factory and moved in with a Christian family named Skok.

It was in the Skok home that she again encountered the evangelist, Jakob Kovac. He was preaching in a Baptist church in Zagreb and he lodged with the Skoks. Jozeca was delighted.

Jakob preached and afterwards held a baptismal service in the river Sava. Jozeca was baptized that day; and looking up into Jakob's praying face as he lowered her into the baptismal waters, she thought for certain she was beholding the countenance of the Lord himself.

"Today all is different," she told him. "I am quite certain God will help me so I can be as you."

He looked at her clear blue eyes which shone like bright coins and smiled. "I do not understand, Jozeca."

"My mother has sent for me to marry a factory worker in one of our villages in Slovenia," she explained.

"Ah, *ja*. And you wish to remain unmarried."

"*Ja! Ja!* I wish to be as you!"

In Jugoslavia in 1934, dreariness, poverty, unrest and hostility filled the lives of most men and women. King Alexander's reign brought many hardships to the people. The members of the little Baptist church in Zagreb lived under the threat of being arrested. Their meetings were looked on with suspicion and they were accused of anti-government activity.

There was little money for food. Jozeca earned 12¢ a week working ten hours a day in the factory. She sent half of this home to her mother. Her dreams of going back to school had faded permanently. The only brightness in her life was playing the piano in the Skok parlor at night by the flickering light of a candle. As the shadows and dull glow of the candle darted across the pages of music, Jozeca soothed herself with the sweet strains of Mozart and Chopin. She taught herself hymns and sang and played until she was too tired to continue any longer and softly made her way to the room where she shared a bed with the three Skok children.

One day the women at the factory were told they would not need to return again because the factory was closing down. Many of the women supported families with children on their meager earnings and they were now left destitute. Jozeca longed for her mountains and forests of Slovenia and wrote to her mother asking to come home.

In two weeks she was on a train to Trbovlje.

"You were a foolish girl not to accept the marriage I had arranged for you, Jozeca. You would now have a roof over your head and an honest, hard-working man for your husband."

"Mama, you have too many worries. I am strong and I can work. I do not need a man."

"There is a farmer's son in Lasko who is not married. Perhaps I can arrange—"

"Mama! Kindly do not speak of it."

"Such a daughter I have. Twenty years old and still unmarried. Ah, Jozeca, you are almost a spinster!"

The town of Trbovlje hugged the side of a mountain and spread down into the valley between the wooded hills and surrounding mountains. The hills were white with snow and in the distance the mountains shredded the sky—blue, silver and white. Jozeca felt at peace climbing again the slopes she had loved and grown up with. Looking into the browned and deeply lined faces of the peasants, she was happy to be back among her people.

There were no fine pastries and no comfortable bookstores here; no grunt of trolleys, nor strands of telephone wires. Here there was the smell of woodsmoke, the honk of geese, the clop of horses and oxen pulling wagons up and down the narrow hilly roads, the sloshing of feet through the mud as the men made their way to and from the Trbovlje coal mine.

It was the sight of the men on their way to the coal mine that halted Jozeca in her path early one morning as she was gathering wood. She recognized the large loping figure of one of the men. His head was bent slightly upward, his hands swinging at his sides. There was no doubt who that man was—only one man in the world had such a presence, only one man in the world could stand out in a gray and black string of shadows as he did.

"*Gospod! Gospod* Kovac!"

She ran down the hill toward him. "*Zdravo!*"

"Ah, Jozeca," he smiled. "*Zdravo.*"

"You—you are here in Trbovlje!"

"*Ja.* And you—you are here also."

"*Ja. Ja.* I am living in the house of my mother and my stepfather."

"It is pleasing to see your face again."

Jozeca ran along beside him, taking three steps for each of his one. Her face was flushed. The basket bounced on her back, the wood clattering, with each step.

"You are welcome in our house, *Gospod.*"

"Thank you, Jozeca. Kindly greet your family."

"*Na svidenje.* Good-bye."

"*Na svidenje.*"

Jozeca sang all the way back to the tiny house. The basket of wood on her back was decidedly lighter. "Such good fortune," she mused. "God has smiled on me. I have once again met with the man of God. This is a good sign—I am sure of it."

Two days later the evangelist came to visit the Podgornik family. Jozeca dressed in a flower printed cotton dress with a full skirt and lace bodice. Over it she wore an embroidered white apron. Her thick brown hair was tightly braided around her head and on her feet were the same shoes she had been wearing and polishing since she was fourteen years old. She sat eagerly awaiting his arrival, holding her book of prayers in her lap.

There were apples in the bowl to eat and later her mother would prepare *turska kava*, Turkish coffee. Though the single room of the house was scrubbed and polished, drifting across the room, permeating the walls and the fabric of the quilts was the acrid smell of the animals. The little pig stall was directly under the window by the door and its inhabitant lived practically as one of the family. It freely wandered into the house and out to the road near the house. The hens also were part of the family and came inside the house to lay their eggs by the stove and at night sat upon them there.

The stove was in the corner of the room beside the wooden table, around which were three painted wooden chairs and a small wooden stool. Jozeca's father had painted the delicate designs on the furniture, and it was a happy reminder to her of her childhood when she lived on the big farm set in the hills beneath the mountains in Brice.

The plaster walls were covered with newspaper pictures, an old calendar, a photograph of King Alexander, a picture of the Blessed Virgin, a crucifix and several rugs placed to keep the cold from blowing through the cracks. The rest of the room was taken up with the small wooden beds piled high with mattresses and counterpanes.

Jozeca was usually tired at the end of the day, but today she was excited and anxious. She was aware of herself and surroundings and felt, in her anticipation, that all would be well with Trbovlje, her troubled family and herself because, after all, there were men such as the evangelist on the earth, a man who walked with God and whose heart was like rubbed gold.

He arrived. Jozeca's mother answered the door. "*Dober Vecer*, Good evening, *Gospa* Podgornik," he said in his fine clarion voice.

"Good evening, *Gospod* Kovac," answered Jozeca's mother. Jozeca sat clutching her little book of prayers, her knees pressed together tightly and her mouth dry. The sight of him in the doorway made her blush. He was dressed quite differently from the last time she had seen him. He was clean-shaven, wearing a crisply pressed white shirt, a woolen jacket which smelled of the forest and on his feet were high shiny boots. She quickly rose to remove his boots and fetch him a pair of slippers.

He smiled at her. In a brief glance Jozeca was lost in the muted greenness of his eyes and she felt his smile, like a warm coat covering her. He was taken unawares by her nearness, all fresh and sweet. Looking at her he was reminded of ripe red strawberries. Her hands were not yet rough and her fingernails were still pink because she had not been back in the country long. Soon they would be muscular and worn and the nails black with dirt, as the hands of all the country women were.

The evening passed quickly. Jozeca spoke little, sitting stiffly on the wooden bench by the window. Her mother and father and the evangelist spoke of the hard times in Slovenia and of rumors of a coming war.

"Ah, the devil," muttered Lojze, her stepfather. "Our earth is fertilized with the blood of our people. The Austro-Hungarian Empire walked on our backs and the Ottoman Turks on our bellies. Now we have a country of our own and we have a king. But we still have the same ways as when we were ruled by barbarians."

Gospa Podgornik sighed. "A thousand years of Germans dominating us as well as the Austro-Hungarian rule is bound to leave a deep scar on Slovenia, *ne*, no?"

"We have been known simply as 'the Balkan people,' " the evangelist said, his face bright in the yellow glow of the fire. "Our Jugoslavian men have fought on the battlefields of Europe under the Hapsburgs and under Napoleon. We fought at the battle of Nordlingen where seven regiments of Jugoslavian troops under Hapsburg flags defeated the Swedes; our men fought in the Seven Years War when Jugoslavian regiments occupied Berlin." His face was serious, the eyes somber.

"In the Napoleanic wars and before, even at the battle of Valmy, up to Leipzig, the regiments of Jugoslavian military frontier fought on the side of the Hapsburgs and later in Napoleon's Grand Armeé. The first two regiments under the French flag who entered Moscow in 1812 were composed of Jugoslav soldiers. In the battle of Leipzig, Jugoslavs fought on both sides against each other for the glory of European courts."

Lojze grunted. "Huh. And the reward, I ask you? We are cursed and resented by all of Europe."

"But now we are a nation," said Nezka, his wife, "and the world will know that we are a nation."

Her husband laughed and lifted his wine glass to his cracked lips. "What makes you think the world would care about us?"

The evangelist shifted his weight and a gray shadow slipped across his face. Now the glow from the fire struck his shoulders, chest and hands. "We must always remember, the strong are many. The weak are few. We Jugoslavs must be strong and many. God gives us strength, not the sword."

"Huh!"

"Will there be a war, *Gospod* Kovac?" Jozeca asked, finally stirred from her silence. "Fascism is on our doorstep, I hear. Even now the Italians are moving across our Slovenia."

The evangelist did not answer. He looked at Jozeca, his face losing its creases and crevices. The taut expression melted away and in spite of her question, he looked at her tenderly, silently. Her stepfather spoke.

"Ah, the devil," he growled. "The Italians will come, the Germans will come and the Russians will come. The earth will be stained red by our blood under all of their boots."

Nezka interrupted, "Please. You will have *kava*?"

"*Ja. Ja.* Thank you."

They drank turkish coffee and ate the brown and yellow apples, swollen and warm in the bowl. Jozeca watched the evangelist chewing the apple, his large strong jaw clamping down on each bite. Everything in his hands became important for the simple reason they were *his* hands. He teased her, tossing an apple toward her and catching it himself.

Her laughter was sweet, like clear water of the river Sava. He didn't want the sound to end. He threw another apple and this time she caught it and tossed it back at him. He whooped as it struck him on the chin, tossing it quickly back to her. The apple flew back and forth across the room until it landed on Lojze's sagging lap. He popped it into his mouth looking like a stuffed pig, then ate the squashed thing, nearly swallowing it whole.

When it was time for Jakob to leave, he gave a tiny pull of Jozeca's braid. "*Lahko noc.* Good night," he said.

Jozeca raised her eyebrows and pulled at his shirt-sleeve as gingerly as he had tugged on her braid. "*Lahko noc, Gospod* Kovac."

Chapter Three

It was becoming more and more difficult for the peasants to sell their products. A calf sold in Ljublijana for 3 dinars a kilo, 2¢ a pound. Chickens sold for 20¢. The people living in the city could not afford to buy things with their reduced wages and salaries. The people called the situation the *kriza*, crisis.

Nezka Podgornik wanted to hear how it was for the people in Zagreb. "Was it a fine house you lived in, Jozeca?"

"A fine house, Mama? It was a flat in a block[1] with many other flats."

"The sitting room, Jozeca. Tell me about the sitting room."

"Yes, Mama. In the sitting room was a plump old sofa which smelled like wet beech leaves and it was piled high with blue, red, pale yellow and gray cushions. There were vases painted with flowers on little tables and in the corner was a glass cabinet from Vienna with a silver tea set inside."

Nezka sighed with delight. "Imagine my daughter living in such a rich man's house."

"But Mama, they ate lentils and black bread like we do. There was very little money."

"Ah, the *kriza*. . . ."

"I heard many things in Zagreb which trouble me, Mama. On the streets I saw many young people rushing and screaming 'Long live liberty! Down with the dictatorship!' And they carried signs and placards. 'Down with the bloody dictatorship of King Alexander the Last!' "

"Hush, daughter. Not so loud. If anyone were to hear—"

"Mama, I heard it said that our king is the highest paid head of state in the world. Is this true? I heard he receives a million dollars a month, more than the president of the United States! Also, I heard that he has twelve brand-new Packard cars. O Mama, imagine! And our people are starving!"

"Jozeca, you could go to prison for the words which you have just spoken. Have you no respect for your mother? Be at peace with yourself now and put your worries aside."

---

1. A block is an apartment building.

"But Mama, is this how we solve our problems? Do we simply put them aside? *Ne*, Mama. This is not our way."

Nezka raised her eyebrows. Jozeca recognized that look. When she was younger it made her heart shrink in fear. Many were the days when that very expression on her mother's face would be followed by a fast yank of Jozeca's collar. With her feet scratching and scrambling behind her, she would be positioned in the corner of the room, forced to kneel on the floor spread with beans.

Every morning Jozeca hurried with her large straw basket on her back to a small hill behind the winding muddy road. Here she had a perfect view of the men on their way to the coal mine. Though it was dark and the cold wind blew against her legs, chilling her entire body, she didn't even notice as she tried to single out the evangelist in the silent, slow-moving line of men. Sometimes she thought she spotted him, and when she did, she felt as though God had blessed her specially that day.

"I have seen him. Surely this is a good sign. Like a blessing fallen onto my doorstep, I am quite sure God will help me and He will help our Trbovlje and our Jugoslavia."

But then she saw him less and less. Several days passed and she did not see his form in the line of men. And on Sunday he was not in the church. She was troubled and prayed for his protection and help. A few days passed and a letter arrived at her mother's house. It was addressed to her. Opening it quickly, she read,

"Dear Sister in the Lord—and something more . . ."

A newsy letter followed. The evangelist was working in a coal mine in Zagorje and he was sending his greeting to her and her family.

Jozeca could see no other words but the greeting: "*and something more.*" Her face flushed so that even her ears were red.

She carefully answered his letter, telling him he was welcome in her house, and signed it with trembling hand,

"Your Sister *and Something More*,
Jozeca Podgornik."

Chapter Four

Jozeca's next days were spent in a cloud. The words *"and some-thing more"* buzzed through her mind like the flies in the butcher shop. She questioned, worried, pondered and blushed until she wearied herself. Finally she decided to pay the evangelist a visit at the Zagorje mine.

"Jozeca, I do not approve," her mother said sternly.

"I ask your permission, Mother. Please grant it."

Looking into her daughter's bright blue eyes and seeing her face, red and round as an apple, she sighed. "It is against my good sense." Then shrugging her shoulders, added, "Give him my greetings."

Jozeca was ready to go before the sun was up. She packed a chunk of cheese and a small loaf of black bread which she had baked before the morning hours. She watched the sun pull itself up out of the darkness behind the mountains and poke its yellow and white rays onto the cold of the earth like the tongue of a snake.

The sun did not brighten everything at once; it came in streaks and rivlets because too many mountains hid its full light. She loved the shadows and the streaks of light in the early morning. She was enervated by the smells of the trees, the steam of her breath upon the air, the layers of white snow brighter than the rays of light and the high stretch of mountain before her ready to be climbed.

"Surely God is with us," she hummed. "In such beauty and peace, He could not withhold His presence."

The trek took six hours. She climbed across the dark mountains covered with patches of snow, some spotted with dead leaves. She scaled the riverbanks, singing as she walked steadily and evenly through the thick trees. Emerging onto a straight little flat plain dotted with farmsteads and snow-covered trees, she looked straight at the entrance of the coal mine where the evangelist was deep within the stony blackness.

The hills had been steep and, in her anxiety, she had climbed too quickly. She knew the wisdom of the mountains, "Slow and steady," and "Never be in a hurry on a mountain." She was trembling, flushed and breathless. She waited near the entrance of the mine until she had caught her breath.

A man in black, coal-stained clothing pulled a loaded cart from the elevator. Jozeca approached him shyly. "*Zdravo.*"

"*Zdravo.*" He gave the cart a shove down the tracks to another man waiting at the curve.

"I am looking for Jakob Kovac."

"He will be up in a quarter of an hour. You can wait." He pointed to a corner out of the way of the heavy machinery and the loaded cars of coal. She watched the cars roll down the tracks into the pitholds and disappear.

Shortly a familiar voice was very near to her. "*Zdravo.*"

"Ah! *Gospod* Kovac. *Zdravo.*"

He stood beside her, tall, strong and covered with black coal dust. His eyes shone from out of the black and when he smiled, his teeth looked white and clean.

"This is a great surprise, Jozeca, and an honor."

She waited while he washed and changed his clothes. It was the pride of a Slovenian to look his best. When he had washed and changed into a heavy woolen jacket pulled over a white shirt, gray Austrian pants tucked into high polished boots, he took her to a smoke-filled *restavracija* nearby. She gazed up at him, unable to say anything. He looked at her without a word.

They sat that way for several minutes, neither of them speaking. He looked bigger than she remembered sitting across from her at the white-covered table. His large rough hands lay flat on the table-cloth and his eyes looked directly into hers. She was blushing but she held his gaze. She felt a kind of pink shivering sensation and she could hear her heart pounding heavily beneath her wool coat.

"Jozeca," he said. "I am an old man."

She held her breath. A waitress, wearing a white apron tied around her stomach and miner's shoes with the toes cut out, brought them two large cups half-filled with thick black turkish coffee topped with a dollop of whipped cream.

"You are such a young girl. . . . You are just—how old?"

"I am twenty, Jakob."

"Ah *ja*, twenty. And you called me 'Jakob.' "

She twisted the end of the tablecloth in her fingers. "*Gospod*—uh, Jakob. If you would be so kind, would you explain to me the meaning of the greeting in your letter?"

He watched her face. Her small mouth was trembling and her eyes were damp. He swallowed a tiny spoonful of the whipped cream.

"I travelled this far on foot that I might know the answer to that question, Jakob," she continued.

He touched his chin with two fingers, looked at her deep and long; then he said quietly, "Jozeca, you are my heart."

She gasped. Her face turned crimson. "I have been miserable without the sight of you," she blurted. "There is no cheer whatsoever. All is gray and misery."

She was overcome. Surely it was God who gave her such feelings.

Jakob spoke softly, his voice cracking slightly. "I am thirty-five years older than you."

They were quiet again. Then Jozeca pulled in a deep breath, fastened her eyes on his face and said, "We Slovenes are not known for being coquettish, nor do we falsely represent our hearts. If you love me and want to marry me, you have my permission to tell me so."

His expression did not change whatsoever. He sat very still, his face placid. "Should an old and weary oxen frolic with the young ponies?"

"Should a sapling die in the forest without the protection of the strong oak?"

Jozeca was accustomed to proverbial exchanges. It was the way with Slovenes. Often these exchanges would go on for hours, with the discussion carried on in axioms and stories and never discussing the real issue.

Jakob spoke. "Can you put old wine into new skins?"

Jozeca answered quickly. "Permit me to put to you a question." He nodded. "There is a small yellow flower growing in the shadows near the barn."

"Ah, *ja.*"

"This little flower goes unnoticed by all who pass by. The farmer does not notice the flower, nor care about it, and the flower is forsaken by all, even by the sun, which rarely shines upon it."

"Ah, *ja, ja.*"

"One day a child comes along and notices the flower. In joy, the child picks the flower, to enjoy for a time until it fades and is gone forever."

"*Ja. . . .*"

"Now my question: Is it better to remain without love alone in the shadows or to be enjoyed for a time in the light where joy is gained?"

He wanted to grasp her hand, hold her face, stroke her rich brown hair. She, at that moment, became a part of him, that part of him which would never be empty again, that part which would forever pulse with fresh strawberry sweetness and the life he had never had.

"I will love you forever," he said simply and his eyes were moist.

The walk back to Trbovlje seemed endless. Jozeca could hardly wait to get home with her news. She would shout it to every cottage in the town. She would ring the bells, shoot the guns, strew the road with ribbons. She stopped to sit on a rock, laughing and swinging her feet. She poked at a crusty patch of snow surrounding a weak winding stream, then peered up through squinted eyes at the trees.

"Friends," she shouted, "I have important words to impart!" She began to giggle. "There is great joy within my heart! There is such a joy!" She hopped up from the rock, leaped across the stream and threw out her arms, shouting, "*And something more!*" She collapsed against a birch tree, happily squealing with laughter.

Chapter Five

"Why, the old fool," they said. "Imagine a sensible and reasonable man like Jakob Kovac marrying a woman thirty-five years younger than he!"

"She will grow tired of him and he will be all the worse off in his old age."

"Jozeca, why do you marry that old man? You are young. Think of your children. Do you want them to have an old grandpa for a father?"

To all the derisions Jozeca calmly tossed her hand in the air. "I will love and serve my husband as Christ himself."

Jakob received the criticisms of his friends soberly. "What you say is true. I am an old fool. But I believe it is God's will that I marry this woman."

They were obstinately happy. Not even the most malevolent comments discouraged them.

It was not so long ago in Slovenia that marriages were arranged by the parents of the bride and groom. The prospective marriage partners did not usually lay eyes on one another until the wedding day. Nezka told Jozeca about her own younger sister who refused to marry the man her parents had arranged for her. The pretty, dainty girl took one look at the groom on the fateful wedding day and burst into tears. He was a withered sour-faced man with a long nose and unintelligent stare. She ran from the room sobbing, "I will not marry him!"

But her father caught her and whipped her with a thick wet rope. So severe was the beating she received for shaming her father that she fell unconscious to the floor. When she revived, she no longer protested the marriage.

Jozeca's grandfather had arranged her mother's marriage also. Her mother was barely fifteen years old when she was told that she would soon be getting married. Happily, the young man who was chosen to be the husband was honest, hardworking and, as a bonus, attractive. He had just turned sixteen. Their marriage was a fruitful and happy one and lasted until Jozeca was thirteen years old when he died of pneumonia in the big bed on the farm in Brice.

Jozeca could never really understand why her mother married

a drunkard like Lojze after having been married to such a kind and good man as her father for so many years. She wondered if perhaps loneliness caused people to act foolishly and regretably.

Four months after their meeting in Zagorje, Jozeca and Jakob were married. It was the talk of all Trbovlje as well as the surrounding towns and villages.

The wedding was held in the Baptist church. The building was not really a church but a house. There were no markings to tell it was a church. Jozeca wore a long-sleeved white dress buttoning up the front, with a large white collar reaching to her shoulders. Around her waist was a white satin belt. She wore white stockings and black shiny laced shoes. Her hair was parted in the middle, hugging her head in thick waves which met at the back of her neck in a knot.

She blushed when she saw Jakob. Somehow he looked twice as big in his black, neatly pressed wedding suit. He had a high forehead and Jozeca realized as she looked at him that his hair was receded and he was bald right at the top of his head. A crop of thick dark hair covered the back of his head but the front was bare. She couldn't help but smile at her discovery. Why was it she had not noticed before? She felt as though she knew another secret about him and he became all the dearer to her.

She lowered her eyes shyly as they caught his glance. "So this is how it is," she thought. "I, Jozeca Podgornik, becoming the bride of Jakob Kovac, Sent Man of God."

And then she prayed. "Father, you have looked down upon your servant and blessed her beyond her imaginings. You have answered her prayers and blessed her above all other maids in Slovenia because you have chosen her to be the bride of Jakob Kovac. I will try to be worthy."

The days when weddings were festive occasions celebrated by all nearby villages were over; the gala wedding celebrations of past days when the feasts went on for several days together with gay costumes, wine flowing like the river Sava, frenetic music and dancing were now gone. Even rich folk no longer had enough for such extravagant doings.

The ceremony was short and when they were man and wife he leaned toward her, his eyes crinkled and smiling, the palms of his hands damp; then slowly and gently he placed upon her tiny heart-shaped lips the very first kiss she had ever received from a man.

It was a simple celebration. There was the table in the big room of Jozeca's mother's house. It was covered with a white cloth upon which sat a wedding cake decorated with the words "God bless us all." Jozeca had baked the cake herself. Overhead hung chains

of flowers and green twigs symbolizing the beginning of a new life.
Friends and relatives pressed into the tiny room. An accordion played
and there were toasts to the new bride and groom and speeches
made by everyone wishing to extol the virtues of a good wife and
the duties of a husband.

Although many people had ridiculed the wedding couple, on that
day there were no protests or dispersions. When Jakob's turn came
to give a speech, his face shone and his eyes danced. He said in
a soft voice, "I am the happiest man in all the world today," and
turning to a blushing wife he said, "My bride is God's gift to me."
He smiled then and whispered close to her cheek, "My sister and
something more, eh?" Jozeca, her face crimson, laughed, showing
two rows of small, uniform white teeth. There was a whoop of ap-
plause and the accordion played a *valcek*, a folk waltz.

Chapter Six

They moved into a one-room *hisica* at the bottom of the hill. The widow lady who owned the small house lived in adjoining rooms. They were fortunate to be able to find a place of their own because the *kriza* made housing scarce. Many people were living with as many as six people in one-room dwellings.

"I believe that God has blessed us! Our *hisica* is a good sign," Jozeca said happily. "It means our marriage will be blessed and happy."

"And does it mean we will be without troubles as well?"

"Only a fool expects life to be without troubles."

Jakob folded her in his arms. "My little strawberry," he said, "sweet and perfect. You must be brave, I tell you. Harder times will come."

"Harder times?"

"News has reached us here in Trbovlje that our king, King Alexander, has been assassinated."

"The King assassinated!"

The news rippled through the town. There were feelings of fear, happiness, worry, rage and grief. Jozeca listened to the talk with a solemn face. "What kind of a world do we have? This is the eighth monarch in a hundred years. All were autocrats, and King Alexander, God rest his soul, they called a cruel dictator. Our kings are either killed or exiled. What can we expect next for Jugoslavia?"

Jakob stroked her round cheek. His strong body near her, the smell of him, the presence of him, was comforting.

"We will have sons, Jakob. What kind of world will be here to greet them?"

"I believe that mothers and fathers everywhere ask that question."

"Even in places such as America?"

"Ah, even in America, I believe."

She listened to the commotion outside the house. Men and women were running and shouting. Shadows were playing on the wall and they could hear the widow lady in her rooms moving about preparing her dinner. Soon smells of boiled cabbage filled the air.

"Jozeca," he said quietly.

"*Prosim?*" she responded, "Please?"

"I would like to put to you a question."

She waited.

"Can peach on the vine be sweet and salty at the same time?"

"No, it cannot."

"You have answered right. Now let me put to you another question."

"*Prosim.*"

"Is it good for a Christian to have fears and worries in the heart at the same time as trust and faith?"

She was still. The smell of the cooking cabbage was thick in the air.

"Ah, Jakob." She reached for his hand, kissing it. "Jakob, forgive me."

"Little heart, let us trust God. Let us always trust God."

"Yes, Jakob."

He took both her hands in his and kissed them and she breathed the cabbage in the air and heard the pounding of her heart against his smooth long forehead.

Every day the news was worse. On Sunday Brother Zevnik told them what he had seen in Ljubljana, the capital city of Slovenia, Jugoslavia. "It was an exhibition," he said. "In Russia there is an anti-religious campaign. A newspaper, *Bezboznik*, The Atheist, tells the people:*You will not get a good harvest by praying to God, but only by deep ploughing fertilizers. Electricity and hygiene will improve our health, not prayers!*

Brother Zevnik shook his head. His broad cheeks were deeply lined and his eyes hidden in many creases. "I am afraid many are falling from the faith. Exhibitions such as this are very dangerous to the faith."

Jakob, who had been listening quietly to Brother Zevnik, rose to his feet. "Dangerous to the faith? My dear brother, for twelve centuries we have been a country and a people who have suffered much bloodshed; our lands and provinces have been passed from hand to hand like small change, yet truth has always proven more powerful than the sword. The truth cannot be altered no matter how many newspapers they print!"

All eyes in the room were upon him. Jozeca sat upright and still in her chair. He continued, "Let us remember our Serbian brothers. What do you suppose gave them the will to go on existing as a people during the many centuries of Turkish invasion and dominion? I will tell you! Faith! They believed in liberty! Belief in victory over evil!"

"This is folklore, Brother," said a large, black-haired, mustached man sitting by the wall. "Let us also remember that partial freedom is no freedom. It is complete or it does not exist." Heads nodded in agreement.

"Our whole mentality is inclined towards slavery! We are filled with fear, pessimism; we despair so easily." Jakob's voice was loud, sure. "Do we not realize we are a new generation? We are in Christ Jesus new in every way!"

"Our brother speaks the truth."

"Why are we speaking of despair and doom? Our hope is in Christ! Our faith is in the eternal!"

The large man with the mustache stood quietly and recited the verses:

O you, young corn, your harvest has to be premature,
You have to bow your ears before they are ripe. . .
But your sacrifice will not be useless . . .
One day on your graves will grow the flowers
For a faraway generation. . . .[1]

They were still. They felt the words of the poet were prophetic somehow. World War I was over, the economic depression that had swept the United States and western Europe had tattered Jugoslavia as well; the King lay dead on foreign soil; and a devastating price was yet to be paid for freedom, the desire for which was a gnawing sore in every Jugoslav heart.

Someone in the back of the room began to sing softly, then others joined. The voices mingled and swelled into a crescendo: "God is Lord over all; we shall cling to Him. . . ."

Walking home, a warm breeze blowing, they climbed the hill together. Jozeca thought on the words of the poem Brother Ruglj had read. "It is a beautiful poem, *ne*? But our people suffered generations ago as they do today. Which generation receives the flowers?"

Jakob's face was flushed with emotion. "God is our strength as well as our wisdom. Our people must be brave," he said. "We must look toward God who is good and merciful. We must believe in Him. Our people must believe in Him and we must trust Him."

Now events of the *kriza* occurred in rapid succession. In Maribor, an industrial center of Slovenia, the plight of workers grew worse. A young man came to Trbovlje and was found near the coal mine nearly dead from starvation. He told Jakob, "Living is terrible. We are all hungry. Twenty-eight railway cars and three small huts are housing 650 men, women and children. . . ." They had carried the man to Jakob's house where he rested and drank some soup. He told them about a new public beach which had been opened in Maribor. "It is so strange—everything is crazy. We are starving

---

1. Prince-Bishop Petar Petrovic-Njegos, *Mountain's Wreath*.

and an entrance ticket to this beach costs ten dinars. This is what a worker earns for one day's work.''

It was a gray, misty day when the workers at the Trbovlje coal mine declared a hunger strike and refused to come out of their pits. Wages had been reduced by six percent, and, to make matters worse, the French bank who owned the mine had fired many workers. The Trbovlje mine had the biggest coal output in Slovenia.

Jozeca stood with the hundreds of women and children who were gathered at the pitheads. Her mother stood beside her.

Jozeca looked at the faces of the women. They were tense, grim, but not maudlin, nor self-pitying. They wore dark clothes and were huddled in clumps around the mine, some carrying babies, others quietly fingering the beads of rosaries. There were no displays of emotion. They stood silently, shrouded in shawls and babushkas, their eyes fixed on the openings of the mines; their jaws were tight and the deep lines and wrinkles of their faces hidden by gathering shadows. A few children whispered and played quietly near the gate.

Days later, after threats and decisions were made, the men emerged from the pits without their requests granted. They were gaunt, weary, looking like black phantoms. Slowly they dispersed with their families, each to his own home, moving unhurriedly, silently, like falling sand.

The soccer triumph in the summer of 1935 gave a slight but much-needed recreational relief to the country when Jugoslavia won the International match against Poland at Katowice by 3 goals to 2. But there was unrest everywhere. The people's hunger for freedom growled from every corner of the country. Peasants tried to rebel in Croatia and paid for it with their lives when police opened fire upon them. The prisoners in Sremska Mitrovica jail rioted in an effort to obtain certain requests and police beat them into servitude. There was a general election but the government managed a majority, though small.

The little Baptist church in Trbovlje struggled with its handful of members. Strongly Catholic, any other religion was considered pagan in Slovenia. Baptist children were teased and bullied adding more burdens to the already bent backs of these church members.

"We must never speak against our Catholic brothers," Jakob admonished. "We must not forget that every one of us here was born of Catholic parents, reared in Catholic homes, educated in Catholic schools. My own wife was planning to be a cloistered nun at one time. Let us speak and act with love. Find Christ as your Lord and Savior and it doesn't matter what church you belong to. In Christ Jesus you will find love and hope and eternal life. This is what matters.''

Chapter Seven

Jozeca began praying for a son. They had been married two years and were without children. Her mother was certain it was because they did not have the ear of corn, symbol of fertility, hanging from their rafters.

Croatian neighbors brought Jozeca hard-boiled eggs decorated with wheat. "Eat," they told her; "then you will have a child."

She was given pillow cases embroidered with ears of grain for fertility. Jakob received hard-boiled eggs decorated with figures of roosters. Jozeca accepted the gifts reluctantly.

"The Croatian people believe in these superstitions. It is a pity. For hundreds of years they have believed in these superstitions. It is their way," Jakob explained. "Our children will come from God, not from a hard-boiled egg." They laughed together. "Tonight we shall pray for a son and then we shall pray for our Croatian friends."

Then earnestly each morning she and Jakob rose from the bed and knelt on the floor, clasping hands and asking God to bless them with a child.

"I believe God will give us children, Jakob. I believe it."

Jakob held her in his arms, breathing in the smell of her skin and her hair. He kissed the tears rolling down onto her small chin.

"And God will not turn His face from so dear a heart," he said.

One evening when Jakob was still at the mine, an old woman named Nata came to the door. Jozeca was surprised to see her. Nata was rarely known to visit anyone. She kept to herself in her one-room house at the bottom of the hill. They said she could remember the revolution in Europe and the signing of the Paris treaty in 1856. She stood there in the shadows, her eyes peering up through folds and creases. "*Gospa* Kovac," she said in a high, whining voice.

The sound of her voice sent an ominous chill through Jozeca's body. "*Dober vercer*," she said, "Good evening."

She motioned for the old woman to enter the house, and once inside she brought her a chair to sit on. The old woman walked without lifting her feet. She lowered herself slowly into the chair. Jozeca stood by the door staring at her. She looked more than a hundred years old. She had only one tooth which protruded upward over her

44

lip in the front and her eyes were red-rimmed and hidden in the stretched and puckered skin.

"*Gospa* Kovac, so it is," she began again in the high, whining voice.

"I am pleased you have come to visit," said Jozeca.

"I did not come to please you, *Gospa*, but to warn you."

The light was dim and the old woman was swallowed in shadows. A shaft of light struck right above her head in a jagged line.

"You have sinned against God!" Her voice cut through the air like a scythe. "God is punishing you! You shall never bear a son because of your sin!"

As is customary in Jugoslavia, the conversation is usually held in a series of soliloquys. Jozeca did not interrupt, but stood waiting for the old woman to finish her speech. She was trembling and near tears.

"You married an old man and you will pay for your sin," the old woman continued. "You have sinned against God!"

Jozeca defied custom by interrupting. "You are wrong! I will give my husband a son, you shall see. God will answer our prayers!"

Jozeca did not tell Jakob about the old woman's visit, which was a mistake. The awful memory of her face leering at her and the sound of her high thin voice remained in Jozeca's mind. She felt the old woman's terrible words, like a curse, wrap themselves around her neck and begin to squeeze. Days passed and the words of the curse held her like a vise. Hope and beauty and love seemed further and further away. She lost track of the days and became absorbed only in her own thoughts. Even her vision was impaired and on some days she would see only black spots and shadows. When Jakob was not at home she sat by the wall and wept.

Somehow she managed to keep her suffering from Jakob. He could tell there was something wrong but he was silent about it, waiting and watching. It would pass if it were only a trifling matter.

On a spring morning when the carts drawn by mules clacked past the cottage on their way to the market, Jakob was surprised when Jozeca refused to get out of bed. Her face was to the wall and her body curled in a moon. He touched her shoulder gently, "*Screce*, little heart." She did not respond.

She was always first to rise and the happy presence of her would fill the little room as she lighted the fire for the stove for cooking and brought in the water. He loved the sound of her high clear voice singing hymns as she worked.

Again he touched her shoulder. "Jozeca?"

She turned, looked at him with tormented eyes. He tickled her neck with his fingers and blew softly into her ear. "My beloved."

She wanted to press her face to his chest, hold him, but she only looked at him and did not move.

He smiled at her, "My beloved has blessed me because she has rested herself."

She groaned, almost hating his kindness. It made her own miserable state more obvious. Her thoughts were like heavy rocks and her body felt heavy too, too heavy to move out of the bed. This was the first of many mornings when she would remain in bed brooding and depressed.

Summer, hot and torpid, moved across their lives like a long empty road. Jozeca walked through the hills listening to the high-pitched, persistent ringing of the mowers as they reforged the cold iron of their scythe blades. She watched them mowing beneath the high grasses beneath the trees and on the mountainside.

She liked mowing time and the swinging of the short scythes among the tall grasses. She squinted as she recognized her stepfather, Lojze, among the mowers. Behind them followed the women who put the grasses in rope cradles and carried them stretcher-like down to their farms. Her mother was among them. She walked down the hill and asked if she could work also. The farmer's wife nodded "yes" and Jozeca joined the women in their labor. She helped weave the grass into tall drying racks. She was silent and spoke only when it was necessary. It was the first work she had done in weeks.

The workers talked of the kriza, of the Fascists who were attacking from Italy, and of more war. The women gossiped among themselves, pretending they did not notice Jozeca's peculiar indifference.

"My daughter is still like the river before the storm," her mother told her husband.

He grunted.

"It is not well with her," she said.

Grunt.

"Perhaps she is tired of her husband."

"Ah, the devil," he said, being tired and of nasty temper. "Mind your own house and you will not get my neck into trouble."

It was on a hot July evening as they sat in the whitewashed room of their cottage finishing their meal of sour milk, black bread and bacon, washing it down with linden blossom tea that Jakob said, "Now I am listening and you will explain to me what is in your heart."

Jozeca looked at him surprised and a little frightened. "Today I tied twenty bundles of grass."

". . . And your heart, Jozeca?"

"It will pass, husband. I am sure of it."

"A teapot is not meant to hold tea forever, for it will spoil and be good for nothing. But when the teapot is emptied of the old tea, then it is cleaned and ready to hold a new pot of tea."

"Ah, Jakob, I cannot . . ."

He took her hand and began to pray. It was sudden and the force of his hand and voice was startling. "Father, in Jesus' name!" he began.

She hardly heard his words but she felt them raining around her, engulfing her. The horrible words of the old woman which were meant to wound and oppress had come at her like furious darts, and Jakob's words now filling the air were waging war against every vestige of evil. They were good words, and their Author was beauty and love. They were ringing through the air, slicing to bits of dust the cursing railing of the old woman. Jozeca closed her eyes and leaned into the warmth and safety of Jakob's words. It was as though the room was filled with something sweet smelling, golden, wonderful.

He took his Bible and began to read in a loud and excited voice. His arms tread the air as he read. She realized he was not just reading to her, but to invisible forces as well. "Listen!" He read the words of Jesus in the Gospel of John, "The thief cometh not, but for to steal, and to kill, and to destroy: I am come that they might have life, and that they might have it more abundantly!" [1]

He waved his Bible in the air. "We are the children of the Lord God! We refuse to allow the thief to enter and steal! Our hearts are the Lord's! The thief may not enter and steal what belongs to God!"

Jozeca rode on the crest of his voice and could actually sense herself being released from a dark grip; she could sense the heaviness dropping from her. Fear, self-pity and anger had held her captive, but now they were being smashed to bits. More powerful than a two-edged sword, the words sliced through the air, and Jozeca knew that a great invisible war was being won.

She closed her eyes and joined in Jakob's prayer which seemed to fill the room. It was the first time she had been able to pray with her whole heart since the old woman had come to her house that day long before. "I thank you, my Lord God," she said simply, "for you have saved me from the thief, the murderer and the plunderer. My heart belongs to you."

Then she turned to her husband. "I am sorry, Jakob," she said to him. "I have been slothful with my heart."

---

1. John 10:10

"Jozeca—"

"No, Jakob. Hear me. I have been swallowed up in self-pity, in fear and in anger. Forgive me. Please forgive me."

Together they slid to their knees. They prayed and sang together, and she told him of how old Nata had come to their cottage and how she had allowed the woman's words to bind her up like one of her hay bundles. She told him that Nata had said Jozeca had sinned and would never bear a child.

"Our people are riddled with superstition and fears," he said.

She showed him the shocks of wheat which well-meaning neighbors had presented to her for fertility. They were tucked under the bed.

Gently he took the wheat. "Wheat is for bread," he said. "It will not become bread under the bed. Let us trust wheat to become bread and trust God to answer prayer."

He held her hands, plump and white, and smiled at her. His smell, acrid and leathery, his body, large, muscular, tough, became all her senses. They sat quietly in the heat. The room was hot and they were wet with perspiration, but they felt as though they had just taken a long, cool swim in a river of living water. Gently, very gently, he reached for her, kissed her lips and she knew again with every fiber of her being that she was born to love him.

Chapter Eight

Everywhere they were, they were praying, those Christians. Under bridges, in houses, in small groups, large groups, alone or with a church; they were scattered from Slovenia to Macedonia in Jugoslavia. There were not many of them but they were there and they were praying.

And as they were on their knees praying to God, a man named Josip Broz Tito was rising in power in Communist ranks. He had been born the seventh son of peasant Catholic parents in Kumrovec, Croatia, and one of his best subjects in school had been the Scriptures. He went to church regularly as a boy, but he had been mistreated in the church and he allowed it to put a cold wedge between him and God. He earned his living as a metal worker. He fought in World War I in the Carpathian front, where he was wounded. In March 1915 he was captured by the Russians. In 1917 he joined the Red Army.

Between the wars Josip Broz Tito was arrested and sentenced to five years imprisonment for subversive activity, and when he was released he went to Moscow where he worked in the Comintern's Balkan secretariat. In 1936 he was sent to Zagreb and Paris to organize recruitment for the international brigades fighting in Spain. In 1937 he became secretary-general of the Jugoslav Communist party, making his headquarters in Zagreb.

The praying people in Jugoslavia did not know that Josip Broz Tito would lead the most courageous guerrilla war against the Axis in World War II, nor did they know that under his leadership, Jugoslavia's republics would be united into one nation under the Communist flag, separate from the Soviet Union.

In 1938 Tito said, "Communists must live with the workers. Communists must be the best workers, the best students, the best members of the family. It is very important that the men with the best human qualities become Communists."

Because of this political and social structure, the Christian's best example was in the excellence of his character, his work and his social usefulness, which had to outshine even the most dedicated Communist. This was no small task.

They prayed. They prayed for strength, for perseverance; they prayed for mercy, for freedom to worship God, for bread; they prayed that their children would have food to eat, land to tend and jobs to perform. They prayed for peace and the privilege of life.

These had been the prayers of their ancestors and few had seen all of them answered.

But one prayer was answered in Jugoslavia that year. It was August of 1938 and Jozeca knew, knew for certain—the doctor in Ljublijana had confirmed it; she was with child. She had moved so carefully, so gently these last two months as she waited almost breathlessly to be sure, to be certain. Now it was sure. There, housed within her womb, was a baby, safe and clinging to her body. She could be sure now. Yes, the doctor said so. It was there, inside the soft walls of her belly, another new life.

She had decided on the train that she would walk home steadily and slowly from the station. Then she would sit down on a chair and wait for Jakob to arrive. She would prepare supper as usual and she would tell him the news after he had taken a wash. She would help him. It would be orderly, perfect. She had dreamed it a hundred times, a thousand times. She pointed her face toward the coal mine and walked calmly, evenly. Then her pace quickened and her step was brisk. She broke into a full run, running, running, to the father of their baby who now grew in her womb.

He was leaving the coal mine, walking with a firm, strong step, his muscular body moving rapidly over the stones and dust. Then he saw Jozeca, braids flying, running toward him. Her thick, short legs paddled the air and he smiled at her youthfulness, her seeming unconcern at how she appeared to anyone else. Her face was flushed deep red and perspiration ran down her neck and her dress.

"*Zdravo!*"

"*Zdravo*, little flower."

She breathed heavily. It would be improper to come right out with the news. First you engage in polite exchanges.

"You are well?"

"*Ja, Ja.* I am well. And you?"

"I also am well. Is it good with you?"

"*Ja, Ja.* It is good with me."

"Praise be to God."

"Praise be to God."

She could stand it no longer. "Jakob! I am with child!"

His mouth dropped, his eyes widened like suns. "With child! Jozeca! Is it true?"

Her cheeks were red and shiny, her mouth like a small flower, trembled, and her wide, blue eyes were moist. He wanted to hold the moment forever. She grinned, showing her little teeth right up to the gums and bobbing her head up and down, and said, "It is true! You will be a father!"

They walked side by side to their *hisica* at the bottom of the hill. He walked more slowly and steadily. "But you must not run and wear yourself out!"

She bounced along, taking two steps to his every one. They clung to the golden closeness of God, so special at times of answered prayer. The honk of geese and cluck of chickens were the only sounds they heard and the heavy sweet smell of the fields and woods filled their nostrils. He knew at that moment that he would thank God with his every breath until he breathed no more. God had given him a new life, a life of youth and laughter and vigor. When others his age were reeling at the end of a plank, he was at the center, snug and loved, and now a new life would bear his name. He was dizzy and from his eyes there came long tears, like fingers.

Chapter Nine

"Do you trust God, Jozeca?"

"I do, Jakob."

"Then let us go to our knees and pray together. We will not lose faith—no matter what happens."

She seized the last words of his sentence: "no matter what happens."

"Jakob, I will not lose this baby."

He patted her eyes and smiled patiently.

"My baby and I will be together in this life, Jakob."

His smile faded.

"Jakob, do you believe this?"

He said, "I believe in God and His holy will. Whatever happens, I will praise Him and thank Him for it."

The doctor in Ljublijana had examined her and then, with a stern face, drew Jakob into the gray light of the corridor. "She must have an abortion immediately," he told him in a voice so dispassionate he could have been ordering soup in a *restavracija*.

"An abortion?"

"Her body is not strong enough to carry a child full term. I tell you, if she does not have an abortion, either she or the baby will die."

The days passed slowly and painfully. Jozeca hemorrhaged and could not move from the bed, but there was no way to convince her to have the operation. The doctor insisted she be operated on immediately, explaining to Jakob that he may lose both his child and his wife if she continued with the pregnancy.

"My baby and I will be together in this life," was her answer.

They continued to pray health into their child who was curled within her, although every day her own life hung on a thin string. Jakob prayed for Jozeca, determined to see the Lord accomplish what the doctors could not. Many times in the night Jozeca awoke to find her husband kneeling beside the bed praying for her. During the day he withdrew apart by himself where he insisted God breathe life and health into his wife and his child.

The months passed. The heat of summer gave way to the cool breezes of the autumn and then winter snows and freezing rains covered their mountains. Finally on a cold, drizzling January morning in 1939, icicles hanging from the window by the bed and the road outside hard with frozen mud, her time had come. She wrapped her coat around her, tied a babushka under her chin and walked to the hospital. Her white breath on the air streamed from her lips like knives as she made her way between pains up the steep hill. She sang softly to herself, struggling not to fall on the slippery ice. "*Osamljen nisem, osamljen nisem*, I am not alone, I am not alone. . . ."

Jakob came quickly to the hospital when he heard that her time had come. He rushed to her in hope and fear. When he found her room, he paused at the door to pray and catch his breath. Then he entered, his back tall and straight.

He found her lying in a bed, a child in her arms. She smiled brightly when she saw him. "Here is your son," she said, presenting to him his gift; and then, hearing only the sound of his handkerchief wiping the tears from his eyes, she closed her eyes and slept.

The peasants and townsfolk came to congratulate them. The women clucked and cooed over the baby and over Jozeca for being so brave and trusting her God.

"I was certain God would give them a son," said a past opponent. "And furthermore, see how healthy the child is and how Jozeca, pleased as a cat, is blessed with strength!"

"Did I not tell you so?"

"The evangelist is a man of prayer—Sent Man of God he is. God listens to his prayers from heaven and He answers."

Old Nata shrugged when she heard the news and shook Nezka's hand. "Now you are a *stara mama*, a grandma. *Srecno!* Good luck!"

But the special attention was short-lived. There was little time for celebrating events like the birth of a child, particularly when such events were not usually considered a blessing. The *kriza* was now like a fierce spider's web and it drew more tightly around the towns and villages every day.

Two years earlier the League of Nations had failed in Ethiopia, and the growing strength of Mussolini and Hitler was advancing Fascism on all fronts. The baby, Jakob Josip Kovac, was born the same year Stalin signed the Non-Aggression Pact of friendship with Adolph Hitler. It was also the year of the outbreak of World War II when Germany invaded Poland, and Britain and France declared war on Germany.

Jozeca's faith was at a crescendo in spite of the darkness which circled them. She exclaimed to everyone who would listen, "God will answer all our prayers. See how He has blessed my husband's house and given him a son! Surely He will look down on our village and our people and have mercy upon us!"

She felt happier than she could remember. With barely enough food to eat and the sound of marching jackboots in the distance, she rejoiced as though she were in a country without war and in a world without hunger or fear. "Our God hears our prayers. He is a God who loves His people. You shall see!"

Jugoslavia was still nursing its deep and bloody wounds from World War I. That war had struck Beograd, the capital city of Serbia, with ferocious blows, as well as all Jugoslav cities and lands. Serbia alone lost 40 percent of all the soldiers she had mobilized at the beginning of the war, which is two and a half times more than France, three times as many as Great Britain and Italy, and four times as many as Belgium lost. The combined loss of civilian soldiers throughout Jugoslavia in World War I amounted to two million human beings, almost every fifth inhabitant.[1] Many had perished of hunger and disease.

Now, only twenty-three years later, another world war was about to fall upon them. Like a comet disengaged from the heavens hurling earthward, there was no escape from it, no running from its deadly blow.

It was a country where cars were not yet produced. It was only twenty-six years since Austria had captured Beograd right in the middle of a gross typhus epidemic. Serbia was crushed to bits and wiped off the map for three years.

At the beginning of World War II Jugoslavia was prepared with only sixteen frontier battalions spread out to form the cadres of the newly mobilized reserves, sixteen infantry divisions, three mountain divisions and two cavalry divisions. What could they do against the Italians from the west and the Germans from the north and east with their guns, aircraft and panzer divisions?

Operations were begun before Jugoslavia was in the war. As early as 1940 they had begun Partisan factions which were to characterize their battles throughout the war years. On February 25, 1940, the Slovenes of the Julian March fired an Axis military dump at Klana. On June 25, 1940, they began to disrupt Italian communications, springing the railway at Trbizh. These Julian March Partisans damaged enemy railways during the war 960 times. They derailed 125 trains. They sprang 88 bridges and made 2,570 attacks on enemy transport—without sophisticated weapons, artillery and aircraft. They cut off the German-Italian enemy free use of the Julian March, an essential link between Italy and Germany. Beneath the humble surface of the Jugoslav people there were torrents of enormous pride and courage.

---

1. Dedijer, Vladimir, *The Beloved Land*.

Chapter Ten

After work in the coal mine Jakob packed his rucksack and walked to other villages to preach and to bring Bibles to the people. Before he was married he had walked throughout Austria, Germany and the Jugoslav states of Slovenia, Croatia, as far south as Bosnia and Serbia, with his Bibles and the message of good news. He couldn't stop now, even though his bright-eyed young wife was the joy of his life—far dearer than the blisters and blood on his feet which the hard unyielding mountains gave him, and the cold refusals of many villagers snarling, "Ingrate! Son of a Protestant she-dog!" Her breath and gentle words would hug his thoughts as he walked.

"It is a soft, unfortunate man who refuses to give something of himself for what he believes, Jozeca. Pray for me." And he would be on his way.

Jozeca waited for him to return, though not with the longing loneliness of a wife who depends too heavily upon her husband to fulfill her life. She busied herself with prayer, with rounding up village children and teaching them songs and scriptures; and she even began a little women's group in her cottage. They met in the evenings and in the mornings when they could and they prayed and studied the Bible. Many of the women found the Bible brand new. Its words of freedom and life were something like sudden tingling to a paralyzed body.

"*Je mogoce?* Is it possible?"

"God is a God of love!"

"It is too wonderful!"

Even old Nata came once. Her gray, shrunken face, lined like Mt. Triglav, peered out of her black shawl. She said nothing, but her eyes, rimmed in red, were wet. Jozeca was polite to her, forced herself to extend a hand to her. "Welcome, Nata, to my house." Old Nata grunted, did not take her hand, and sat in stony silence throughout the meeting.

Jozeca's mother was horrified. "Jozeca, as certain as the nose is in the center of my face, that woman is up to no good. She's come to bring another curse upon your house, maybe upon us all. You must forbid her coming into our midst."

"We shall take the matter to God, Mama. He will instruct us."

Jozeca did not sleep that night. She remained kneeling by the bed praying until her arms were numb from clenching her palms together. She begged, she pleaded, she moaned and insisted, "O God, our God, our people are overtaken in superstition and fear!" It was not only old Nata; it was the very town itself. It seemed so much easier for the people to believe in witches and goblins than to believe in God, His Son Jesus, and the Holy Spirit of power and love.

Only last night a woman had rushed into the cottage with her eyes wild and her face as white as birch syrup. "They're knocking again!" she gasped.

"Who is knocking?"

"The spirits. They are knocking on my window!"

"What spirits are knocking on your window?"

"The spirits of my husband's dead brothers. They are seeking revenge. Oh, help me! Help me!"

Many of the villagers believed the souls of the dead returned to torment the living. Some of the women even left food on their doorstep for the spirits, food which they could not afford to take from their hungry families. The souls of dead children were believed to remain near the family to protect them from harm, and many of the people prayed to them, made shrines and left clothing on doorsteps for them. Some people left pans of water out for the dead souls to wash in and they set a place for them at the table. At the death of a family member, all mirrors in the house would be turned toward the wall so the soul of the departed would not catch a glimpse of himself and decide to stay longer in his spirit-state haunting his own house.

"All this superstition and hokum-pokum!" Jozeca cried. "It grieves me, Lord, to see my people so bound up in deception and lies."

The St. Nicholas festival was the worst. Jozeca trembled when she remembered her own childhood and the village men dressed up as devils, coming to each house looking for the children. She hovered fearfully on the stove with the other children. "Have you been good?" And if the child had not been good, the man dressed as a devil would threaten to come and take him away forever.

Her friend Zorka, who lived on the next farm over the hill, was a beautiful, black-haired girl with fiery blue eyes. She was twelve years old when she was taken to the river's edge and tied up with wet rope—all in fun by these devils. She would not bow and pray to the men robed in black, so they decided to play a little trick to teach her a lesson. They left the poor screaming girl there at the river's edge all night.

Jozeca could still hear her pitiful screams, "Do not leave me! Please do not leave me here! I am cold! I am afraid!" But it was no use. In the morning, laughing and joking, the men returned to untie the girl and send her home to her parents. But when they found her, she was dead. Struggling to get free, she had rolled into the water and drowned. Her hair was floating like moss in the water, tangled in the weeds. She was stiff, her skin blue and her eyes and mouth were frozen white. They told the girl's parents that their daughter's death was a certain sign that she had been possessed of evil spirits.

"O God, God, dearest God of mercy and love, look down upon us! Look down upon our Jugoslavia! With your heart, so filled with tenderness and love, see our people and lead them out of darkness!"

While Jakob was gone on his preaching trip, a village woman named Sofia was struck with the fever. Jozeca went immediately to the little house to help care for her. She bathed her with cold wet rags and tried to feed her chicken broth. She sat by the delirious woman's bedside at night praying and changing the cold compresses on her head and body. The woman's babies cried and whined and the husband paced back and forth nervously until exhaustion claimed him. He slumped into a chair, put his head on the table and slept.

By sunup of the third day the woman's fever was no better and she was nearly unconscious. The husband ran on foot to the doctor who lived six kilometers away. He returned with him in the afternoon. By this time the woman was barely breathing. Jozeca was sweating and weeping, her face pale and her body shaking from lack of food and sleep.

Her prayers were almost frantic now. She was no longer entreating; she was begging, desperately begging. The woman's babies sat outside on the doorstep in silence, their wide eyes staring outward at nothing, sensing the tragedy that hovered over their lives. "Mama," cried the youngest. "Mama, want Mama!"

The doctor looked at the small form in the bed, now shrunken with sickness, a wet mass of hot skin and bones, and shook his head. His wide head and large jaw moved slowly. "I can do nothing more," he said.

"God have mercy!" cried the husband. Jozeca grabbed his hand. "Maybe the doctor can do nothing more, but God can! God will heal your wife with His own hand! You will see!" She fell on her knees by the bed, resolving not to rise until Sofia opened her eyes and lifted her head.

The afternoon faded. Evening floated across the mountains and filled the tiny town. At seven o'clock Sofia was dead.

The wake and the funeral for Sofia passed and Jozeca barely

realized what was happening. She was hardly conscious of anyone else's grief. Why had not God answered her prayers? Why had He not shown this family mercy? Was it because of sin in her life? Was it because of sin in the life of Sofia's husband? In Sofia herself? Oh, what was the reason? Why had God turned His face and not answered her prayers?

Jakob's return brought Jozeca back to a sense of reality again. Her cheeks were pink and puffed and her eyes swollen. "Why, Jakob, why?"

"The Lord is God. He is all majesty and all power. His greatness is beyond our knowing. His glory is beyond our understanding. The Lord is God. He created all things. He created every breath that is breathed. He is the source of all life and energy. He is God."

That was his answer. Jozeca lowered her head. She wanted to cry out in anger and frustration.

He held her chin. "We want faith to be like a wooden door behind which is a table laden with bread. You stand in front of the closed door and proclaim to everyone that you know there is a table filled with bread on the other side of the door. The people do not believe you. They say, 'Ah, it cannot be true.'

"You say, 'Yes, it is true. I will prove it to you!' And you fling open the door and there is the table filled with the finest and most wonderful bread. But faith is not like that. Often we must believe in the bread, and tell people about the bread without ever seeing the door flung open."

"I wanted God to prove himself to Sofia's husband. I wanted her to live!"

"It is enough of this pity now, Jozeca. Press your hands together and turn your eyes to heaven and with your very heart and soul you thank God for taking Sofia because you know that this was His choice and He knows all things."

She hesitated.

"Do it, *moja srcek*," he said. "Do it now, my little heart."

She closed her eyes and very quietly formed the words on her lips.

"Thank you, Lord. Thank you, for you know all things."

Chapter Eleven

She couldn't have known how Sofia's death prepared her for what was to come.

The Italians were attacking many of the villages. Fighting had broken out in Montenegro and slogans were everywhere, *MUS-SOLINI HA SEMPRE RAGIONE*. These slogans would be replaced by *EIN VOLK, EIN REIGH, EIN FÜHRER*; and these in turn replaced by *ZIVIO TITO, SMRT FASIZMU*.

On a trip to another village ten kilometers away, Jakob knelt down in the pine needles to pray. The hours passed and soon the day had melted behind the mountains. He remained on his knees, not conscious of time. When the sun rose in the east, causing the sky to tremble and the mountain to burn as though struck with a match, he arose from his long vigil and continued on his way.

He knew that when God calls a believer to prayer, it is always for a magnificent purpose, far beyond reasoning. It was well past noon when he reached the next village. The first house he came to he knocked on the door in his usual fashion and announced, "I am Jakob Kovac, evangelist, and I have come to tell you the greatest news in the world."

The large-boned woman in the doorway stared open-mouthed. "Enter, please," she said.

It was a cheerful afternoon and the family of the house seemed friendly and genuinely pleased he had come to them. He gave them a Bible and told them of the love of God. He prayed with them and then for each one of them individually.

But as he sat in the house with them, watching their smiling, friendly faces, he knew there was something wrong. He didn't know what it was. He could sense something in the air that was insidious, cunning; it was there as he sat with them, feeling their breath upon him and looking into their small eyes.

They offered him supper and although he felt he ought not to, he accepted their invitation. He ate goats' cheese, thick chunks of bread and drank hot *kava*. It was a feast for a king, he thought. But why did he feel so uneasy? He prayed as he usually did, but he felt his prayers were hitting a tin roof and falling back upon him. Something was definitely wrong, and he wanted only to get out and away from that house.

He left quickly, saying a quick prayer with the family before going out the door. The children hugged his knees and the woman shook his hand vigorously. "Come again to us, soon. You have brought us good news this day. God bless you!"

They offered him their house to sleep in, but he refused their kindness and that night slept in a field alongside the road.

He awoke to the sound of distant voices. It seemed to Jakob, still enclosed in the cool grasses and sleep, that they were coming from another place and another time. They were angry voices, all talking at once. Finally reclining where he was, he lifted himself up onto his elbows and squinted in the brightness of the white light of morning. There was a wagon pulled by a donkey and there were one, two, three—four men sitting in it. Two in front, two in back. He pulled himself up to his knees, and then he recognized the man driving the wagon. It was the man whose house he had just come from. He rose to his feet and waved his arms. "Brother!" he shouted in a friendly greeting to the approaching wagon. "*Zdravo!*"

He hardly expected what happened next. The men in the wagon became wild. They leaped from their seats and rushed toward him. "That is he! That is the man!" screamed the driver. Before Jakob knew what was happening, two men had him hard by the arms and were bending them behind his back.

"That is the man, all right! It is the Bible Man! That is the one!"

"So you thought you would get away with it, did you? Well, we know what to do with your kind!" The tall man who was sitting in front with the driver jumped from the wagon and shook his fists in Jakob's face. Then he began punching him in the chest and stomach.

Jakob tried to ask what was going on and why he was being treated this way. They were all shouting and talking at once and taking turns hitting him. The tall man now struck him in the head and face. Jakob could feel the blood running from his nose across his mouth and chin.

The men pitched him into the back of the wagon after tying his hands and feet together. Then they took him to the police, where a fat-jowled jailer and mayor sentenced him to three months in prison for barn burning. Jakob protested feebly but his words fell on deaf ears. Did he not know that animals were a man's livelihood? How could he do such a dastardly deed, "Protestant dog!"

"You do not deserve to call yourself a Slovene."

"I call myself a Christian and do not deserve to kiss the feet of my Lord."

"Dog! Barn burners ought to be hung by their noses."

"I have committed many sins but barn burning is not among them."

"Ah! So you admit that you commit sins!"

"*Menda ja*, of course! And so do you. We are all sinners."

"There you have it. The Protestant dog admits to committing this sin against an honest and hard-working man. Shame! You are a disgrace to our people. Son of a Turk!"

"I am neither a son of a Turk nor a barn burner."

"Shame! God will punish you!"

Jozeca waited for Jakob to come home. She did not know if he was living or dead. She kept herself and the baby alive by gathering and selling kindling wood and by carrying a basket on her back and knocking on doors and asking for bread. Some days there was only one piece of bread between them.

Italy had attacked Greece, and Germany had invaded Roumania. Jugoslavia was remaining neutral. But the days were numbered.

Jozeca was hired to drop seeds in furrows in a nearby field and she was overjoyed. For a day's labor from sunup to sundown she would receive a can of milk or another day it would be a basket of apples, a head of cabbage. She praised God because now she and her son would not starve. And every day she prayed for a sign that Jakob was alive.

At last, after he had been in prison over a month, she received word that he was alive and well. The following day, the baby on her hip, she walked eight kilometers to the prison to see him. She brought some apples and a cheese wrapped in leaves.

He looked gray and gaunt, but although he had lost weight he had not lost the look of strength and largeness. She grabbed his hands and kissed them.

"It is well with you, my beloved?"

"It is well."

"You are not ill?"

"*Ne*. And you?"

"We are well. The child grows daily. He is strong and healthy."

"Good."

Finally she shook her head and flapped her hand at the wrist to emphasize her words. "Jakob, how could this happen to you?"

"God has many enemies, my soul. These enemies strive to hurt God by hurting His people. Ah, my love, take heart. I pray daily for the man who deceitfully put me in this prison. If God will touch him and one man is brought to the knowledge of Christ, I gladly endure this suffering."

Jozeca shook her head.

"Look upon me. God will not leave us alone. Look for Him, Jozeca.

He is in everything. Everything. He is in this, also, even though it is hard for understanding."

She tried to smile and said cheerfully, "See how fat your son is!"

"Ah, *ja!*"

"I am working in the fields and the Lord provides enough to eat for each day. For this we are grateful."

She gave him the apples and the cheese. "They say that the German army is crossing the border into Serbia. They are coming from Bulgaria and Hungary and also from Roumania and Albania. The Italians support them."

Jakob took an apple and one small bite of cheese and gave the remainder back to her. "This is for you, for the child. Please take." She protested but he insisted in spite of the fact that his diet consisted mainly of cabbage and water. "You must eat and be healthy. It is my joy to see you well."

The visit was over too quickly and Jozeca found herself back on the road to Trbovlje. The baby cried unhappily and she gave him a piece of the cheese she had brought for Jakob. Her own tears bit at his face. "Lord God, he is old. Do not punish him so. Have mercy on him, dearest God of all there is. Have mercy on my Jakob! Oh, have mercy. . . ."

Chapter Twelve

It was on April 6, 1941, a week before Jakob came home, that the Germans bombed Beograd without any warning or even a declaration of war. In its history of more than 2,000 years, the city of Beograd had been destroyed by invading armies 37 times. But no destruction had been so horrible, so effective or so swift as on Palm Sunday, April 6, 1941, at the hands of the Germans.

After waiting for help from the Soviet Union which never came, Tito called upon the workers and peasants of Jugoslavia for a guerrilla war against the Nazis. The first Partisan detachments were formed of untrained and determined men and women who spread into the hills and forests, armed with cudgels and axes, old sporting guns, and anything else they could lay their hands on. They were determined to fight the Germans by any means. For supplies they depended on what they could capture from the enemy and what the country people could give them. Tito was frankly fighting for a Communist Jugoslavia, even though he called the Partisan struggle a People's War and welcomed all anti-Fascists. The Partisan slogan was "Attack the enemy wherever you can, however you can!"

Jakob was released from prison before the end of his sentence. He had grown thin and sickly and the jailer worried he might die. The jailer tossed Jakob's personal belongings across the low metal desk. "We are not Serbs," he said. "We do not torture our prisoners and send them home in boxes. If you must die, die at the hands of the Germans," and he let him go.

The long walk home was slow and difficult. He met men and women who were on their way to mobilize with the Partisans. They told him that Beograd was in shambles. In Zumin there had been an aircraft factory, an ideal target for the German Stukas. Now the streets of Beograd were crawling with Nazi-helmeted soldiers with their submachine guns slung across their chests. The Beograd National Library was a charred ruin. Rare books, medieval manuscripts, priceless documents of Jugoslav history were strewn in the rubble of the library basement. He wanted to weep as he heard this news.

A young girl, about eleven years old, drove her geese along the road with a long stick. She wore heavy wooden clogs on her feet and her long skirt and petticoats were gray and colorless. Any goose who made a noise or was the least distracted received a quick tap of the stick on the head. Jakob watched her as she hurried along with her geese. "This is our Jugoslavia," he thought. "Now what will become of her? God have mercy."

He passed dark-clothed men and women walking along the road, old women with their heads tied in black babushkas, men wearing knickers, high boots and small Austrian caps. All of the talk was about the bombing of Beograd and the plight of Serbia, the little province which had been occupied and torn apart by large and small empires alike—the Turks, the Austrians, the Germans, the Hungarians, the Bulgarians and the Italians. The land survived for five long centuries solely by the efforts of a handful of rebels and a few songs.

He prayed with every step. "God have mercy. God have mercy. God have mercy." He thought of the beautiful "white city," Beograd. He remembered the Cathedral and the University, the National Library and National Theatre, the new Parliament House, the Theological Seminary, the old Turkish Kiosk, the Royal Palace, the Botanical Garden, the exposition grounds and buildings, the museums of Prince Paul and King Alexander, the zoo and the Tomb of the Unknown Soldier on the hill of Avala. It seemed as if it were not so long ago that he had been in Beograd preaching the Gospel. He felt hunger and fatigue slowly overtaking him and he trembled and wavered. He imagined the broad and beautiful streets of ancient Beograd stretched before him. No, he would not stop to rest, nor would he fall to the ground. He lifted his head and prayed louder. His legs were numb with pain and the soles of his feet were bleeding. But soon he would be home. Though his mouth was dry and hot, slowly and softly he began to sing the old Slav song:

O Slavs, you are still alive,
The Slav spirit will survive centuries. . . .

He was joined by others and soon it seemed as though the whole countryside resounded in the words of the ancient song. The voices of men and women and children with Slav blood running in their veins were singing and sobbing all at once. Those who were still there on the tortured soil and those who had gone to other lands, even lands as far away as America, the Slavs now hiding in the charred ruins of Beograd—now their voices could be heard singing in the hills and in the fields, in the mountains and in the cities . . . singing and sobbing for their beloved land—

The Slav spirit will survive centuries. . . .

When he opened his eyes, Jozeca was there, her face very near to his. Her voice came from somewhere out of the dimness. Lojze, of all people, his own father-in-law, had found him on the road. Nearly ready to collapse, when he saw Lojze he did collapse.

Jozeca's mother carried in the bowl of steaming broth with chunks of bread floating on top: "Get some food into his belly and he will be as good as new," she said.

Jakob's energy did increase and his body grew stronger. He rose in the morning at three and prayed on his knees until four. Then after a breakfast of hard bread crumpled in black barley coffee he went to work in the mine until sundown. At night after their evening meal he prayed on his knees for another hour or longer before retiring. This was his schedule as he worked from sunup to sundown at the mine six days a week.

At night Jozeca positioned herself at the door of their cottage to watch for his coming down the hill. In the center of the room was the bucket of warm water waiting, and the chair for him to sit on. She watched him walking so tall and straight, his clothes and skin black with brown coal and lignite dust. One hand swung at this side and the other held a little bouquet of wild flowers for her. As he drew near, he hid the flowers behind his back.

"Zdravo!"

"Zdravo!"

"You are well?"

"I am well."

"And the child?"

"A gift from God. Like an angel."

Then he would tease, "What do you think we have here behind my back?" She laughed, reaching for his hand. He jumped to the side with a loud, "Oooo! Is it a turnip? A dove? Ah, no! It is a cat's nose!"

And she would run circles around him giggling and trying to catch his hand until finally she would turn and discover a bouquet of wild flowers stuck in the pocket of her own apron.

"Ah, Jakob, they are so beautiful!"

His face rippled with dust and sweat and laughter. He smelled of brown coal, dirt and lignite. No matter how hard she scrubbed his skin clean, he always smelled of the mine, of sweat and dirt and coal. It was in his skin, muscles, tissue; in his breath and hair, always there; it was part of him. Foul, acrid, wonderful. It was a smell hard-earned, paid for with every strained ligament and driven bone. Oh, she would love that smell forever.

"Come, sit," she said as she kissed the tips of the flowers and put them in the jar on the table.

"Is it well with you?"

"The day is long but in it there are treasures from God."

"Ah, *ja.*"

He watched her strong sure movements as she removed his jacket and stained shirt.

"Jozeca, my love," he said. "The flowers blush in your presence. They blush to be in the presence of such beauty."

She pressed her face against his sleeve and blushed.

Then she removed his boots and placed them carefully beside the bucket on the floor and kneeling before him, she tenderly and thoroughly washed his feet.

Chapter Thirteen

Slovenia was not the scene of the heaviest fighting during the war but it was hit hard. The lush, vernal fields of Slovenia strewn with daisies and buttercups became targets for the German Luftwaffe, which circled and strafed whatever it spotted that moved. Then the field would be stained red and the dead left—a young boy and his cow or an old man carrying a basket of straw on his back for his geese.

Young Josip was growing up to the morbid music of gunfire, air-raid sirens and bombing. He had his father's broad, full face, his deep brooding eyes, and his wide, crooked grin. "Will he grow tall as you are tall, Jakob?" Jozeca wondered as she sewed in the light by the window. She sewed clothes for the baby by cutting up her own dresses and camisoles and petticoats. She sewed trousers for Jakob out of old overcoats and blankets. Now that the *kriza* had bloomed into a war, there was even less to live on, less money with which to buy food and clothing. But God would take care of them, yes, He would—God would not forget them. He would look down upon them with mercy. She believed that, and she told everyone who would listen to trust God, to have faith. And she invited everyone she talked with to come to the church.

It was a one-room church in the back of an unmarked two-story red building near the center of the town. The believers gathered each week with Jakob, the pastor, to pray, learn about God and encourage each other. Jakob preached every week, insisting that the believers take care of each other. So here they exchanged food also. If one family had butter and the other had bread, they would trade so each would have a little of both.

"This is what our Lord would have us do. If we eat bread when our brother has none, we are to be shamed."

But the people hardly needed a sermon on how to give. Giving was in their fiber and bones. If a stranger came to a Jugoslav home and there was nothing to eat, the man or woman of the house would rush out to sell something in order to get food for the guest. It was a great shame not to offer gifts and food to one's guests, although during the *kriza*, mutual understanding sufficed when friends and neighbors came to visit and there was little to eat or drink. Still, what one had, one shared.

Jakob told the story of the Serb who was sentenced to death. On his way to the gallows a spectator shouted to him, "Ah, Vlado, this is a terrible thing that has happened to you! It is the worst shame ever brought to your name."

But the Serb jerked up his head and with eyes filled with sudden fire said, "But you are wrong! This is not the worst thing to happen to me. Many years ago a visitor came from afar to my house and I had nothing to offer him. That, my friend, is the worst shame ever brought to me."

Jakob preached in a loud and emphatic voice. "We must not forsake love! God is love. Remember, He loves all people. He loves the Italians and He loves the Hungarians and the Greeks; He loves His children of the Balkans and He loves the Germans, too."

He was the pastor of the little church in Trbovlje and, in addition, travelled on foot to other towns and villages. "All around us is destruction," he preached. "The ugly arm of war is rushing toward us. *Cuj! Cuj!* Listen! Listen! In times such as these we must hear the voice of God! We must hear Him and trust in His holy name. We must believe with all our hearts and souls that He is with us! He is a God of love!"

These words he spoke as the battalions of 22-ton Wehrmacht German tanks roared across Jugoslavian soil. The Christians sang "God Is Love" beside a cold stove, holding hands, trembling. And motorized anti-aircraft units, armored cars, machine guns, tommy guns, hand grenades, gas masks, motorcycles, Stukas and Messerchmitts screamed in the hills.

Lojze pulled the donkey's ear and gave its neck a slap as he hitched it up to the loaded wagon. His wife, Nezka, bustled back and forth giving orders, inspecting every parcel and bundle, and pausing only to sniff upwards at the sky and mutter, "May God keep us from robbers and Germans along the road."

Lojze had eaten his breakfast of fig preserves washed down with a glass of water and several glasses of plum brandy. His stepdaughter, Jozeca, stood by the door of the cottage, her face red and blotched from crying. She held her baby, Josip, in her arms.

The wagon was loaded. There was not much left to do now except say good-bye.

Lojze knew Jozeca believed that her mother's bones belonged in the coal black soil of Trbovlje, not the gray sullen earth Celje was built upon, but, then, who was she to make decisions for him? She and that preaching devil of a husband. If he worried as much about Lojze's stomach as he did about his soul—ah, now there would be a fine kettle of cabbage.

"*Mamica*, dear little mama," the braided round-faced stepdaughter cried, "The city of Celje is not for you. The people are like those in Ljubljana—they are intellectual and book-minded."

There she was again—meddling. Right where her nose did not belong! Was he the head of his house or was he not?

Nezka hoisted herself up onto the wagon. "Intellectuals must eat, daughter, and books need dusting. I can both cook and clean."

"But, *Mamica*, there is the *kriza*, the war—"

"We must follow the bread, daughter. What can we do? We will starve here. Please understand."

"Yes, Mama."

Jozeca kissed her mother on both cheeks and embraced her. Jozeca did not want to see her leave. She drew close to her and whispered, "What about Lojze? Will he try to find work at a factory in Celje?"

"It does not matter, daughter. I will work. Listen. One day Lojze will die. And when he does, I will be able to look up into the face of God," she paused to cross herself, "and I will say boldly and without fear, 'the blood of this man, Lojze, does not stain my hands. I have cared for him as a mother!' "

She watched them rolling forward. "But what will you do if you meet the Germans?" she shouted.

"I will pray for them!"

Lojze, his woolen cap sitting crookedly, scowled. Her mother reached down and kissed Jozeca again and said, "God bless you."

"*Na svidenje*, good-bye, good-bye!"

"*Na svidenje*."

Lojze sat upright in the seat looking determined. His red face and even redder nose poked forward, and through his brown-stained teeth he mumbled "*Na svidenje*" to Jozeca and wiggled his fingers at the baby Josip. Jozeca followed the wagon for a few meters and then stood to watch them vanish around the curve in the road, the loaded wagon bumping and rocking back and forth in the mud.

"I will not rest until I know they are safe in Celje," she told Jakob. And she got on her knees and stayed there praying until the sun shone no more through the little window where the jars filled with wild flowers stood.

Chapter Fourteen

Newspapers abroad reported that Germany conquered Jugoslavia and Greece in three weeks. Dive bombers saturated Beograd and Sarajevo; and forty German divisions, including five armored ones, blasted the Jugoslavian frontier.

Jugoslav towns and villages were now German occupied. In the Bosnian town of Jajce, young girls tossed flowers to the German soldiers in passing motorcycles, trucks and transports. Many of the townspeople wore Nazi arm bands, and the Nazi flag flapped in the breeze from almost every house and building. There was even a German army band to thump out the *Horst Wessel* song in the town square.

Newspapers in America said, "The Yugoslavs, in defying the Nazis, are as a shepherd boy facing a Goliath. There are only 16,000,000 Yugoslavs, mostly peasants, surrounded by 140,000,000 German, Italian, Hungarian and Bulgarian foes."[1]

The Germans bombed and destroyed bridges, railroad lines and communications behind Jugoslav troops so that drives in the north across the flat plains beyond the river Sava were delayed and the Jugoslavian army was unable to defend their land.

King Peter of Jugoslavia fled from his throne like a frightened bird. This flight of a monarch, as interpreted by the rest of the world, spelled defeat. But the Jugoslavs had resisted invaders before, whether Teuton, Latin, Magyar or Turk, and it would take more than three weeks to grind them under foreign boots, though this invasion would be even more cruel than last year's blitzkrieg in Western Europe.

Hitler's goal was to use the Balkans as a base from which to launch an attack on British communications in the eastern Mediterranean. He did not want to lose the raw material reservoir of the Third Reich; the oil of Roumania; the wheat of Bulgaria; the hogs, bauxite, copper and lead of Jugoslavia; and he wanted to stop the British from getting a foothold in the Balkans where they might launch an attack on Germany from the rear.

The peasant families of Kranj, Celje, Kamnik and Slovenian vil-

---

1. *Christian Science Monitor*, April 7, 1941.

lages such as Lasko and Trbovlji wanted only to live, to eat, to raise their children and one day to lie down in the soil with their fathers before them. But the black, monstrous Wehrmacht were tearing up the countryside, and Stukas and the yellow-nosed junkers '87 bombers made the sky a black mass of rips and cuts. Machine guns, grenades and mines tore holes in the earth and left towns a mass of smoking pits and graves. Men, women and children who were once alive were now pieces of raw flesh and splintered bone. Some of them hung from trees like old rags.

This is what Lojze and Nezka saw on the road to Celje.

It was getting warm, the sun white and hot. Nezka was silent beside her quiet, brooding husband.

The road was dotted with travellers in carts, bicycles or walking. Men of all ages were hastening to join the Partisan army.

"The Jugoslav army will not win the war," a young man explained as he rode beside them. "*Nemogoce*, impossible!—not enough firepower, equipment, or material. There is not enough organization or trained officers! Look at the Germans with their powerful army and their tanks and bombs! We are as peas in their hats." Then his face brightened. "But in the mountains! In our mountains we will fight with our bare hands. We will fight for freedom and liberty. *Zivio Tito! Svoboda narodu!* Long live Tito! Liberty to the people!"

He told them how Beograd was in rubble and in twelve days the Wehrmacht, with the assistance of the Bulgarian, Hungarian and Italian forces, overran the entire country. Lojze was quiet until he heard that Zagreb had fallen to the Germans and in the same breath heard that an independent state of Croatia had been created with Ante Pavelic as its leader.

"Zagreb . . . the beautiful capital . . . Croatia an independent state. . . ."

In the drive on Zagreb, 100 kilometers away, the capital of Croatia, the Germans took 15,000 prisoners, including twenty-two generals. [2] It was an ancient separatist dream of the Croats to establish an independent state of Croatia, to be separate from the rest of Jugoslavia.

Lojze half-turned his head, and looking at Nezka he snarled, "Where is your God now, eh? Where is your good God now?"

She did not blink at his accusation; not a tiny shimmer of her eye indicated the remark had reached her ear.

They stopped to water the mule and talked with a Croatian man and woman huddled beneath an oak tree with their family of six or seven children. They spoke Serbo-Croatian. Their teenage sons,

---

2. The United States Dept. of the Army, *German Campaigns in the Balkans*.

thin, with a faint black shadow growing above each lip, eyes brown and frightened, stared helplessly at them.

"In Slovenia and Serbia," the old man remonstrated, "you have native sons defending native soil and perhaps you may meet with some victories here and there—and your sons can be buried proudly." His face was gray and his eyes dull. "In Croatia the troops are of mixed nationality. Our sons do not know whom to fight for; they are confused."

Many of these people believed that if they collaborated with the Germans against their own people, it would bring fulfillment of their dreams to become an autonomous state. They saw the futility of fighting against so big a power and were confused over what they were dying for.

On April 3, a few days before the German invasion, a Croat air force officer had flown from Beograd to Graz in Austria and turned over to the Nazis a list of all airports where Jugoslav army planes were dispersed. In fact, whole units of Croat soldiers mutinied, abandoned their positions, threw away their weapons, surrendered or simply went home.[3] Complete companies surrendered to German planes overhead. An entire brigade, including its commanding officer and his staff, gave up to a German bicycle company.

"What shall I tell my sons?" the old man wept. "The Jugoslav army is disillusioned. In one town, a group of Croat soldiers was in the midst of an officer's party when suddenly they were attacked by a German regiment. The men stopped the fun-making long enough to surrender and then they went back to their party as if nothing unusual had happened."

"*Pri moji duse!* By my soul!—"

"It is not unusual to find Croats fighting Serbs who are Jugoslavs, instead of fighting the Germans. You see these, my sons; they will not fight the Serbs. We will not kill our own kinfolk. So we flee to northern Jugoslavia, to Slovenia."

When they parted, the old man saluted and shouted, "Long live the King. Long live King Peter!"

On April 12 when Beograd fell at 5 o'clock in the afternoon to 1st Lieutenant Klingenberg and an SS infantry platoon, there was a prayer vigil going on at the tiny one-room church in Trbolvje. And Nezka, sitting in the wagon beside her husband, now drunk with *slivovica*, prayed also.

The dead were counted much later, but even now there were 254,000 Jugoslav soldiers who fell into German hands during the twelve-day campaign.[4]

---

3. Hoptner, J. B., *Yugoslavia in Crisis 1934-1941*.
4. The United States Dept. of the Army, *German Campaigns in the Balkans*.

Chapter Fifteen

"Ah, the devil," spat Lojze. "I will not go to war. I have my own worries."

"They would not have you, old man," Nezka answered. "You would be as a burning lantern to show the Germans where the army was located."

"Ah, what do you know, daughter of a vandal?"

"No, a farmer."

"Eh?"

"Daughter of a farmer, Lojze. And a widow of a farmer also."

"Ah, the devil."

The sun was bright and the trees and fields sang with birds and butterflies. Juniper and hemlock woods filled the air with sweetness; poplars swayed in the gentle wind, and the silver and green light reflected the sun in the woods. They were nearing a village. Although the mountains would hide a village from view, you could always hear it at least two kilometers away. In the stillness of the countryside or in the penetrating dark forest or standing in the stillness of the countryside, you would recognize the sounds of an approaching village—the honk of geese, the cluck and squawking of chickens, the barking of dogs and sometimes the voices of children. There were the smells too, the smells of woodsmoke and animals.

It was peaceful, and they rocked back and forth with the clop of the mule. Ahead was another wagon; its wheels creaked and rattled and the mules' hooves clopped and slapped on the muddy road. It carried turnips and cabbages and empty milk cans which clinked together as the wagon jostled lazily along. Its driver was a fat, sleepy old man wearing a three-cornered hat and a loose-fitting shirt belted at the waist.

All at once out of the sky came the blast of several Stukas. Their sloped wings and slim undercarriage were easily seen as they took a preliminary high run and then immediately turned and roared toward the wagons. The leader plane peeled away from the formation and, sunlight sparkling on his wings, came whining downwards towards the village to send his bombs crashing. Then he pulled out of his dive as the next, then a third and a fourth Stuka followed him down, dropping bombs. As quickly as they had come, the raiders were swallowed into the sky, leaving only sounds of the shouts and wailing of women and children and the barking of a single dog.

Lojze sat upright in the wagon, unable to move during the whole attack. Nezka had darted under the seat and pulled her shawl over her head. The wagon in front of them had been hit and the donkey lay dead in the road beside a shattered milk can. The driver was lying mutilated in the brush and trees at the side of the road.

Lojze's mule was uncontrollably terrified. Lojze struggled with the reins, but it was no use. The mule ran in circles, snorting and steaming at the nostrils and kicking frantically. At last it crashed into a tree, tipping the wagon onto its side, and fell braying into the ditch. Nezka tumbled out unhurt, but Lojze found himself pinned under the donkey.

He cursed and shouted and kicked the beast with all his might. "Ungrateful animal! I will kill you with my hands! By my soul, I will kill you!"

Then two men in gray uniforms emerged from the trees and pulled him out of the ditch. "Save your energies to kill the Germans, Comrade," one said.

The men were Partisans. There were others with them. They wore gray uniforms with pants stuffed into their boots, grenades tied on their belts and carried Italian guns. "We have need of the wagon and whatever supplies you have," the first man told them.

Obligingly Lojze indicated that the men take what they needed. The officer in charge, a fiery man with wide Slovene jaw and small brown eyes, bowed politely. "German troops and columns will be marching these roads," he warned. "I advise you to catch the train if the railroad station tracks are not destroyed. . . . Ah, supplies. Those Germans have heavy transport and we have only ox and mule-drawn wagons. But they will see what kind of blood flows in the veins of the Balkan people! They will see! *Zivio Tito!*"

Nezka stared at the dead man at the side of the road. The soldiers inspected the destroyed wagon and the corpse and picked up the cabbages and turnips from the ground.

"We should never have left Trbovlje," Nezka moaned, still staring at the corpse at the side of the road.

"There is no place that is safe now," said the officer. "This is the *borba*, the war. The only place you will be safe is in the grave."

Nezka and Lojze slowly made their way toward the smoking village. Their faces were covered with dust and sweat and they barely breathed for fear of the sights they would see. Children ran burned and naked and screaming. A mother lay bleeding at the doorstep of her burning house. It seemed as though there were fire everywhere, as if even the dirt were burning.

"Dear God! *Jezes,* Jesus!" Nezka cried, crossing herself. She ran to the door of a burning house where she heard the sounds of a woman's screams. It was too late. There was no way to reach her in the flames.

Lojze was suddenly sober. His mouth was wet and hung open stupidly. He stood stunned and unable to move for several minutes. All around him the earth smoked. Piles of wood, straw, refuse were strewn everywhere. Bodies of men, women and children lay crumpled and broken in the dirt. Finally able to connect his will to his body, he moved his foot forward and took a step. Then he took another and his foot landed on something soft and pliable. He looked down and saw he was standing on the body of a dead dog. He screamed in horror. And then suddenly he began running toward the burning row of houses. At the first house he rushed inside. In less than thirty seconds he emerged carrying in his arms an old man wrapped in a scorched blanket. He lay the man down on the street and ran to the next house.

Nezka helped drag the wounded bodies to shady spots beneath trees. They wrapped wounds in leaves and rags.

Then the gunfire began. They ran for cover behind a tree and then kept running. They ran straight through the low brush and thicket, crawled around gulleys and slopes, crossed a brook, and waited in the washed-up silt in the heat of the sun. What was left of the railroad tracks lay ahead of them. They had been blown to bits. They would have to walk to Celje.

The smell of smoke and burning flesh stuck in their nostrils. Their hands were blood-stained and burned and their bodies and clothes reeked of smoke, burning flesh and sulphur. Nezka shuddered and tears streaked through the mud and dust on her face. She knelt in the dirt and began to pray. "Thank you, Lord, for saving us from death. Our bodies are not suffering because you have protected us. But, Lord, please, look down upon these others. O dearest Savior, dearest Lord!"

Lojze was huddled beside her. His breathing was irregular and his body jerked spasmodically. His hands, arms and face were burned and his skin and clothes were covered with streaks of black blood, soot and dirt. He vomited without even making an effort to turn his head. Nezka reached her hand to him and held his neck.

It was hot and there was little breeze in the forest. All around them was the sound of gunfire. Nezka remembered the last war. Soon it would stop. Then the soldiers would come in with their monster machines, take what they wanted, clean up the bodies and move into the village. That's how it was done.

Lojze sat with his head between his knees whimpering. Nezka scooped up some swampy water and dampened his head and face.

But the pain was more than he could bear. Remembering that the *Partizani* had taken his brandy, he cried, "Ah, the devil!"

"No, husband," she answered, "not the devil! It is God who has saved your skin! It is God!"

He turned angrily and, with a blow from the back of his hand, hit her across the face. Tumbling backwards, she fell into the stream with her head facing upwards toward the sky. Lojze was immediately sorry. He needed her.

On June 22 the German blitzkrieg rolled across the Soviet border. Josip Broz Tito was not a man to allow Jugoslavia's defeat. He called upon the workers and peasants for a guerrilla war. In a proclamation printed on secret presses and carried to all parts of Jugoslavia he declared:

> The hour has struck to take arms. . . . Do your part in the fight for freedom under the leadership of the Communist Party of Jugoslavia. The war of the Soviet Union is your war, because the Soviet Union is fighting against your enemies, under whose yoke your neck is bent.

And he gave Jugoslavs the fiery war cry: *Better grave than slave!*[1]

At first the Partisan guerrilla fighters were like troublesome mice. The warfare they waged was small-scale, like vermin chewing the flanks of stallions. Attacks were coordinated so that German troops walked into traps or were mined in transit. Partisan sabotage squads cut phone lines, attacked Nazis in dark streets of occupied cities and stole their weapons. They set German vehicles on fire by dripping delayed incendiaries into gas tanks. They dynamited trains and bridges. They blew up airfield hangars and burned Nazi newspapers.

Celje's streets were dark and still. The houses, closely fit together, lined both sides of the narrow streets. Lojze was too sick to walk another step. Nezka, her face swollen up to her eyebrows, held him up with his arm around her shoulders. That night they slept without food or water in a field by the road to Maribor.

"I think your stepfather would have died," Nezka wrote in a letter to Jozeca, "if it had not been for a man on a bicycle who was riding through the field on a little path. He took us to his home where your stepfather received first aid and some of that devilish liquor which he craves. I also received first aid for a wound on my face and head and some burns. Praise be to God, we can thank Him for all things. But I shall never forget the sound of those women crying in that burning village. . . ."

---

1. Archer, Jules, *Tito of Yugoslavia*.

The bombings were now frequent. And people were dying not only at the hands of the enemy, but also of disease and starvation. The Partisan activities were horribly punished by the Germans. Wall posters went up all over Serbia and other parts of Jugoslavia: FOR EVERY GERMAN WHO IS FOUND KILLED, ONE HUNDRED JUGOSLAVS WILL BE SHOT.

Anyone suspected of helping the Partisans was shot and his home burned. Soldiers would open fire with light machine guns on suspected Partisan saboteurs.

In the town of Kragujevac in Bosnia the Partisans dynamited a train and killed fifty Germans, injuring one hundred more. The German district commander was enraged and arrested all men between sixteen and sixty years of age in town. Groups of one hundred and one hundred fifty at a time stood before firing squads and were mowed down with machine guns. It was estimated 9,000 civilians had been killed. There was mourning in every house in the town. In another town in Bosnia, Kraljevo, 1,700 people were executed by the Germans. They sang as they died:

O Slavs, you are still alive,
The Slav spirit will survive centuries. . . .

Many women joined the *Partisanom*. In fact, one out of four of Tito's volunteer guerrillas was a woman. A pretty young neighbor of Jozeca's explained to her, "I love my country as much as the men do. Why should I not fight for it?"

Jozeca struggled for words, "I want to bless you, but it is difficult for me to bless killing."

"You would not defend freedom for you and your children? Look at your son! Do you want to live under tyranny or freedom?"

Jozeca paused. "I want him to live under the laws of God and to know and love Him."

"Fffff on your God!" the young woman spat. "Do the priests not bless and sprinkle holy water over the guns and planes of the enemy? Do the priests not kill with one hand and hold the Scriptures with the other? How can you talk of such nonsense?"

"Man makes the nonsense, not God. He does not start wars, man does."

"And which side does He bless? Tell me that."

"God loves all men, all. But He especially draws close to those who love Him, those who choose to be His children."

"We are under the thumb of the invader! Do you forget the history of our country, Jozeca? Long live the Slavs! Long live Tito! If it had been up to God, we would have perished as a nation!"

"*Ne! Ne!* It is because of God that we survive today. And I believe we will survive this war! and I believe that our country will prosper and that the Swastika will not fly over our land."

The woman spread the palm of her hand before her face. "You may stay behind in the village, but I will suffer and fight with the *Partizani*. It is far better than being captured by the Nazis or their Ustase pigs."

"Everyone is killing everybody else," Jozeca exclaimed in despair. "It seems like nobody can trust anybody anymore. Husbands cannot trust wives, parents cannot trust children, brothers cannot trust brothers."

It was dinner time and she sat with her hands on her apron staring at the empty table. She had made some soup out of a cabbage and onion at noon and that was all they had to eat that day.

"Jakob," she said, "today a young boy, ten years of age, led the Nazis to his father's house and showed him the wireless hidden there. The father and mother were both shot and the child was taken to a work camp." Tears hovered at the edges of her eyelids. "Do you know why the boy did it? He wanted a piece of bread."

They held hands and got to their knees on the floor. "Almighty God! Holy Father! Look down upon this people!" They prayed into the night. There were no easy answers in this *borba*, this struggle, such as can be decided in times of peace. Perhaps in times of peace it is easy to say, "We do not receive the blessings of God because we are not doing such-and-such right. If we want God to bless us, all we have to do is thus-and-so."

But here there were no prescriptions for answered prayer and prosperity. Prosperity in itself was a word unknown to the peasants and workers of Jugoslavia.

Jakob and Jozeca prayed and believed that if the Balkans would turn to the Lord, turn to Him who stood with His arms outstretched, then He would prosper and bless them with peace. They knew the greatest joy above joys—that of belonging to perfect love, perfect wholeness, perfect eternity in Christ. The burning desire of their souls was to see Jugoslavia know the Lord God and love Him who sent His Son to die for them and make them truly free.

The German Panzer divisions were roaring toward them, yet Jozeca and Jakob believed passionately that they would not be overcome. Man makes war. God makes love. The enemy could burn their cities and towns, but they could not take their soul, their spirit. This they knew and believed.

Hunger, disease and fear spread through the towns and villages, one being worse than the other. There were not enough hospital facilities for the sick and wounded and there was not enough food for the people. There were the continual air raids, the sound of Stukas dipping and screaming overhead. The bombs fell, killing many and leaving many homeless.

Work in the mine ceased. It was not uncommon for families to separate during the *borba*. People had to "follow the bread," go to where there was work and food to eat. Often the Germans split families apart, removing fathers and mothers to different cities to work in German factories or to Germany to work in labor camps.

The morning arrived when Jozeca had no choice but to pack a small grip with her belongings and prepare to leave her husband and her house to find work. Both she and Jakob knew it was the only thing to do—they had known it for some time. The thought had been a dread but now the reality of that dread was here. "Just for a little while, Jakob, my love," she said, not looking at him.

He could not answer. The letter from her mother was still on the table. There was work for women in the factory in Celje. Jozeca should come at once.

Young Josip sat on the bed by the wall. His cheeks were scrubbed clean and he wore pants Jozeca had made from a shirt of Jakob's and a bright green sweater she knit out of yarn from a shawl.

Jakob could not leave Trbovlje because of the people in the church. If he were to go away, there would be nobody to lead the church, to encourage and help the people. Pastors were as rare to find as a Viennese pastry.

"Ah, Jakob, my love, my dearest, we will be apart just for a little while, just until things are a little better, *ne*? When things are a little better—in a month or so, I will come home to you and we will be once again together."

"Yes," he answered dryly, "when things get a little better. . . ."

But things were not going to get better. They both knew it.

He held his son fiercely and kissed him on his cheeks. "Be a man, my boy," he said, struggling to keep a smile on his lips. "Take care of your *Mamica*."

He raised his eyes to Jozeca. In the pale early morning light his skin looked yellow and ragged, and he suddenly seemed older than he was just yesterday. "Wherever you are, my love," he said quietly, still holding onto his smile, "you take me with you—for you are my heart."

She kissed his hands and his face, spilling her tears onto his wrists and neck. "It will not be for long, my husband . . . it will not be for long."

Chapter Sixteen

The flat in Celje was on the third floor of a crude low building behind a factory. The stairways were dark and unlit and dirty, not at all like the homes in Trbovlje where the people took pride in their dwelling places, keeping them spotlessly clean. There were several other small buildings like this one, forming a kind of square around a concrete block. Josip followed her quietly up the steps. Cousin Andrej answered the door when she knocked. He was a short, muscular man with thick brown hair and small green eyes. He shook her hand. The others inside welcomed her with sober faces, each shaking her hand and then shaking Josip's hand.

"Welcome."

There were seven of them already living in the tiny two-room flat, including Jozeca's mother and Lojze. The five cousins, her mother's actually, sat on the beds and leaned against the stove. Now there would be nine of them crammed into this tiny space. It was the war, though, and one must not think only of one's own skin.

That night she slept on the floor with a brown frayed greatcoat wrapped around her and Josip. She prayed as she listened to the sounds of the others breathing.

"Thank you, Lord," she whispered into the sleeve of the coat. "Thank you for bringing me and my son safely to this place. But Lord, do not be angry with me. I confess I long for the presence of my husband. . . ."

The next day after registering with the police, she went to the factory where her mother had arranged a job for her. She was stunned to discover the factory was German-run and her job was to stand in an assembly line and put together German hand grenades. The pinkness in her cheeks faded when she realized what she had to do and she trembled so badly she could not hold the instruments in her hands. After a few days she was transferred to the department which made ceramic dishes. In spite of her knowing that God loved them as well as he loved the Jugoslavs, it still made her sick to be working for the Germans. Though the workers at the factory were Jugoslavs, many of them spoke German.

"Mama, how could you—you, a Slovene—how could you work for those Germans who are here to take our country from us—take

our language like the Italians tried to do? Mama, do not you remember when you were a child what they tried to do to our country?"

Her mother licked her lip. "Ah, Jozeca, you know so little. Have
you ever gone without bread so that your belly swells up to your
chin? Have you?"

A voice startled them. A man was sitting by the window near
Lojze and holding a bottle of plum brandy in his hand. He was
a giant of a man with black hairy arms and hands. "Foolish women
with foolish talk!"

"Ah, Screcko, it is you sitting in the shadows," said her mother
sourly. "Why do you not let yourself be known instead of scaring
two tired women out of their wits?"

The hairy giant grunted, "What difference does it make which
side you make the guns for? Everybody will kill everybody else
off in the end anyhow."

Her mother put her face close to Jozeca's. "Watch out for this
one," she whispered. "He is famous around here for being a bully.
He loves a fight and beats up anybody he can get his hands on."

"What is he doing here with Lojze?"

"Your stepfather finds him amusing—besides, Screcko is also
a drunk. Drunks like to drink together but in reality they hate each
other."

Days and hours and weeks went by, each one bringing more
terrible news. Always stuck in their nostrils was the smell of gun
powder and sulphur and always in their ears the sound of air bombers,
mortars, tanks and machine guns. Jozeca ached for Jakob, for his
strength and wisdom. Every night she prayed the war would end
so she could go home to him. But it would be one year before she
would see his face again.

Although they worked hard, there was never enough food. There
were not enough beds, chairs or water for everyone and often out
of frustration and weariness, voices were raised in anger. It was
usually Lojze who started the arguments. He was the only one in
the family who did no work. He sat in a chair by the window all
day with his bottle of *rakia* until he was too drunk to sit up any
longer. Jozeca hated to be near him when he was drunk and especially
if that hairy beast, Screcko, were with him.

Jozeca spent many hours in prayer. "I know, Lord, that if I
do not hear your voice, know your will, there will be no peace for
me. All that my eye sees is destruction and death. In you is life
and love. I must hear from you and know you or else I perish like
rot."

More and more men and women were joining Tito's National Liberation Army. A new patriotic fire was kindled as a result of the atrocities committed by the Ustase and the Nazis. Fighters numbering in the thousands joined the guerrillas.

Both male and female Partisans had to take the passionate oath Tito had written:

> . . . In the name of liberty and justice for our people, we swear that we shall be disciplined, persevering and fearless. That we shall spare neither blood nor life in fighting the Fascist invaders and all traitors to the people until they are completely annihilated.

The Germans retaliated viciously for their losses. In Macra the Nazi soldiers slaughtered men, women and children, then covered their bodies with flour to dispose of them to hungry pigs. At Cajetina, German tanks wounded sixty Partisans, then deliberately ran over them with tanks as they tried to crawl away.

Jozeca continued to watch and pray, though the faith of many of the believers waned. She must remain strong for their sakes. She realized that God prevailed in spite of circumstances, in spite of the turmoil of the world.

One night she was walking home from the factory. The street was so black she could not see but a few steps in front of her. All around she could hear the sound of other footsteps. People were walking home to their own flats, but she could not see them.

"O God, O Jesus, Lord!" she prayed quietly under her breath. "I love you in spite of the *borba*. I love you in spite of the blood on the streets and the machine guns and the tanks and the Swastika. Yes, Lord, I love you in war and I love you in peace. I love you even though my husband is far away from me. I love you even if I never see his dear face again. . . ."

When she arrived at the flat her son, Josip, was sitting on the outside step waiting for her. A broad grin stretched across his face when he saw her and he scrambled to his feet to run to her.

"Josip!" she cried, "what are you doing outside like this?"

He was surprised at her outburst.

"You must never sit outside on the step like this! It is dangerous!"

He shrank, the smile on his face faded.

"Never go outside alone, Josip! Never!" and she whacked him across his backside with the palm of her hand.

Josip was hurt at this reception. He turned his head, fighting tears, and answered, "Yes, Mama."

She took his hand and led him up the stairs to the little flat.

After the formal *Zdravo's* and How are you's, Jozeca cried, "My little boy was outside by himself in front of the building!"

Her mother answered curtly, "Jozeca, you must train your son yourself. Is it our fault? He is four years old now, old enough to take care of himself."

In spite of her warnings, Josip would still sneak away from the flat during the days and find his way to the factory where his mother worked. Passing the German guards in search of her, he would, at last, find her at her work. She would be horrified to see his little blond head moving between the rows of workers. "*Moj* Josip! O God! O Jesus! O Mother of God!"

One cruel morning when Lojze fell asleep at the window, Josip put a small loaf of bread into his coat pocket and left the flat. He had not gone more than a block when he met a German soldier with a rifle strapped to his back. Josip stopped in his tracks, frightened. The German shouted, "Halt!"

Josip was terrified and ran. The soldier was amused at his impudence and playfully chased him. Josip could not outrun him. When the soldier caught him he picked him up by the pants and laughingly swung him through the air. Josip screamed and writhed and spit in the German's face. At this the soldier became outraged and heaved him through the air like a toy. Josip hit the wall of a building and then fell into a heap on the ground. The furious soldier gave him a kick with his jackboot; "I ought to kill you, you dirty little mouse. I ought to peel your skin and roast you like a potato."

Josip lay there some time before he tried to get to his feet. There was a large lump on his head and he bit his tongue so he would not cry. Then he limped toward the factory where Jozeca worked. Not daring to go inside, he hovered in a corner until noontime when she would come outside to sit on the grass. He held his tears until he saw her and then he could not be brave another second. He ran to her, clutching her legs, and to her horror, fainted in her arms.

That was the beginning of Josip's strange behavior which lasted for several years. It began slowly at first, almost unnoticeably; but if Jozeca was there when it happened, she would see the boy's skin suddenly turn pale and his lips begin to tremble. His hands would tremble and then his entire body would start shaking until he was almost in a state of unconsciousness.

"What happens here when I am at the factory?" she demanded of Lojze.

He glared at her out of his red-rimmed eyes. "Who allows you to speak with me in this way?" he growled. "I will put your nose where your ears are if you speak to me like this."

"I ask you what I want to know! Have you been beating my son?"

He sneered.

"Answer my question. Have you been beating my son?"

Lojze tipped his bottle to his chin. "Only if he deserves it. And you would hardly call a few light taps on the head a beating."

Jozeca gasped.

"That boy needs to learn respect," he continued, "something you, Jozeca, and your dear mother never learned."

Jozeca drew close to Lojze, her body shaking in anger. "I will protect my son from you! It does not matter the cost."

His lips puckered in an odd smile. "Ah yes, it is most amusing to live with these dear and blessed saints of God! So pure and holy they are—never losing their temper!"

She ran from the room in tears. "O God, O Jesus, forgive me. Forgive me."

Later that night they gathered in the kitchen to pray, the five cousins, her mother and two neighbors. Jozeca confessed to the family how she had lashed out at Lojze. Again she was admonished, "Josip is old enough to take care of himself."

The next morning Jozeca brought Josip to the kindergarten instead of leaving him home with Lojze. When she asked the boy if Lojze beat him, he only stared at her with wide, frightened eyes.

"God of heaven, look upon this child and heal him of these evil memories."

Then they heard the awful sirens of the Gestapo. The sound always made her heart stop beating. Josip clung to her.

Chapter Seventeen

Lojze sat quietly by the window drumming a finger on his knee. They had all left. "Ravens, all of them. Out to have me killed. That fool wife, forever whining and nagging. What good was she to a man anyhow? What man could put up with such a woman? And that disgusting daughter!"

The first swallow of *rakia* burned his throat and he sighed and made a clucking sound in his throat. They will all have me killed— raving fools—all of them raving over a book. Bible fools. They will get my skin boiled.

He stared across the room at the Bible by the bed against the wall. Maybe it will burn like dead leaves—yes. . . . He stood to his feet and walked haltingly, legs stiff, to the bed. Then he heard the cries of women, the barking of dogs, he felt the flames surrounding his back and his neck. It seemed as if the bombs were falling all around him. He stood on the backbone of a dead dog; its blood was still warm. He fell on his knees, the Bible tightly in his hands, and wept like a newborn baby.

That is how the Gestapo found him. He did not realize they had him by the arms and legs until he tried to stretch a muscle in his back. "But what is this?"

"Is this the one?"

"*Ja. Ja.* This is the one. He fits the description."

"But what—?" Lojze could not tell whether he was still dreaming or if he were actually being yanked down the steps of the building toward the waiting Gestapo truck.

They struck him on the head with a stick. "We shoot your kind," said the big one wearing the rubber coat.

"Huh?"

"Leading Partisan meetings here, are you? And calling them religious prayer meetings!"

Lojze was dumbfounded. "Have you a drink?"

"Do not deny it! Did we not find you on your knees with a Bible? And last night did you not lead a secret Partisan meeting right here in this building?"

They shoved him into the wagon and, before anyone in the neighborhood saw what was happening, the wagon was gone, its sickening siren honking in the distance.

"O God, have mercy!" Jozeca prayed as it drove past, not knowing that the man inside was her stunned stepfather, accused of being a Bible believer and organizer of illegal meetings.

He sat in the police station looking small and shriveled, smoking a cigarette. He stared at the floor and would not look at Jozeca when they pushed her into the cell at the end of the hall. Her mother followed, stumbling into the wall from the force of the Nazi police captain.

It seemed that Lojze had "confessed." Under a bit of Gestapo persuasion, he said that the people he lived with were definitely enemies of the Führer. For his patriotic gesture he was awarded ten German cigarettes, a litre of rum, and released.

Jozeca was frantic, "My son! My son is alone!" She knew Josip would try to find her. "Oh, please, please, have mercy!" she called to the German guards. "I am a mother and my son, my little boy, is alone with no one to care for him! Please, please, have mercy. Think of your own mother! Do you have mothers? Mercy, I beg you, mercy!"

Her own mother snorted and waved her hands at her. "For the love of Mary, will you stop, Jozeca?"

"Mother, my little boy! My son!"

"*Ja, ja*—so he is alone. What can you do about it? You are here in this jail. Here you will stay. Now quiet down so your mother can rest and think."

"O *Jezes, Marija*. O Lord, help me. Help me!"

She clenched her fists together and waved them above her head. Back and forth she paced. "Hear me, God! Hear me!"

All night Jozeca paced and cried out. The thought of Lojze alone with Josip was too terrible. Supposing he beat little Josip. God only knew what he might do to him with nobody around to stop him.

"O Jesus, sweet Lord, hear me! This is the son given to me by your own hand—so that he would bless my husband and me. O God! Dear holy Jesus!"

The guard shouted for her to be still. But on and on she raved. Her hands were numb from clenching together so tightly. "Hear me, Lord! Help me!"

She did not stop calling out and crying for two days. She refused food and at night would not sleep.

Chapter Eighteen

It was cold, that morning in Trbovlje. Jakob walked passed the women who were digging the trenches in the side of the hill. Their faces were lined with dirt and sweat and their arms were thick with muscle and sweaters. "Our women are like none in the world," he thought. "They are strong, hard working, good—like my Jozeca."

These women were digging trenches for the Germans, the only work there was for women in Trbovlje. Jakob prayed for his wife who he thought was now at her job in the factory in Celje. But he felt uneasy, uncomfortable. He tried again to pray. "Lord, bless my wife—" but he had the feeling of a person on a train going in the wrong direction, or when the soup is without salt. Then, there in the field, to the chinking sound of shovels hitting gravel, he got on his knees. He prayed out loud, "God, have mercy! Mercy!" He did not understand why he wept or why he prayed as he did, but he continued to pray out loud, not caring who saw him or heard his words.

That afternoon, without any explanation, Jozeca and her mother were released from jail. Their names were called, the door was unlocked and they were set free.

"It was a miracle, Lojze," Nezka told the stupified man hunched in his spot by the window. "God himself released us from that hell of a place."

His mouth hung open and then he said, "It is hot—the fire—the fire is burning my mouth, my throat. Do you have something to drink? God in heaven, I'm burning up, woman!"

Josip had waited on the steps for Jozeca to come home, and a woman with four sons of her own found him sleeping with his head in his arms, still sitting on the steps in the early hours of the morning. She quickly brought him inside before the Gestapo found him and he stayed in her flat for the next two days while Jozeca was in jail. Jozeca wept with joy when she found him. "I thank you with my whole heart," she told the woman. "God will bless you for your kindness."

"My name is Franciska," the woman said, "and I know you are a praying woman. Will you pray for me?"

"Yes," answered Jozeca, not anticipating what lay ahead. She sat on the chair by the bed and listened as the tears rolled down the woman's face and she told her story. "I am a Serb. My husband is a Slovene. Recently I received the news that my six brothers were killed—" she stopped and sobbed vigorously. "My six brothers—living in Kordum in Serbia—were murdered in cold blood—by Ustase soldiers!

"But that is not all." She paused to blow her nose. "After the killers had murdered my brothers, they pushed out their eyeballs with spoons and—" She could not continue.

"How horrible!"

"My brothers were Cetniks; they fought under Mihailovic. O God, they pushed out their eyeballs—and when my old mother came home, these killers met her at the door and presented her with a bread basket covered with a handkerchief. She removed the handkerchief and found the eyes of her sons."

"God have mercy."

"Then they took my mother away—those Ustase. Oh, how they hate the Serbs!"

The woman was sobbing wildly now. She put her face in her apron. Jozeca sat frozen, clinging to the edge of the chair.

"They carried my mother off in a wagon, God knows what they intended to do with her—but the *Partizani* captured them. My poor old mother was insane with grief. The *Partizani* executed the Ustase for what they did and my mother threw herself at those Ustase screaming—and, O God, she beat at them and clawed their faces. After they were dead and the bullets were rammed through their bodies, she lifted her skirts and danced in their blood."

"O Jesus, Mary and Joseph."

"What am I to do? She was released by the *Partizani* and they knew she was insane. Now I have her on my hands to take care of. An old aunt who was there saw what had happened. They brought her here to me."

The old woman sat by the stove. Jozeca was startled when she turned and saw the old crone sitting there, glaring into space, seeing things nobody else could see.

Jozeca felt utterly helpless. It was all so terrible. So awful. "Please, *Gospa*," the young woman pleaded, "you are a woman of prayer. I know you are. I have heard. I beg you, pray for my mother. Pray for me. We need your help."

Jozeca could not move. She felt sick to her stomach. She had seen troubles in her life but this was too awful, too awful. She really did not know how to pray. She wanted to run—run home to Jakob and wrap herself in his arms, enclose herself in his voice, his strength, his wisdom. The old woman leered at her from across the room and began to rock and moan.

Then Jozeca rose to her feet and raised her hands to the ceiling. "Jesus!" she shouted. The sound of her own voice startled her. "I am praying for these women now, Lord! Do you hear me, dear Jesus? Look down on me here! These women need you! Hear me!" She prayed for a full twenty minutes. Then she ordered the women on their knees. Josip got on his knees also and so did the four little boys who had been cowering against the wall. "I command peace and beauty here in the name of Jesus!" She had never prayed with such authority and power; it was overwhelming. The presence of the Lord was so near in the room that they could hardly keep their balance. Jozeca felt herself toppling to one side, but she held on and prayed even louder. "Lord! Lord Jesus! Help us! Restore this old woman's senses!"

Ah, the Serbs and Croats—would they ever stop killing each other? It was so terrible, so disgusting. God alone could help these people whose hatred spread across generations and God alone could heal this mad woman's mind.

She prayed through the night for the two women. When they heard the shuffle of feet outside on the pavement, they knew it was morning and the workers were going to the factories. Jozeca stroked the face of the old woman who closed her eyes and seemed to be at peace. Franciska cried in a very small voice that she had not seen her mother with such an expression of peace since the beginning of the *borba*. She lifted her hands to the ceiling and exclaimed, "God of All, you are God! I believe you and I worship you!"

Every night Jozeca visited the two women and the four little boys. They read the Bible together, prayed together and Jozeca taught them some little songs. Then a miracle happened that was to change Jozeca so drastically that she would never be the same again.

The old woman, her face deeply furrowed and so thin that her bones rubbed against each other, called Jozeca to her side. "I am going to lie down soon," she said. "I am going to lie down and when I do I will never rise up again. And they will lay me into the earth."

Jozeca murmured and took her hand. "Now listen to me, child," the old woman continued in a deep throaty voice, "I will die with a heart that is not blackened with bitterness. God is the avenger. I forgive the Ustase for killing my sons."

Jozeca gasped and then wept uncontrollably. She held the old woman in her arms and knew without a doubt that God is a great God and that nothing, utterly nothing, in this world is impossible to Him.

Chapter Nineteen

News got around quickly about Jozeca, the woman of prayer. In the complex of workers' flats, gray dull buildings surrounded by little rivers of concrete and empty lots strewn with garbage and litter, they heard of the woman who prayed and miracles resulted. They heard about the old Serbian woman's tragedy—how the Ustase had boasted over the eyeballs of her sons; they had seen the old woman, mad with grief, and they had kept their distance from her. But now she appeared at the market with her basket under her arm and she seemed peaceful. She now walked with a calmness about her and her eyes were no longer crazy. The people were amazed. God had performed a miracle and restored her mind.

Soon mothers were bringing their children to Jozeca for prayer, wives brought their husbands, children brought their parents.

Late one night Jozeca and the others were sleeping and awoke to the sound of knocking. They were silent, listening, not sure if it was the Gestapo or not. Whoever it was continued to rain blows against the door until cousin Andrej answered it. A small boy stood timidly in the dark hallway.

"It is Screcko's son!" Andrej told the others in the darkness.

"*Zdravo*, forgive me for alarming you at this hour."

"*Zdravo*. Yes, boy, please? what is it?"

"Help me! Help me!"

Andrej pulled him into the room and closed the door. In the dark the boy cried, "My father is killing my mother. Please come. Please, I have come to fetch the praying lady."

Andrej turned to Jozeca who was now out of bed and standing in the middle of the floor near them.

Her cousin spoke in her direction. "I will go. I know this man, Screcko. He is a brute with the temper of a wolf. I had better go."

"*Ne!*" wailed the boy. "Only the praying woman can help! *Please!* Before he kills my mother!"

Jozeca dressed with fumbling fingers and followed the boy to his flat in the next building. They had to be careful not to be seen by the Gestapo because the penalty for being out after the curfew was prison.

"God, help us," whispered Jozeca.

They arrived safely at the flat and found the woman lying in a heap on the floor and Screcko sitting at the table with his head in his hands.

"God, help me!" whispered Jozeca again.

Hairy arms matted with sweat and blood, he looked up, startled to see Jozeca there.

"What do you want?"

"Shame on you!" Jozeca said loudly, surprised at her boldness. "Shame!"

"Huh?"

"You heard me! I said shame! You oafish brute! Beating on a small creature like this woman. You call yourself a man?"

No one spoke. The woman rose slowly, painfully. She was bleeding from the mouth. "Do you not know this is the *borba*? How is it that you make such a disturbance? Do you want us all to be thrown into prison? Where are your senses?"

"This lazy woman—" he started.

"Shame on you! Shame! God gave you this woman. What is her name?"

"Ana."

"God gave you Ana to love and cherish, and you treat her like a goat, abusing her honor, disgracing yourself! Now what do you suppose God thinks about that?"

"You speak of God?"

"Shame, I say! Here is the woman who bore you this son, this woman who is your wife and your companion, who serves you faithfully—yet you beat her!"

Screcko struggled for breath, staring at Jozeca in disbelief. He knew that if he were a man worth his mustache he should strike this intruder down dead. Who did she think she was, intruding in his home like this? A woman! But somehow he could not move. He stared, dumb-mouthed.

Jozeca waved her finger in his face. "Listen to me, Screcko; if you ever touch this woman again except with the hands of love, God will punish you. Do you hear? Do you?"

"*Ja. Ja.*"

"Before the eyes of God and the eyes of the holy angels, take her up and tell her you are sorry for what you did to her."

Rage covered his face. To do such a thing would be out of the question! No man could think of being called a man if he apologized to a woman. Ridiculous! He would rather eat poison. Yet he slowly reached out his hand to the woman cowering against the table. His face softened. He stammered, then said, "I am sorry, I am sorry. God, forgive me."

The change in Screcko was apparent to everyone who knew him. "Impossible!" the neighbors clucked, wagging their heads. "It is impossible for such a man to change."

But it was true. The violent and nasty-tempered Screcko who beat his wife as frequently as he urinated had actually become a quiet and gentle man. He had surrendered his heart and will to the Lord Jesus Christ, and the change was miraculously sudden.

At first he found himself weeping each time he tried to pray. He wept as he walked the dark streets to the factory in the morning and he wept at the machine he operated. He wept at his evening meal sitting beside Ana, his wife, and his son, Stane. Often he wept late into the night as he lay trying to sleep with the moonlight playing on his forehead.

God had touched Screcko and it was something glorious, something that affected his entire being. He knew that night in the dim light with Ana lying bleeding on the floor that something was happening to him. That woman, that praying woman, had caused it. She brought God into the room with her, she did. She stood there with her eyes flashing and her lips trembling and he knew he could not argue—he knew the fight was over. A new fight was beginning.

The *borba* had been hard on Screcko—not only physically but mentally. He had nightmares that he was transformed into a skunk and the boots of Bosnian Partisans were trampling him to death. He would have joined the Partisans long ago but he was afraid to die. This fear of dying plagued him until the only peace he found was when he passed out in a drunken roar. When he was drunk he hated everything because he related everything to himself. But now God had touched him. Now he had the freedom he had craved. Now he was released from the heavy chains of his own fears. God had done it. God had done it.

Ana, his wife, was the last person to understand the change which had taken place in Screcko. She goaded him, prodded him. "Are you a man?" she gloated. "Are you a man to sit weeping at the table like an old woman? Are your eyes damned that they can only shed tears? Answer me! Answer me! By the eyes in your head, say something."

Screcko endured her nagging calmly. For years she had cried out to heaven to have mercy on her and change her husband. Now that her prayers had been answered, her longsuffering righteousness vanished, poof, like smoke from the barrel of a gun. She needed to suffer. It was her way of proving that she was good, remarkably good. Without realizing it, she really wanted her husband to renounce love and decency and return to his old beastly ways, which eventually would lead him to his own demise. Then she could again righteously weep for his rotten soul and love herself for enduring with patience.

Perhaps Ana typified the anguished women of the Balkans who for centuries lived as chattle and only now in the *borba* were able to receive status and recognition as human beings equal to men. It was hard to adjust.

But at Petrovac in 1942 Tito called a conference of women patriots, anti-Fascists and Partisans from all over Jugoslavia. He thanked them not only for being magnificent fighters but also for being an indispensable supply corps. He promised women complete equality with men in a postwar Jugoslavia. "You have more than earned it by shedding your blood, too, in combat on the battlefield," he said.

News reached the workers in Celje of events in Serbia, Bosnia and Montenegro. The Anti-Fascist Council of National Liberation (AVNOJ) met in Bihac on November 27, 1942, and the delegates were moved to tears as they heard the testimonies of the mountain peasants.

Srecko knew a Partisan named Ivo who had been at that conference. Ivo was a Serb and he had fought with the Cetniks who were on the side of the Nazis, at the beginning of the war; but then, like many others, defected to the Jugoslav Partisans. He told Jozeca and the others one night in the dim light of Srecko's flat what he had heard and seen at that conference. When he was finished there was not a dry eye in the room.

"An old Serb limped up to the platform. He looked vaguely familiar but he was so disfigured. He began to speak and he told us how the Ustase came and gathered his whole village into the little schoolhouse.

"He told us how our people were bound up with ropes and then divided into categories. One group was to have their throats cut, another group was to be thrown into pits and killed with grenades. Another group of girls and women were to be raped and then pushed under the river ice. The children were smashed to death against rocks or else they were impaled on hayforks."

The Serb stopped there to wipe his eye with the back of his hand. "The old man told how his own little grandson, brown as a walnut, eyes as black as the earth, was run through with a hayfork and left hanging against the barn wall."

Srecko pushed his face into his hands. "Somehow the old man lived," Ivo continued. "He was thrown into a pit but he got out, badly wounded but alive. It took him a day and a half to work his way out of the pile of mutilated dead bodies and rubble."

Nezka crossed herself. The room was still. The Partisan breathed deeply, and pulled a gray cap out of his pocket, a red star sewn on the front.

Srecko was the first to speak. It was a prayer, really; he spoke softly, and gradually his voice rose in a crescendo. "Help our people, Lord Jesus, help our people. Our brother here is an Orthodox, others here are Catholic. Our people are also Moslem. You and you alone know how desperately our country needs you! You and you alone, Lord God! No political system will save us from ourselves!"

The Serb's head bobbed up. Screcko praying? And as profoundly and sweetly as jam on a spoon?

The next morning Screcko packed his socks, boots, heavy sweater and coat and left with Ivo to join the *Partizani* in the mountains. His son, Stane, watched him prepare to leave, his face solemn.

"I will not kill," Screcko told his son, "but I will work like ten horses and I will also pray. Only God can help our Jugoslavia. Only God."

"Yes, Papa. I believe also."

Ana wept bitterly, angry that he would leave his family, hurt that he did not realize she had needs of her own. How would she live without a man?

"Woman, you do not need a man. You need the Lord Jesus Christ."

She blew her nose on her apron.

"Ana! Listen! I can face the bullets without fear. The Lord has given me courage. Ah, I see it so clearly. I see it with the eyes of my heart. There is no courage without God. To give my body to be burned means nothing if it is not given in love. I give myself gladly in love. Can you understand? I give myself gladly because I give myself to the Lord! In Him there is no death!"

Jozeca, her cousins, her mother and the other believers gathered to pray for Screcko and for Ivo. They blessed them both and hugged their necks. "Carry us in your hearts," Screcko said. They held their arms up with their fists clenched in the symbol of prayer, and were gone.

Screcko became a well-known name in the workers' blocks of flats and in the houses along the road and in the *kavarna*. The story of his conversion gained broader proportions with each telling. Some said how an angel of God appeared and covered Screcko with sunbeams from heaven and anointed him as a prophet to his people. Others said he was really St. Paul come back to earth.

Jozeca listened to the stories with a heavy heart. The people desperately wanted to believe in a God of miracles. They had for so long believed in the power of men and armies and governments; they were so full of longing to know the Lord that they were even willing to make up stories of His miracles.

She began to pray that the Lord would really show himself in miracles, real ones, ones that were true and directly from the gates of heaven, so that the people would not have to make them up out of their own minds.

"Nevertheless," she prayed, "if you choose not to move in

94

miraculous ways with this stubborn but hungry people, I will love you, Lord! I will love you!" Her arms swayed above her head. "Nothing, no nothing, will take my eyes from the One Way! The one living and holy God! Not war, not suffering, and not even silence from heaven!"

Chapter Twenty

Winter was folding in on the city and the hills and mountains. There was no heat in the flat except for the heat from the cooking stove. They were cold but not as cold as the people in the mountains where the soldiers were freezing and starving to death—Germans, Italians and Jugoslavs alike.

One night after they had eaten their supper of chicken soup and black bread, cousin Andrej took out the worn Bible and began to read aloud. Jozeca sat on the floor holding Josip in her arms. Nezka was by the window near Lojze. The shades were drawn and the light was dim. He read in a low voice:

He that overcometh, the same shall be clothed in white raiment;
and I will not blot out his name out of the book of life, but I will
confess his name before my Father, and before his angels. [1]

Then they heard a soft tapping on the door. It could not be the police. They do not knock so gently. They sat utterly still. Then another knock.

"Brothers," a voice whispered, "it is I, Jakob."

Jozeca scrambled to her feet. "Jakob!"

Andrej opened the door slowly, carefully, and a large, dark figure quickly entered the room and pushed the door closed behind him.

Jozeca held her hands to her mouth and Andrej fell on Jakob's neck kissing his cheeks. One after another they embraced him and kissed him until at last his rough tear-soaked cheek was pressed against Jozeca's and she was crushed between his two arms to his half-frozen body.

He had come on the train but the tracks were blown up at Lasko, so he slept outside for the night while they were repaired. The following morning, he walked on foot to the village to preach and tell the people about the Lord Jesus. Then he walked the remaining eight kilometers to Celje.

"I promised the Lord that I would not rest until two families gave their hearts to Him. Oh, I tell you, God is good! In spite of the propaganda against God and Christianity, God's power cannot

---

1. Revelation 3:5.

be squelched. The governments can teach that God does not exist all they want to, but they cannot fight a supernatural power who will make himself known in spite of all attempts to deny His glorious existence!"

Nezka poured linden blossom tea and heated up some chicken soup. Jakob ate hungrily.

In typical Slovenian style, he continued telling his story. "I visited a man, an old Moslem, who lay dying on his bed. Ah, death was so near, the room stank of it. He lay on a pile of dirty old Moslem tapestries. On the wall all around his bed hung old dusty, ragged tapestries. His wife, a Macedonian—somewhat of a Christian believer—was scurrying around him, nursing his needs and praying for him. She squirted perfume in the air to rid it of evil spirits. I entered the room, which stank of rotting flesh and sweet perfume, and I began to pray. 'God! O Jesus! Lord Jesus!'

"And suddenly the man began to squirm in his bed. The woman was on her knees on the floor. There were pots of different foods standing around on tables and flies buzzed over it all. I tell you, the room was dirty. I could see the man was breathing his last. The Catholic priest was on his way to forgive him his sins and send him to purgatory even though the man was a Moslem and not a Catholic at all.

"'God! Lord Jesus!' I was really shouting. Then all of a sudden, the man rose up out of his bed. He rose right up! The poor woman nearly fainted away on the floor. I continued to pray. Loudly. Then the man got right up out of bed and walked over to the door and back again. He looked like Lazarus must have when he rose from the tomb, I tell you. He was as thin as a hop pole and his skin was gray like mud. On his head he wore his fez. Well, then suddenly the priest arrived and observed this wife on the floor crying and the old Moslem walking around the room with a pleasant smile on his face—and me, standing in the center of the room shouting to high heaven. He did not know what to make of it.

"I tell you, God hears the prayers of His people. I know it. Yes, I know it. The priest invited me to come to his church and speak to the congregation. He opened his home to me where I slept that night. We were like brothers."

Andrej threw his hands up toward the ceiling. "Praise be to God!" he exclaimed. "In our Slovenia to see Catholics and Protestants love each other as brothers—it is a miracle!"

"Praise be to God!"

"Praise be to God!"

Soon everybody was talking at once and for a few short hours the war vanished. Joy and hope filled the air. Jakob shared the

Scriptures with them and taught them all a new song he made up on the way to Celje. They laughed, hugged, wept, kissed and they thanked God.

Jakob was well loved most places he went and Celje was no exception. His years of travelling and preaching had brought him more friends than he could count. In earlier years he had preached in Celje when he was on his way to Ljublijana, and there was great rejoicing among the Christians when they knew he was in their midst.

"Ah, the evangelist! God has blessed us. He has looked upon us and given us mercy. He has sent the evangelist."

"God himself speaks to *Gospod*, Mr. Jakob."

"*Gospod* is 'Sent Man of God,' I tell you!"

Jozeca had not had more than five minutes alone with her husband since he arrived. But she was so happy she could hardly swallow, hear properly or think a sensible thought. It would not be decent to kiss him or stroke his dear body in the presence of others; such demonstrations were only for those who were unsure about love. So she would wait until the time was proper.

Little Josip clung to his father. And Jakob produced a small treasure for him. First he sat him down and then he told him there was something in his pocket just itching to find his little hands. Which pocket did Josip think this something was in? The boy jumped and ran circles around his father until suddenly he found stuck in the suspender of his own trousers a chocolate bar.

Chocolate! He shared it with all nine of the family so everybody had a bite. First they smelled it, "Ah, it is fine chocolate." Then they each took their little bite and broke off crumbs to let melt on the tongue. "Ah, fine, fine." It was an exquisite treat and nobody was more proud or thrilled than little Josip who had never tasted chocolate, even though it was *ersatz*, a wood pulp substitute.

Chapter Twenty-one

The following evening Jozeca and the others returned to the flat from the factory and had barely gotten inside when they heard sirens. The deadly honking stopped directly in front of their house.

"O Jesus, Mary and all the saints," cried Nezka, crossing herself. Andrej hurried to hide the Bibles. Jakob and Jozeca fell to their knees.

"Dearest *Jezes*! Dearest Lord!"

The pounding on all the doors with the butts of guns sounded like machine gun fire. Everyone was ordered outside.

"*Macht schnell!*"

Little Josip was horrified at the sight of the Gestapo policemen. Crying, he ran to Jozeca. She bent to pick him up when suddenly a rifle butt came down on her shoulder and she sank to the floor. Josip screamed and the policeman picked him up and slapped him across the face.

"*Stoj!* Stop!" screamed Jozeca.

"I could kill you," the man spat and heaved the boy against the wall. Josip fell to the floor unconscious as the Gestapo marched everyone out of the flat single file with their hands over their heads.

"My son!" Jozeca pleaded, but a Mauser barrel was placed at her ear and the heel of a jackboot pushed against her spine. Then she was outside on the pavement with the others.

"You are all accused of collaborating with the enemy! You have aided the Partisan army and are guilty of holding secret meetings against the Führer and the Fatherland! You will march through the streets of the town with your hands over your heads as an example to the people!"

They marched in a line through the streets of the town. If one of them dropped his arm even slightly, a rifle butt on the back of the head reminded him to lift it up high again. Jozeca noticed the leader was a young man of maybe nineteen or twenty. This member of the master race had pimples on his nose and one crossed eye.

The march ended at Stari Pisker prison, where they were ordered to stand outside with their hands over their heads for another hour. They were exhausted and frightened. Most of the people in the morbid procession were hard workers who labored daily for the Germans in their factories. Ordered inside, the women were marched to one section, the men to the other.

Jozeca's grief was deeper than the pain in her arms and shoulders. Where was little Josip? There was nobody left in the block to watch over him. He was all alone. Was he hurt? Where was Jakob? "Ah, Jakob, my Jakob!" and she wept.

When she drew herself up and dried her face, she looked around her and saw the pitiful state of the others. They were shocked and frightened; some were sobbing, others pleading with the guards.

The cells, which were hardly big enough for one person, held eight women in each. There were two pallets to sleep on and two blankets. There was a drain in the middle of the floor and one window near the ceiling with bars across it.

"I shall not shed another tear," she vowed and she kept that vow for the next thirty days spent in that cell.

They received their first meal the next afternoon. The guard threw it on the floor by the drain which also served as their toilet. The pot of gray liquid had fish scales floating in it.

"Ah, stew!" exclaimed Jozeca. "Come on, girls, let us eat."

But the smell was so pungent they could not lift the cup to the chin without wincing.

"Rotten fish!" one of the girls wept. "They are feeding us rotten fish!"

"Do they call this food? This is food for the pigs!"

"It is garbage!"

Jozeca's eyes flashed. "And we will get down on our knees and thank God for it!"

Jozeca held the cup in front of her mouth and kissed it. "Thank you, Lord," she prayed, "for this food which will keep us alive." The others got on their knees also and they ate the stinking soup without another word.

The guards did not allow the women to sit down except at night when they slept. They were kept walking all day in a small circle around and around in the tiny cell. It was the only way they could keep warm because there was no heat in the prison. All day long the women moaned and wept. Some had come with only slippers on their feet and most were not dressed adequately.

Jozeca thought about her mother whom she had not seen since the morning they were arrested. In the march through the town they were not allowed to turn their eyes to the left nor to the right and so she did not know where she was.

Her biggest worry was Josip, however. Where was he? Who was caring for him? "O God, O dear Jesus!"

Hour after hour the women in the cell walked in circles, back and forth, around and around. They were cold and some were sick. Jozeca taught them some songs and they sang softly until the guards would tell them to stop.

They were nearly paralyzed with fear. They knew that if any Germans were killed in the town, prisoners would be marched in groups to the courtyard and shot. Some rumors had it that for every one German killed, fifty Jugoslavs would lose their lives. Others said it was a hundred Jugoslavs. One thing was certain, prisoners were shot daily. The drains in the floor served not only as a toilet but also as a convenient place to sweep blood into.

A young, plump-cheeked Nazi policeman came to the women's cell one evening, eyeing the women smugly. He was not German, but a Jugoslav quisling who had defected to the Nazi side. He spoke Slovenian but with the typical bloated words of a person who had been a nobody all his life and now was important because of the importance of his associates. The brass Swastika at his throat gave him newly found stature and a puffed-up chest, the price of betraying his own people.

He grinned at Jozeca and taunted, "We are shooting all of the *old* people who are of no use any longer."

"What do you mean?" demanded Jozeca.

The quisling guard looked directly at her and answered, "The old people, *Frau,* the old ones—especially the men, the men who have more than sixty years."

Jozeca bit her tongue. Jakob had sixty-four years. O God, have mercy.

The fat-jowled guard licked his lips.

"What good are old men over sixty anyhow, eh, *Frau?*"

She did not answer.

"Especially to the young women. Ha ha!"

She turned her head away.

"But my dear *Frau,* you need not trouble yourself. We will take care of you here. Ah, let it never be said that here in Stari Pisker we do not take care of our little neglected *Fraus,* eh! Such a young, ripe plum needs plucking. Do you not agree?"

He laughed and walked away, his fat sides wobbling. After he was gone, Jozeca began to tremble in anger, fear and horror. She raised her hands and clenched her fists.

"God! Look down upon me! Hear me!" And she prayed in a loud voice until she closed her eyes to sleep. Nobody stopped her. In fact, the women prayed with her. And before the morning sun rose, everyone in the cell knew that Jesus Christ was real and living and that in spite of every atrocity of man, He was a God of love.

It was about three o'clock in the morning when the fat guard had come for her. With him were two other guards, both German.

His chubby hands unsealed the lock on the cell door and he motioned for Jozeca to follow him. His face was pink and greasy in the pale green light. Jozeca did not move. The cell, heavy with the smells of perspiration, tears and human excretion, was silent. The fish smell from the day before still lingered on the women's clothes and hair.

Again he motioned for her to follow him.

She did not move.

He entered the cell and took her arm. As he touched her, he recoiled as though burned. "Acht!"

He grabbed her arm again, and again he recoiled.

"Devil!" he snarled.

"Jesus!" she answered.

He stood glowering at her and she remained unmoving. His face was a deeper pink. He pulled out his Luger and pointed it at her temple. Then he laughed nervously and wiped his wet mouth with his hand.

"Now you will come, *Frau*," he said.

She looked him straight in the eye and did not move. He cocked the hammer of the gun.

"Move! Now!"

Jozeca's eyes narrowed as she kept them on the quisling Nazi. He pressed the gun to her head and then he suddenly recoiled again as though singed by fire.

"Devil!" he cursed.

"Jesus," she repeated.

He humphed and grunted and jammed the gun back into his leather holster. Then with his high, black boots squeaking beneath him, he turned to leave the cell. The two guards with him snickered at him.

His pride deeply wounded, he angrily twirled around and told Jozeca, "Tomorrow you will be shot!"

Jozeca immediately raised her hands to heaven and praised God. "O God! Jesus! Dear Holy Spirit! You have delivered me from the destroyer! Praise the name of the Lord! O God! Thank you, Lord! Thank you with my soul! And if you would will it so that I once again will see my son and my husband, do not allow me to die tomorrow."

She slept peacefully that night.

There were no shots heard in the courtyard during the entire month they were in the prison. And that month not one person over sixty years of age was killed.

Chapter Twenty-two

Time, dragging on and on, was a bitter enemy. The days were endless. Several of the women fainted as they were kept walking back and forth. The guards kicked them in the ribs and threw water on them until they staggered to their feet, chattering and fumbling for something to cling to.

Jozeca prayed and preached adamantly. "Dear girls, do you think it is an easy thing to follow the Lord Jesus Christ? Eh? Did He ever tell us it would be easy? Listen to me, I tell you, God is with us! He is in this prison with us! He sees everything! Everything! Be strong. Do not give up hope!"

"The Lord tells us in His Holy Book that if His people will obey His commandments and follow His ways, He will pour out His blessings upon them."

A thin gray-haired woman asked, "What means this?—Blessing?"

"The blessing of knowing Him, that is what. There is only one blessing—the blessing of knowing Him! To live with a cleansed heart; to be free from fear, hate, pride, bitterness, anger, jealousy—this is knowing Him. Then our imprisonment, hunger and diseases we can bear because He bears them and us! Oh, to know Him!"

Then a young woman with pale yellow skin spoke.

"And we who are in prison understand best the blessing of eternal life."

The women turned to look at her. "All of this will pass away and soon we will be in the arms of Jesus," she continued. "How very real and very true is eternal life. Perhaps we learn this best in prison."

Jozeca sighed and thought of the difference between this woman, weak and dying but shining for the glory of God like a sun which never sets, and the Jugoslav quisling soldier, stuffed into a Nazi uniform, guarding the prison.

"Praise God," she breathed. "Praise God for lifting us up—miserable and imprisoned, hungry and cold. Thank you for lifting us up high above the world—high above all that can kill the body. Thank you, Lord, we are risen with you! We are free!"

They became acquainted with death in a bizarre sort of friendship. Jozeca forced herself not to despair. She stopped worrying about little Josip, about Jakob and her mother. She rested in the grip of eventual death which hovered over them all. It was cold, bitter, the biting winds snapped at their bodies, and on some days there was only one potato to eat all day.

When the guard threw potatoes into the cell, spilling them in the excretion on the floor, Jozeca bent down and kissed them and thanked God for the food.

But then one day, in the same manner they had been herded into the cells, they were suddenly ordered to line up with their hands over their heads and were herded out. She crossed the courtyard where many prisoners before them had been shot. There was blood splashed, some black, on the walls and pavement.

They were being released.

"And the men? What of the men?" asked a woman from another cell.

"Shut up or we will put you back inside where you can rot."

As she walked through the door Jozeca glanced back at the quisling sergeant. He averted his eyes as he caught her glance. He stood with his chin high and his neck stretched upwards and on his face was an expression of smug contempt. "Forgive him, Lord Jesus," she said under her breath; "he is deceived."

They were anxious to know if the men were being released also, but they did not dare ask questions nor wait to find out. If the men were released, they would return to their homes. It would be best to get away as quickly as possible.

Jozeca found Ana and Franciska who had been in another cell. They embraced and did not bother to wipe away the tears from their faces. They were all thin and sickly. Franciska's face was covered with sores. They walked back to their flats together. As they walked, a large-framed woman wearing a babushka, black coat and apron tied around her stomach quietly approached them.

"You are from over there, are you not?"

"Over there?"

"Ja. Ja. The prison. Stari Piskar."

"We were there."

"I live here," the woman pointed in the direction of some houses across the street from the prison. "And I tell you, it is terrible. I cannot sleep at night with the screaming coming from that place. It is terrible. I hear the screaming and I hear the weeping. All night, all night!"

Jozeca looked at the woman with a stony expression. "And you have shared our sufferings?"

"What goes on over there? Tell me that, will you? I cannot

sleep. It is terrible. The screams! The crying!"

Ana spoke in a patient voice. "Those are our people in that prison, *gospa*, Mrs. Our Jugoslav people suffering and being tortured under enemy hands. Remember that as you sleep tonight. People are suffering so that Jugoslavia can be free."

Jozeca felt pity for the woman as she watched her slip away into a doorway, still crying, "I hear them during the day also!" She thought how the Lord Jesus had suffered so that all people everywhere might be free.

"We are blessed," she said softly. "We are blessed to have tasted a little of what our Lord suffered for us."

Ana and Franciska were silent. "Do you understand me, my friends? We are honored and blessed. We have received strength and courage from our Lord."

The women squeezed her arms. "We understand."

"Ah. Then let us walk as honored vessels and let us be blessed."

As they neared their block, they asked everyone they saw about their children.

"Have you seen my son, Josip?"

"Stane—have you seen my Stane?"

Jozeca knocked on the doors along the road. "Pardon me, have you seen my little boy? He is small, blond hair, he is Josip."

Their pleas were met with silence or hopeless shrugs. Everyone was familiar with tragedy by now. The loss of families and children was another one.

When Jozeca arrived at the flat she discovered that a German family had moved into it. Their belongings were gone.

"Josip! Josip! My little boy! Have you seen him?"

No response. She stood outside on the step, her eyes examining the concrete fringed with weeds and scrub brush. She would knock on every door in the city until she found him. She would inspect every clump of weeds. Alive or dead, she would find him.

Late that afternoon she nearly tripped over Stane, Ana and Srecko's son. He was walking toward her on the road.

"Stane!"

"*Zdravo, Tovarisica*! Hello, madame!"

"Oh, dear Stane. Thank God! Your mother is searching for you!"

"Is it not wonderful? I have just left her side."

"Praise be to God." She embraced him and kissed his smiling face.

"You are well, Stane?"

"*Ja. Ja.* And *Stara*, the old woman, is well also."

"Old woman?" She remembered the old woman whose mind God had restored. "*Dobro.* Good. That is good news."

"And *Tovarisica* Nezka, she is well, also," he continued.

"My mother? Stane! Speak you the truth? My mother—she is with you? She did not go to prison?"

"No, she did not go to prison, as old *Stara* did not go to prison. We believe it was the Lord's way so that we boys would not be put in a camp."

". . . you boys . . .?"

"Yes, the sons of Franciska and me and oh! *Tovarisica*! Josip is with us also. He is your son, *ne*?"

She sucked in a gulp of air.

"Josip? Stane, listen, my son, Josip, is safe?"

"Of course, *Tovarisica*. Did you not have faith and believe in God? He watches over all. I go to meet Josip now. He is in the kindergarten. Each day I meet him and bring him home. The others are older; there are four of them, you understand. Even though Josip is old enough to watch out for himself, I feel for him as a brother. Do you understand, *Tovarisica*? I hope you will understand."

Her eyes blurred. "I understand, my Stane."

Chapter Twenty-three

The two women, Stara and Nezka, were living in Screcko's flat with the six boys. Franciska's four boys nearly wore the flesh from their mother with kisses and embraces. Ana held her son, Stane, tightly and whispered to him, "Son, now I believe as you and as your father. I believe in Jesus. Forgive me for my old selfish ways." Tears fell from everyone's eyes.

Nezka stood at the stove with a soup ladle in her hand. Her face was covered with tears and a thousand cracks and creases. Kissing Jozeca on both cheeks and squeezing the breath out of her, Jozeca and Nezka greeted one another with all of the proper questions.

"You are well, daughter?"

"*Ja. Ja*, Mama. I am well. And you—are you well, Mama?"

"*Ja. Ja*. It is well with me."

Then she took Jozeca's hands and asked, "And Lojze, have you heard any word? And what about Jakob? Have you heard anything at all? Did you know that they took Andrej to a work farm in Germany? Took him away the same night they took you and the others away. All of your cousins are now in Germany—on the work farms, Jozeca."

That night as she slept on the floor with the boys, there·was fighting on the streets. They were awakened by gunfire and mortar shelling. The next day it was learned that tlwee Germans had been killed. In reprisal, the Germans marched to the *Okoliska sola*, a neighborhood school on the other side of town, and ordered the children outside with their teachers. Then they lined them up, one behind the other. There in the park, with the white frost sparkling on the branches of trees and the sound of sparrows calling to one another, the children and their teachers were shot down in cold blood, their bodies dropping like apples in a basket.

Jozeca found a kitchen job in a German-run factory. She scrubbed putrid garbage cans, washed pots and swept and cleaned the floors. She was ecstatic to get the job.

"O thank you, Jesus! Praise be the name of the Holy God! Holy and good! Praises be unto His name!"

She was able to bring home food that was thrown into the

garbage. Every day she would discover treasures such as half-eaten pieces of fruit, bones with a little meat or gristle left on, or hard chunks of old bread. She rinsed potato peelings, and brought them home in her pockets. She also brought home scrapings from the bottom of pots. All of this made wonderful soup for which she praised God.

One morning she discovered piled at the bottom of one of the large garbage cans several dozen soaked and dirty biscuits. They had been too stale and streaked with mold to eat so they were thrown away. Jozeca stared at the biscuits with her eyes wide.

The German cook watched her with amusement. Then he signalled with his hand, "*Bitte*, please—"

She did not understand.

"Take. Go!" he said, waving his arms and pantomiming the removal of the garbage.

She understood.

That night at home the boys helped cut out the moldy parts and wash the dirty biscuits, laying them on the stove to dry. Some they put inside the oven. There were biscuits drying all over the flat.

"We will store the dried pieces in the cupboard and we will have food for a year," Jozeca beamed.

"Ugh. I cannot eat this garbage," sobbed Franciska. "It is worse than the prison food."

"Shame, Franciska!" Jozeca drew her hand into a fist. With her teeth very close together and her eyes narrowed, she said, "You will eat this food and you will get down on your face and thank God for it!" Then she kissed the salvaged biscuits, got onto her knees and lifted her hands to the ceiling. One by one, the others joined.

"Thank you, Heavenly Father, for providing for us," she prayed. "We give thanks to you for you love us and care for us. Our hearts are full of thanksgiving to you, most wonderful, high and holy Lord. For even this blessed food, dear Father, we are not worthy of."

Before going to sleep that night they hungrily ate the dried biscuit chunks dipped in linden tea. Even Franciska had to admit it was quite tasty. From that time on nobody went to bed at night with a crying stomach.

They were happy in spite of the events around them, and even Josip seemed to be less nervous. His strange attacks were fewer, now that Jozeca was home again. Every day they counted as a day closer the time when Jakob and the other men would be home and the *borba* would end.

They had just finished reading the Bible to the children one evening and were ready to go to bed when there was a tap at the door. Franciska recognized it as a Partisan signal. "It is safe—open it," she told one of her boys. A well-dressed man with shaved cheeks and a thin mustache entered. His hair was red, obviously dyed. He bowed politely.

The women bowed in return and invited him to sit down. After the formalities he said, "I have brought you a letter. It is from Screcko." Lowering his eyes, he held it out toward Ana.

She rose to her feet, half smiling, wanting to cry out in joy, but not knowing whether the letter held good or bad news. She stood absolutely still.

Finally, "You have seen him, my Screcko? He is well?" her voice was high, taut, tremulous.

"He gave this letter to give to you, *Tovarisica*. He is a brave man."

He extracted a piece of paper from the heel of his shoe and gave it to Ana. Stane moved closer to his mother, staring at the man and then the paper. Ana held the letter in her hand, looking at it for a moment, and then she drew near the light and carefully unfolded it. She read it aloud:

My Dear Wife!

I greet you with love and the prayers of a dying man, both to you and to our dear son.

The war against the enemy of our people has brought me to Bosnia. Ivo and I were brought here on a mission. Since the day I left to join the Partisans, I have seen much hardship and trouble, but I have also seen that the Lord Jesus Christ is the one hope of man.

In Slovenia I carried the gun but I did not kill. In Croatia also. Here in Bosnia I carried the gun but I did not kill. Ivo and I were among 200 men on a reconnaissance party when the Nazis opened fire on us. Shells hit our column and we were scattered like flies. The Stukas and Dorniers swooped over us bombing and strafing. Many of the men and horses were blown to bits but, praise be to God, we went uninjured.

Ivo was hit by antipersonnel shrapnel and lost part of his right shoulder. But being in the First Proletarian Brigade, he was brave to the end and continued on. The Nazis fell on us like wolves.

Still I did not shoot the gun.

On our marches we saw much brutality of men, not only German but Jugoslav men also. All men walk with sin and in need of the Savior. We cannot point the finger at any country of men, for we are all evil and wicked.

We saw entire villages burned to black stubble. Orthodox churches that had been filled with people were then set on fire, burned to the ground. We found their ashes. One morning we came upon a cave filled with 52 dead bodies of women and children who had been murdered. Their eyes had been removed. One of the babies, about a year old, was still alive. A woman Partisan treated its wounds and brought it along with us.

Every day we are joined by whole families fleeing from the Axis. Our numbers increase daily. We have heard that over 100,000 refugees block the mountain paths and our columns are in danger of bogging down. The people are barefoot, hungry, ill-clad and freezing, often unable to drag one foot after the other. Some ride in ox-drawn wagons.

At the time I was struck, we soldiers roasted and ate our pack pony. It was sour tasting meat mixed with burnt skin and dirt. I gave thanks to our God for food to eat so we could continue on. We have kept alive on whatever we could forage, walnuts, dried wild pears, barley . . . but the barley seeds sprout in our bellies. Typhus is spread through the columns by lice.

I do not complain. I am proud to serve God as a Partisan. I volunteered to serve the army in Bosnia, although I could have remained on our beloved soil of Slovenia. Even as the breath is leaving my body I have no fear.

I can thank our God that I have not held the gun at any human head. God is the giver of life! I believe that He has put me here to preach and tell these men about the Lord God. Many of them listen to me. Ivo has heard my words and put them into his heart. He lies near me here in the hospital.

All of this I am writing to you by our friend who bears this letter. He has asked me to keep his name unknown. Believe me, you can trust him. He is the bravest Partisan of them all. Dear wife, pray for him. It is he who writes this letter. I cannot hold the pen.

There are hundreds of men and women Partisans in this hospital in the forest, all seriously wounded. The hands and feet of many have been frozen. There are only a few doctors and they work night and day amputating limbs. There are no anaesthetics.

Wife, I can hear these brave young men and women scream as their hands and arms and feet and legs are sawn off—but not with pain and self-pity. No, they cry, "Long live Stalin! Long live the Soviet Union! Long live Tito!"

I write this to you so that you can tell our son and so that he can tell others. These men and women shout for the victory of man—but we must shout for the victory of God! When I gave my legs to God, I did not shout a political slogan, no, I shouted *blessed be the God of hosts who lives now and forever! Bless the name of the Lord Jesus Christ, our strength and our Redeemer!*

This must always be our cry. Great is the devotion of the unbelievers to their causes, but our devotion to God must be greater than theirs.

You know, my dear wife, your husband was not afraid to lose

his legs and he is also not afraid to die. I am ready. I can go home to our Lord. But I shall be ever near you and our son and also the faithful believers who continue to press on in faith in this troubled world.

By the grace of God, I give up my life to God. Remember always to fight evil with good. Teach this to my son. I allowed many years to pass before I found the Savior. It is my deepest regret. For the evil I have done you in this life, I beg your forgiveness.

I tell you of the events which I have passed through since I last saw you so that you will know your Srecko died without fear and so you will tell this to our Stane. Also it is not my desire to pass from this life to the next without having blessed you in the name of the Lord and told you, *Nasvidenje*.

Your Srecko

Chapter Twenty-four

In July of 1942 about seventy thousand of Mussolini's troops, aided by about three thousand Italian-equipped White Guards, began an elaborate offensive against the Partisans in Slovenia, who were then numbering only about five thousand men and one thousand women. These "White Guards," or the *Milizia Voluntaria Anticommunista*, were almost without exception young Slovene Jugoslav priests just out of seminary. They allied themselves with the Italian Fascists, carried weapons and wore officers' insignias on their priest's tunics.[1] The Italians then, using the White Guards as guides, fine-combed the whole of Lower Slovenia looking for Partisans. They painted slogans on walls: FOR GOD AND THE FAITH—THE PARTISAN MUST CROAK—THIS IS THE WILL OF THE PEOPLE.

The objective was to destroy Tito's bands once and forever. They crawled through bushes, up and down hills and mountains, but Tito's guerrillas vanished out of their hands like sand through a sieve. Furious at the futility of the hunt, the Italians and their White Guards burned hundreds of villages and slaughtered thousands of hostages.

It was not until the end of the war that the Liberation Forces captured the infamous church *Sveti Urh* in Ljubljana after a four-day battle. It was run by a branch of the White Guard organization called the Black Hand. The priest-commanded outfit tortured and killed about a thousand men and women, most of whom were not Partisans, because they might have been relatives of the Partisans or may have been pro-Partisan. The Black Hands' motto was: IN THE NAME OF THE WOUNDS OF CHRIST THE PARTISAN MUST DIE!

This was confusing to the people. Some began to identify the church with killing and brutality.

On September 8, 1943, Italy surrendered and the Allied Supreme Middle East Command ordered the Italian Army occupying Jugoslavia to surrender to Tito. Many Italian units, eager to get out of the war, gladly turned themselves and their equipment over to

---

1. Adamic, Louis, *The Eagle and the Roots*.

the nearest Partisan units. Others who were not quick enough were seized by the Nazis and the Cetniks.[2]

That same month Hitler launched the Sixth Enemy Offensive. The Slovene Army suffered heavy losses as the Nazis drove the Partisans out of their positions gained from the Italians.

Also in that same month Jakob Kovac was released from prison. He had been in Stari Pisker, although the police would not give that information to Jozeca. "They thought I was a dead man," he told Jozeca wearily, "so they released me. This is the second time God has spared me by putting upon me the look of death."

Jozeca stared at her husband, her small heart-shaped mouth trembling. "Ah Jakob, my heart, you are for me the sun which never sets, but you have upon you not the look of death but the glow of heaven."

He smiled. Her lies would not convince him. He was sixty-five years old and he knew he looked more like a hundred. And his young wife, not yet thirty, firm, strong, with cheeks as pink as when she was yet a girl, would with her love, breathe the life back into him.

"Your stepfather, Lojze, I am sorry to say, went to Dachow."

Nezka gasped. Dachow was the most dreaded prison camp of them all. It was there the smoke of the ovens where human beings were baked alive hung over the camp like flags and the screams of thousands of gas chamber victims filled the air to be heard for decades to come.

Jakob opened his arms to the old woman. She fell against his chest. "What happened, Jakob? Tell me all."

Jakob sighed. "He spit at one of the officers during an interrogation. They took him away and that was the last we heard of him. I am sorry, Nezka. Though he rejected the Lord, I loved him."

Jozeca tried to force Jakob to rest and recuperate, but he refused. Every day he made rounds of believers' flats and prayed with them. Every day he prayed on his knees and every day he told somebody new that God loved him or her. He walked the roads and foot paths praying and waiting until he felt the leading of the Lord to approach a person. The praying was very important to him because he knew that if God directed his footsteps and if God showed him the person who was already hungering for Him, then he would see godly results.

---

2. Cetniks were essentially a Serb movement deriving their name from the Serb *cetas*, companies which fought the Turks in the Middle Ages. Led by Draza Mihailovic, they fought for the return of the monarchy and restoration of pre-war conditions in Jugoslavia. They sided with the Axis during the war and violently fought the Croats and Partisans.

A man or woman would pass him and he would pray for them, "Lord, touch that person! Touch them!" And then he would ask the Lord, "Whom may I approach? Which one, Lord?" And the Lord would guide him, gently, gently, and he would approach the person right under the noses of the S.S.

"*Prosim*, please, would you be agreed that I have a few words with you?"

"Uh . . . *ja*, please?"

"I am an evangelist," he explained to the suspicious listener, "and I must tell you now, right now, before another minute eludes us, that God loves you. Today is the day of salvation."

Then within a very short time a new Christian would be born.

With these new converts he started new churches. But his Baptist churches were like a gnat in a bucket of milk. The religion of Slovenia was Catholicism.

One evening, only a month after his release from prison, Jakob announced to Jozeca that they would be returning to Trbovlje.

"*Ja*, husband. When you are well, *ne*?"

"We will return tonight."

"Tonight?"

And so they packed their meager belongings into a dishcloth, stuck a cheese and loaf of black bread into Jakob's coat pocket and they were on their way. The kisses and embraces of the others were still warm on their skin when they walked briskly up the road to the train depot. Jakob looked down at his son trudging along beside him. "Josip, my son, are you a man?"

"Yes, sir, I am a man."

"Then you will walk to Trbovlje also."

They met hundreds of men, women and children along the roads. Some were running from burned-out villages, homeless, and some of the them hoping to join the *Partizani* in the forests and mountains. The German reprisals were ferocious, but for every village they wiped out, another village rallied to join the *Partizani*. If the Germans slaughtered a hundred women and children, another two hundred joined the guerrillas in the hills to counterattack. They had impassioned fervor.

Tito, the leader of the Partisans, refused to be deterred by the Nazi reprisals. To him it meant that more men and women would join his ranks while the Cetniks and Ustase were losing fighters. His guerrilla army consisted mostly of displaced persons—people without homes, men without families, and those who were angry, embittered and in need of a cause. They had one cry: freedom; one cause: nationalism; and one deep hatred: foreign occupation.

Tito realized the real enemy of the Partisan guerrillas was not the Germans at all but the rival guerrilla forces. The Allies were not supporting those forces, Mihailovic and his Ustase, any longer, however; they had switched their support to Tito. His long impassioned cries for help from Stalin never came, and now the United States and Britain were dropping aid, arms, medicines, clothing and food to his National Liberation Army.

The Partisan army was disciplined and had a reputation among the peasants for being honorable. They had been ordered by Tito that it was forbidden to steal from the peasants. In fact, he used terror to enforce discipline among his fighters; it was punishable by death to steal from peasants.

Jakob and Jozeca witnessed a macabre ceremony when a Partisan soldier was discovered stealing food from a peasant farmer. If he had asked the farmer for the food, the farmer would probably have given it to him because the people of Slovenia supported the Partisans unanimously. But this Partisan soldier took without asking. The punishment was death; so, before the entire little village, he was blindfolded and a fellow soldier held an Italian baretta to his head.

Before he died, he made a little speech deploring his actions because he had disgraced the good name of the Partisan movement.

The cold night was closing in. About 100 meters from the road, Jakob spotted a cowshed where they could spend the night. They were still upset from the execution they had just witnessed, and Jozeca felt weak and sick to her stomach. Inside the barn it was quiet and, they thought, empty.

Jakob sniffed the air, looking around. They lay down on the hay and straw on the floor and prepared to go to sleep.

They had hardly closed their eyes when the cowshed at once became alive with human life. The door opened and a burning torch was poked in front of their faces. "*Zivio* Tito! Long live Tito!" said a voice.

"Long live Tito! Liberty to the People!" answered a voice behind them.

They were of all ages—men and women—some wore gray uniforms with the pants stuffed into short black boots and pointed hats with the red star in the middle. Others were dressed in peasant clothing or in loose fitting trousers, boots, tunics, homespun shirts. Grenades hung at their waists and rifles were strapped to their backs. They carried German and Italian guns as well as knives and sticks. One of them was setting up a wireless in the hay behind them.

A tall man, obviously one of the leaders, told Jakob soberly, "There will be combat in this area. You should get your family away as quickly as possible."

A cracking of a twig was heard outside, hardly noticeable to an ordinary ear; and as quickly and quietly as cats, the Partisans positioned themselves in every corner of the barn, weapons poised.

"Long live Tito!" said a woman's voice. "Long live Tito!" was the reply. Another company of Partisans entered the barn, their point of rendevouz. There were about twenty-five of them. They had only a few minutes before dispersing into the surrounding hills.

The guerrillas' first principle is mobility. They would not remain in one place where they could be easily surrounded and sabotaged, so quickly their strategy was discussed, maps examined, orders given and they were ready to move out.

The little family heard snatches of conversation.

"Our food is gone. Are our troops holding up in the south?"

"Our land army against the screaming Stuka bombers—it is crazy!"

"That jackal Mussolini has met his end! Thanks to the *Partizani.*"

"Ah, to be in Milano and see his body hanging by its feet from meat hooks in the marketplace!"

"A fitting end, *ne?*"

Jozeca and Jakob helped load supplies onto the pack ponies and went from one soldier to another tightly tying on backpacks.

But before the *Partizani* moved out something quite touching happened. It was one of the freak incidents of a war such as this one. "Only in our *borba* could such a thing happen!" they were to exclaim later.

The woman who was leading one of the squadrons suddenly whispered loudly in repressed excitement, "Pavel! Is that you, Pavel?"

The tall man with a two-day beard stared across the darkness toward the woman. He could barely distinguish her features, but he recognized the voice.

They moved toward one another in the shadows of the moon shining through the slats of the barn, a man and his wife.

Alongside the woman was a young man who could not have been more than thirteen years old. "Here also is our son. He is a Partisan soldier as you and I."

The moon sparkled in the man's tears. He had not seen his family since the bombing of Beograd in 1941. He held his son tightly and kissed him on both cheeks. Then he reached his hand out to his wife. It would not be good Partisan discipline to embrace her.

"We have been fighting for five months," she told him in a cracked voice. "After our village was bombed there was nothing else we could do. Our house is gone. Our people are dead. We can only fight now—fight for our liberty."

"Liberty to the people," he mimicked dryly.

The woman smiled weakly. Pulling back her shoulders in a gesture of courage and nonchalance. "*Druse*, Comrade, I am happy to see that you are alive and well."

He stiffened. A tear rested on the edge of his nose. "When the war is over, where will we meet?"

"In Ljublijana," she answered. "We will meet in Ljublijana, our white city. Do not worry. *Stari*[3] knows what he is doing. We will win this war. Our people are strong, too strong to die. They kill us and we do not die. Long live Tito."

"Long live Tito."

They shook hands again. Jakob, who was standing in the shadows, asked abruptly, "Are you agreed I pray for you before you part?"

Their shoulders dropped and they turned to stare at him.

"Pray?"

"Yes. You need prayer. Close your eyes. Get down on your knees. I will pray."

Still staring at him in amazement, they obeyed, scrambling to their knees.

Then Jakob prayed. "Lord Jesus! Look down on this family! Have mercy! Protect them from the bullet and the bomb! Unite them again! Keep them alive. Show them that you love them."

He placed his hands on their shoulders. "Peace be unto you, *Tovaris, Tovarisica*! Courage! I say, courage in the name of the Lord Jesus! Do you believe He is Lord? Is He Lord of your lives?"

"Yes," the man said in a small voice. "I believe in Him. I believe in God. He is difficult to find in this *borba*, but I believe."

The three soldiers remained on their knees beside him, not moving, not saying anything. Jakob continued. "Do not forsake the Lord, your God. Do not forget Him. He is Lord. He will help you. He promised He will never ever leave you. Do you understand? He is Lord!"

They rose to their feet and left in separate directions. They parted with the typical Partisan salute, the clenched fist in the air.

"*Zivio Tito!* Long live Tito!" the woman said.

Then the barn was empty, not a single clue indicating that anyone else had been there at all.

The three remained in the darkness for several moments before speaking. Then, rather than speak to each other of what they had seen, they began to pray. Josip fell asleep with his head resting in his mother's lap as Jakob and Jozeca prayed long into the night. They prayed for the Partisan husband and wife and their son;

---

3. Affectionate name for Tito used during war. It means Old Man.

they prayed for the village of Trbovlje, for the roads crowded with refugees; they prayed for the republics of Jugoslavia: for Slovenes, the Croats and the Serbs. They prayed for those in prison and for their family back in Celje, for Nezka, Franciska, Stane and Ana. On and on they prayed and the hours fell by like leaves from autumn trees.

The sound of machine gun fire riddled the air. Josip awoke with a start. "Mama?" he cried with his eyes wide.

"It is nothing, son. There are some soldiers outside fighting. You must pray. Just pray."

"Mama, let us not leave this place. Let us remain here where we are. God will watch over us."

Jakob looked into the yet sleepy eyes of his young son. "My son has spoken the word of the Lord," he said. "We shall remain where we are."

The barn stuck out of the landscape like colored curtains in the window of a peasant's cottage. It was the most dangerous place they could be.

"We shall remain where we are," Jakob said confidently, "and we shall stay on our knees and pray."

And they did.

Chapter Twenty-five

They heard the bursting of mortar shells and machine gun fire all night, but the airplane engines they expected to hear—the roar of the Stukas and the Dorniers—never came, and in the morning the sound of gunfire was distant and they knew the battle had moved westward.

They left the barn in the early light of dawn and climbed the hill through the woods in time to see a battalion of Nazi tanks moving toward them. The sight was startling. The tanks were painted flat black to reflect no light and on each fender they could see the small yellow insignia of regiment and division. Stenciled on each vehicle were the letters WH, for *Wehrmacht*. They watched with awe. The tanks were monstrous looking creatures, crashing along the road like prehistoric beasts.

The crew members of the tanks were young, blond-haired men with sandy skin wearing black rubber coats and helmets. They were poking out of the turrets of the tanks holding sticks with red and white discs at the end and signalling to teammates in the tanks ahead or behind for road discipline.

"And our people have only oxen-drawn artillery."

Jozeca looked puzzled. "But what is this, Jakob?"

"This is *tanki*."

"*Tanki?*"

"*Ja.* German."

"But what are they for?"

Young Josip nodded his head up and down. "Ah, *ja, tanki*," but he did not understand any better than his mother.

Then came the armored cars, most of them six-wheeled vehicles, carrying men and machine guns. There were motorized anti-aircraft units and soldiers armed with automatic rifles and hand grenades. Every tank, armored car, truck and officer's car of the macabre parade carried a huge Nazi flag draped across the radiator. A yellow-nosed junkers '87 bomber roared overhead at about 1,000 feet unescorted by fighters. The three onlookers dove behind a leafy bush.

"God help us!"

The tide of rumbling iron passed and the infantry regiments followed. Men heavily weighed with weapons marched past, their faces muddy with dust and sweat. Then pumping along came steel-helmeted bicycle troops, hunched over their handle bars and struggling with the weight of their heavy loads.

"*Ali je mogoce?*, Is it possible?" gasped Jozeca.

Jakob's face was expressionless. "They are the Germans," he said in a voice like dry weeds, "but they could be anyone. Our enemy is not the Nazis—not these *tanki* and guns and helmeted youngsters. Listen to me, wife, son: Our enemy is the prince of the powers of evil. The devil is a destroyer. He is a killer. He hates everybody and he hates the Nazis as much as he hates the Jugoslavs.

"The names of those who plunder and destroy may change with each generation. But the real enemy, the real power of evil behind hatred and destruction does not change. It is he who turns brother against brother, husband against wife, nation against nation."

They watched quietly. Tears gathered in Jakob's eyes. "By God! We need Christ! Without Christ the world lies like an open play yard for the devil and his demons, and human beings are the toys."

They lay quite still beneath the bushes, staring at the last of the procession on the road below.

"Dear God! Look at them all."

They watched until they could no longer see the dust or hear the clink of jackboots on the stones. Fear glutted the minds and hearts of the refugees who were on the roads or walking alongside the roads in the trees. Would there be more south-bound German troops and what horror did they bring with them? Many people, weak and cold, were escaping from burned-out villages. Most were home-less and exhausted. They shared two things in common: fear and hunger.

When they met along the way, or rested together beneath the trees, they shared conversation. Jakob led his little family to a narrow clearing where others were gathered and motioned for them to sit on the grass. The tired and homeless strangers were in the middle of a conversation.

An old woman from Croatia told them how the Orthodox priests and believers were suffering in Bosnia.

"An Orthodox priest in Rogatica had the misfortune to remain alive after his church was burned to the ground by the Ustase," she told them.

"So what happened?"

"I will tell you. They nailed horseshoes to his hands and knees, saddled him and rode him through town like a donkey."

"Ah, tch . . . tch . . . tch."

"I myself am Catholic and also a Croat. But I have never cast an arrow at an Orthodox Serb or a Moslem."

"And is it correct that you have never done anything to prevent the arrow from striking either?" asked a young man with his face in bandages.

The old woman stared at the man, said nothing.

"How many friends and neighbors have you quietly watched burn to death? Eh? Tell me that!"

An older man interrupted, sensing a battle about to erupt, "Make peace with yourself, Comrade. The woman is as weak as you."

The air was tense, but the old man silenced the young bandaged man. He spoke in casual relaxed tones. "We Slavs have always been animals. The war is just a convenient excuse for us to kill one another—Moslem, Orthodox and Catholic—now we have a good climate for killing. The Nazis do not know what a wonderful help they are being to us. Now we Slavs can kill each other to our heart's content. It is all stupid, all meaningless, all futile and yet we continue on the same—killing, killing and more killing."

The sun was setting over the mountains when Jakob, Jozeca and a weary Josip arrived in the town of Hrastnik. The air was stiff, blue and cold. Jozeca and Josip huddled against a wall while Jakob went to look for food and a place where they might rest for the night. There were *Partizani* slogans painted on the wall, FREEDOM TO THE PEOPLE, as well as those slogans painted by the Partisan Medical Corps: WASH YOUR LINEN, CUT YOUR HAIR, KEEP FREE OF LICE, AVOID TYPHUS.

Typhus was a serious problem in the south. It was spread by lice. And lice was something nearly everybody lived with, especially the army.

Jakob returned in about an hour, his face bright.

"Praise be to God!" he exclaimed.

"Ah, so?"

"Ana, the widow of Screcko, is here in this village, with her son, Stane."

"Ana? Impossible."

"It is true. They arrived four days ago by train. They are living with kinfolk just two hundred meters from where we stand."

They were weak and their faces marked with tears as they embraced Ana and her son, Stane. The tiny one-room house already had six people living in it, but they made room for the three exhausted and half-starved travellers.

Ana told the others how Jozeca had saved her from Screcko's fierce temper, how she had worked a miracle and brought her husband to God. Jozeca blushed self-consciously. Ana explained that Screcko had changed and become a wonderful man and husband and that his conversion was a *cudica*, a miracle.

Then they kissed again and Ana served them hot soup with carrots and dumplings. It was a feast.

"Screcko is now with God in heaven. He died a man and a hero!"

That night before going to sleep in their corner of the floor by the stove, Jakob, Jozeca and Josip prayed on their knees and thanked God for bringing them safely to a place of rest and shelter. They prayed for wisdom and guidance and, with hearts filled with gratitude, they thanked Him over and over again for bringing them to the home of friends.

One of Ana's brothers had recently been in Trbovlje. Jakob and Jozeca eagerly listened for news. "Ja, I know of your church," said the man with his eyes downcast. "News of it reached me through a friend named Adamic."

"Ah, ja! He is one of the believers in Trbovlje. He has been a faithful member of our little church for many years."

"He it is who brought me the news."

"What news do you speak of? Please, what is this news?"

The young man with broad nose and wide cheekbones shifted his weight nervously.

"I do not like to bring you such news, Tovaris."

"I am waiting to hear."

"The man who owned the house where the church was meeting—"

"Tone is his name. Ja, ja. What of him? Eh? Speak up, man. Do not be afraid."

"I am sorry to tell you, Tovaris Jakob, but he has been taken to Dachow."

"Dachow!"

Jozeca shook her head in disbelief. "Is it possible?"

Jakob's face was rigid. "And why did this happen? Can you tell me this?"

The young man's voice was strained. "He was arrested and his family taken to Dachow along with a wagon full of Jews. He was accused of holding secret political meetings. The others of your church are scattered."

"And Adamic, what of him?"

"He is alone, he says. He is praying, he tells me. He is praying to your God."

Their sleep that night was mingled with tears. The brother had also told him that there was no work to be had in Trbovlje. He himself had returned to Hrastnik to work in the mine even though the pay was hardly enough to buy bread.

And so it happened that their overnight stay in Hrastnik lasted ten years.

Chapter Twenty-six

Jakob travelled on foot to nearby villages to tell the people about God's love as often as he could. A young village wife holding her new-born baby sat quietly by her stove as her father-in-law sat at the table with Jakob, pointing his fingers to heaven.

"Ah, *Gospod* Evangelist, you preach to us of a God of love! Permit me to ask you if you are aware of what is being done in the name of your God of love!"

Jakob had walked five kilometers to see old Cimerman and his family of nonbelievers. He was not discouraged by Cimerman's bitter arguments. He railed on, "Do you not know that at Sveti Urh the prisoners who refuse the last sacrament of the church are tied to a steel ring driven into a tree trunk and tortured? Do you not know that every week in the woods on the hilltop where that church stands, another man or woman is shot, hanged or knifed in the name of the wounds of Christ? Have you a head beneath that cap, *Gospod? Ne?*"

This is how it was. Wherever he went he was reminded of the atrocities committed in the name of the Lord. He preached across the countryside and mountains to this and other villages, and people who once loved the sight of him and welcomed him into their homes now were afraid of him. Strangers avoided him. Was he a White Guard? Was he a Ustase? A Partisan? A Cetnik? A Belogardist? Even God himself could not be trusted anymore because nobody knew whose side He was on.

Cimerman continued, his words punctuated with gyrating hands. "These men of the cloth tortured and killed my own nephew before my eyes! Here before you is his widow—a child in the bloom of life and with a babe in her arms! I saw them torture her husband— saw him die in his own blood, and then I watched the killers calmly genuflect before the main altar of the church, cross themselves with the holy water and a few moments later their forks scraped their plates as they ate their supper in the parish house."

The old man was trembling, his face red and wet. "And you speak to us of a God of love! Fffff!"

"My heart suffers with your heart," Jakob said.

Then he said, "Tell me, Cimerman, if I put your coat on my

back and I put my feet into your boots and I go out onto the streets and tell the people that I am you, will I be Cimerman or will I be Kovac?"

The old man nodded his head. "*Menda ja*, of course, you will be Kovac."

"But suppose I steal something from somebody and the people see only Cimerman's coat and Cimerman's boots, eh? And then the officials come to your door and they say, 'Cimerman, you were seen stealing. You must pay the penalty.' "

"Ah, uh."

"But you tell them, *Ne, ne!* It was not I! I have not left my chair. It was not I."

"Ah, but you were seen, Cimerman. You were seen and identified. You are guilty."

They were silent again.

"I do not believe in the name of your God," the old man said in the quietness.

"Then tell me, Cimerman, what do you believe in? Eh? Tell me that. Can Tito give you eternal life? Can Mihailovic? Pavelic? Can a dead Mussolini? Or can the King? Can any of our heroes of the past? Can you give me the name of any person who has put within your soul the peace of heaven?"

Cimerman winced uneasily. "This talk is a worry to me."

He stood to his feet and Jakob stood also. He shook his hand, clasping it tightly. "Are you agreed I pray for you?"

And so it was. He preached the Gospel in every house that opened the door to him, prayed for every person who would bow their head with him. Night and day he preached, prayed and brought to the people the message he passionately believed. He trekked through the mountains and the woods, reassuring Jozeca, "I shall not die by the bullet or at the hands of soldiers. I believe that."

He visited men like Cimerman regularly and faithfully. Without payment, he spent days helping families who needed help; he walked sometimes a day and a night to spend a few hours with just one family. Every week for a year Jakob walked ten kilometers to Cimerman's little cottage to see him and visit him and talk with him about the Lord Jesus Christ.

And then on a clear winter morning Cimerman wagged his head back and forth, his white hair shining in the morning light, and he said, "Kovac, you have convinced me. Your God is real. Your God is God. You wear the coat well."

His widowed niece also bowed her head and knelt on her knees to pray with the evangelist. It was the beginning of a new church. "A miracle," said Jakob.

Within a year he had formed new churches in seven villages. They were small churches with only a handful of believers, and they met in homes. They gathered together faithfully and they prayed for each other and for their country. Jakob visited them every week, teaching them the Word of God and encouraging them. His energy and enthusiasm was like tonic—his strength gave them strength.

Chapter Twenty-seven

Jozeca blushed happily as she prepared the water for Jakob's wash that evening. She hummed and smiled and Jakob observed her with amusement. "My only one, you are as bright as the crown on the angel's head. Can it be you have swallowed a star?"

"It is a secret," she teased.

"A secret. Can it be? The wife of Jakob Kovac keeps a secret from him? Not so loyal and faithful a wife as she! Come. Whisper gold in my ear."

She danced around him helping him undress for his wash. "Can you bear such gold, *Gospod*?"

"If it is gold, *ja*, but tin—*ne*."

"My news is not tin, but gold."

"Please?"

She took a breath. "You shall again be a father."

"*Resnica*? Truth?"

"*Resnica!*"

With one leg still in his trousers and one leg out, he picked her up in his arms and twirled her around in a circle.

"Praise the Lord!"

During the *borba* many people panicked if they learned that there would be a new family member. They feared the agonies which awaited the new baby, and they worried how they would feed another mouth. A little baby became an enemy when he took the food from the mouths of the others. But Jozeca and Jakob rejoiced because they knew that God would have another servant on the earth to bring glory to His name. Little Josip was happiest of all.

"*Mamica*, may it please be a girl. Please make it be a girl!"

"That is a request you make of God, Josip; I cannot help you. I can bear the child and bring it into the world, but I cannot make it male or female."

"I am asking God for a sister. He will answer my prayers, *ne*?"

"I believe He will, my son. I believe He will."

Jakob worked in the coal mine in Hrastnik. When a two-room flat became available in the building, they rented it. It was the most beautiful place they had ever lived in. Two whole rooms! The kitchen was tiny, barely enough room to hold three people, but it was a room. And the sleeping room had enough space for two beds. They entered the flat with their possessions tied in sheets on their backs. After they put them on the floor, they knelt on their knees in the small kitchen.

"Thank you, God! Thank you!" they prayed. "Remember, beloved ones," Jakob told his wife and son, "with such a great blessing as this, we are responsible—responsible to share with others. 'To those whom much is given, much is required!' "

The neighbors in the house already knew about Jakob and Jozeca, the "praying ones," the "miracle lady and the man," the "evangelist and his family." Some also called them the crazy ones.

Ana still considered Jozeca the miracle lady. Her face was worn far beyond her young years, but yet she had a glow on her cheeks that made her seem somehow beautiful. Lately she worried constantly about her son, Stane. He was only nine years old and yet he was growing so rapidly that he was already as tall as a young man.

The Ustase had come to her flat and demanded that she produce her son so he could join them. Then the *Partizani* came and demanded to know where her able-bodied son was and why was he not helping the People's Liberation Army?

"He is only a child," Ana cried. Night after night Ana and Jozeca prayed together, petitioning God on behalf of young Stane. Ana made her meager living by knitting sweaters and selling vegetables from her garden when she could. Now she had to hide her son to keep the soldiers from taking him away. Her days were a nightmare of worry and fear. Jozeca stayed near her to pray with her and comfort her.

They sat by the stove in the tiny kitchen. It was cold and the wind whipped against the windows. Ana filled the stove way up to the top with little pieces of coal, packing it tight and closing the draft. That way it would glow all night and keep out the frost. There were wet streaks on her cheeks as she thought of her son.

Jozeca sat on the wooden chair which had been hand painted by Strecko many years ago. She sat silently in the dark, feeling and sharing Ana's sorrow. Then she said, "God is with him, Ana. Trust God."

"But he is only a boy! How can he live in a cave in this weather? Surely he will die of the cold!"

"You have done what is best, Ana. Should he die of the cold or die in the army of the Ustase or the *Partizani*?"

"His father died in the army of the *Partizani*. He died a hero."

"Truth."

"Ah, but nine years old, my only son. Ah, how could they insist he fight when he is only nine years old? He is as tall as a young man of thirteen, old enough to be a soldier. They do not believe he is only nine years old. Can I sleep at night? My only son, Stane, hidden in a cave in this freezing winter! It was bad enough when the weather was warm and I had to dig holes and hide him for weeks at a time. There he would be, buried like a corpse, unable to move—but now! Now, to force him into hiding in this cold weather! It will be sure to kill him. O God! O Jesus! Soon the soldiers will leave the village and he can be fetched out. Ah, ah . . . look down on my son, Lord! Look down on him in that cave!"

Jozeca joined her, clutching her fists together and shaking them toward heaven. "Look down on that child! Breathe on him in that cave, breathe on him with your breath which is warm!"

"Ah, this war, this war. Why is there war? Can anybody tell me that? Eh? Why . . . ah, ah . . ."

Chapter Twenty-eight

Freezing winds licked at the tall trees and devoured the shrub and brush surrounding the entrance to the cave. Snow swirled angrily through the tiny clearing at the side of the mountain and completely covered the black earth with high mounds, too deep for a man to walk across. Everything on the mountain was white, even the bare branches of the fir and the birch trees were covered with high, white snow shelves. The only sound was the wind and the scratching of some twigs against the side of the cave.

Yesterday there had been a tiny path through the snow and Stane had made small tracks with his heavy shoes in it. He had hurried soundlessly as possible up the side of the mountain to his hiding place carrying a sack with some bread and a small hunk of cheese which would have to last him until his mother could bring him more.

His legs were cramped and sore. He longed to stand up and stretch, but the cave was low and he had to remain in a crouched position. He was cold but not freezing. He could still feel all parts of his body. He remembered that during the night he heard the wind shift, and as he fell asleep he was certain that he felt a breath of warm air cover him.

He rolled over onto one side and wiggled his feet and moved his legs. Then he rolled to the other side. He moved his arms in a tiny half circle and shook his head up and down. This he did periodically in order to keep the blood in his body moving so he would not freeze. He knew that if he emerged from the cave, he would disturb the camouflage and his hiding place could be discovered. He remained in the crouched position for two days before he finally dared to move the stone and brush which covered the opening to his hiding place.

He rolled out, carefully extending his legs and fighting tears as the pain shot through his cramped muscles. It was black outside with only the silver glow of the moon on the snow shining between the shadows of the trees. He ate mouthfuls of the white snow and lay outstretched for several minutes before returning to the cave.

What he did not know was that a Partisan unit had pulled out from his town, and they were making their way up the mountain only a few meters from his hiding place. If he had remained inside the cave just a half hour longer, they would not have found him;

and his mother, who waited at the foot of the mountain at that very moment, would have come for him moments later to bring him back home.

He was shaking with cold and fear when he was discovered. He was pulled out by his heels to face the barrels of three Browning automatic rifles.

"*Zivio Tito*," he cried, somewhat relieved that they were Partisans. They searched him and questioned him. He told them he was hiding from the Ustase and that his father had died a brave Partisan in Bosnia. He told them that he was his mother's only son.

The soldiers, wearing German, Italian and the green Partisan uniforms, with the red stars sewn on their caps, gave him food and put a German great coat on his back.

"Our new comrade. Long live Tito, Comrade."

Stane gave the Partisan salute and stood on trembling legs which barely held him up.

"Can you drive a wagon?"

"*Mendaja*, of course."

"You will drive the supply wagon. Are you familiar with these mountains?"

"*Ja*. I was born in these mountains, as was my father and his before him."

He thought of his mother through the night as he guided the supply wagon along the steep inclines and through the forest behind the Partisan detachment. What would she imagine when she found the cave empty?

"O dearest Jesus, whose wounds my beloved father now embraces, hear my prayer. Have mercy on my mother—a poor widow. Give her courage. Tell her to have courage, to believe in you, and in eternal life. And, Lord, please give me courage, too."

He stopped counting the days of the march. The sun rose and set, rose and set. Cold settled into his bones and numbness owned most of his body. His hands were blistered and raw from the reins of the horse. Many times along the road he saw the bodies of dead Partisans hanging from trees or impaled on posts swaying silently, turning slowly in the icy wind. They were the Nazi's angry examples to the Jugoslav people.

There were many such examples, such reprisals. When the Partisan's enemy armies learned that a peasant family had given aid to the Partisans, the entire family—husband, wife, children, grandparents, aunts, uncles—would be marched out of the house and shot. Then the house would be burned to the ground. If a village was suspected of sympathizing with the Partisans or helping them, the inhabitants would be ordered out of their homes, shot down like ducks in a pond and then all of the houses would be burned to the ground.

Stane saw the black rubble of entire villages still smoking in the freezing air without a trace of human life remaining. He stared, unable to understand what his eyes were telling him. An empty road which had wound through an old and thriving village, tidy gray-roofed houses on either side, now stretched lonely and bare into the distance with ashes like sloping drifts of black snow strewn across it, its life and people and history gone forever.

He was wounded seventeen days later. The Partisans had blown up bridges and railway stations to hinder Nazi advances. The Germans counterattacked with Stukas. The bombs dropped all around them and although none of them made a direct hit, a tree was hurled from the blast of a bomb and crashed down upon the wagon Stane was driving. The horse was killed and nothing was left of the wagon except the axle shafts and springs. Stane lay on the floor of the forest, his ears bursting with the sounds of the falling bombs and feeling something warm flowing over his body.

"I must be dying," he whispered. "O God, forgive me my sins, I confess all—forgive me, take me on my final journey . . ."

He opened his eyes on an operating table in a local hospital in Dalmatia. His shoulder had been severed and he had lost a lot of blood, but he was stitched up and felt almost no pain. The doctor did not believe him when he told them he was only nine years old. They insisted he was lying and wrote on the records that his age was thirteen.

Partisan orders called for fast surprise assaults, night forays and sudden attacks on the enemy from the rear. It was vitally important to gain a booty of weapons and ammunition after each assault.

Each Partisan formation had its own headquarters, and these subordinate headquarters were directly or indirectly responsible to Tito's General Headquarters. Communications were by couriers and captured enemy wireless sets.

There was no fixed front. Fighting was with small arms only and limited stocks of ammunition. Their enemy was well trained, well armed, well equipped, well supplied, motorized and supported by strong armor artillery and aircraft. The aim of the Partisan was to attack when the enemy least expected it, where he was weakest and then quickly disappear into the mountains and forests, leaving no trace of the escape. If, after a battle, the enemy losses did not outnumber Partisan losses by at least five to one, the Partisans considered it a defeat.

Victories were not lasting. Villages and small towns the Partisans captured by sudden attack would have to be quickly abandoned when the enemy counterattacked. In this way towns and villages changed hands again and again, and each harrowing experience left the village more battered and with fewer inhabitants. This is what happened while Stane was in the hospital. Without warning, the occupying Partisans prepared to move out because the Germans were advancing.

"We will leave you here," his officer told him at his bedside. "Give them a good 'Heil Hitler' and they will let you live."

Stane rose up to a sitting position, defying sudden pain in his shoulder and back.

"Never!" he shouted. "*Zivio* Tito! I would rather die a Slovene than live as a Nazi!"

He had heard about the fate of boys whom the Germans got their hands on. They were taken to Germany and worked like animals on farms and in factories. They were forbidden to speak their native Slovene language and their names were changed. An Ivan Smit became Johannes Schmidtt. A Joze became Joseph. Ivica became Johanna. Oh, never. He would never change his heritage. He was a Slovene as was his father and his father's father. He would die a Slovene. Besides, he feared that if the Ustase captured the village, he would be killed. His eyes would be gouged out to roll about in a Ustase pocket and be proudly displayed in some pub.

The commanding officer looked at him with a grim expression. "You are brave. But you must not slow us down. Can you walk?"

"Yes, sir."

"What is your age?"

"Nine years, Comrade."

The commanding officer's eyes narrowed. He stared at Stane with such a deeply penetrating look that the boy thought he was reading the words in his brain.

"Dear God!"

"Sir?"

"Nothing, it is nothing." Then the officer blinked, straightened, and said, "We're pulling out at seventeen hours. You have fifteen minutes to join your detachment, soldier."

Chapter Twenty-nine

The night was black; clouds crowded out the stars and the moon was hidden so there was little light to follow through the woods. They always travelled by night in order to keep their movements unseen. Stane was assigned to an ammunition wagon with an old man whom they called *Stric*, meaning uncle. He was a burly man covered with hair from the finger to the eyebrow. Stane liked him immediately. They would be together most of the summer. Stane took his orders from him.

They travelled all night, behind their unit. They struggled their way through the mud and thick woods, prodding their puffing and snorting horse. They did not sleep; in fact, much of the time Stane had to walk the horse through the thick brush, pulling and coaxing it and forcing it to keep moving. The pain increased with each step. Every shadow and snapping twig seemed to frighten the horse. *Stric* cursed it, snarling that the fool beast could get them blown to bits.

The battle took place at dawn. It was a bloody one, at the village of Gakovo in Croatia. Ustase were garrisoned in the church and their machine gun fire ripped up everything in sight. Stane hid beneath some trees near a pond. Mortar shells exploded around him. He hid his head so he would not get hit with flying splinters.

With added ammunition and more soldiers attacking from the rear the *Partizani* had the stronghold. Burnt powder seared Stane's eyes and throat. There was the stench of burning huts, dust, human blood. In the pond near him he saw weapons of dead soldiers floating like toys, and right near his foot was a human head, its hair tangled in the roots of a tree. He sat very still on the young, white-green beech leaves, remembering the words his father had written. *I carried the gun but I did not kill.*

Those Partisans who had survived the horrors of Kosjeric, Milanovac, Mionica and Valjevo were hardened to war. They had seen enemy soldiers light bonfires on the bodies of their friends, seen lines of bent figures digging their own graves with their hands before being shot. . . . The war to them made human life seem like a dubious commodity.

Killing was more than fighting for liberty. It was fiercely passionate, wild, hateful, psychopathic. The war drew out the human madness which otherwise may have lain dormant. There emerged an attraction to the bizarre, to the beauty of bombs and fire and blood. Men and women were drawn to the spectacle. The men who found a particular love for destruction were the ones who set the fires to the homes of villagers and to churches. One Ustase would actually fly into a screaming rage if he could not personally light the torches to the Orthodox churches which were filled with people. Their screams as the church went up in flames reinforced and spurred him onto further atrocities.

The executioners, the men who lined up the prisoners and shot with guns or stabbed to death with their bayonets, were specially chosen. They were the ones who dearly loved to kill. *Stric* told Stane of the Cetnik whose job it was to make sure the victims were dead after they had been lined up and shot. He leaped upon the corpses with his bayonet, stabbing at them wildly until he fell exhausted. Covered in sweat and the blood from a pile of dead men, he then gave the sign for the dirt to be thrown over the bodies. He did his job well. *Stric* thought he was even decorated for his good work.

And through the stench of death and hate were the prayers and pleas of the Christian believers. In spite of the thud of mortars, clap of howitzer shells, and burst of Nazi leaders, they proclaimed resolutely, "God is a God of love and He loves us."

The battle was so confusing that Stane did not know which soldiers were which. He sat with *Stric* one afternoon, pressed against the side of an old well, when a few Stukas and Dorniers swooped low overhead, bombing and strafing. Stane threw himself face down. Holding his head and trembling, he heard a voice, so gentle and kind that he wanted to embrace it and never leave its sound. The voice said, "Move over there—beside that pear tree."

He grabbed *Stric's* shoulder and shouted, "Come!" *Stric* would not budge. "Please! Come!" Coughing and gasping for breath, the old man followed Stane on his belly as they crawled to the pear tree just seconds before a shell burst directly where they had been positioned. Anti-personnel shrapnel flew through the air, missing them by inches. Nearby were some Partisans lobbing shells into a captured 105 mm gun. Stane, his head covered and his mouth filled with dirt and dust, prayed and thanked God for sparing their lives.

By nightfall it was all over. The airplanes had disappeared into the blaze of a spring sunset and the gunfire ceased. The *Partizani* were lining up the captured Ustase. One young prisoner was yanked from his hiding place beneath some floor boards of one of the houses. He was pulled out to the road screaming, "*Ne! Ne!*" As he got to his feet he pulled the pin of a grenade and blew himself to pieces. So great was his hatred for the *Partizani*, he would rather blow himself up than fall into their hands.

Two Partisans were wounded in the blast and there was much cursing and shouting over it. Several of the captured Ustase defected to the side of the Partisans, however. In fact, many of the Partisans in the unit were formerly enemies of the *Partizani*. Germans, Italians, Ustase and Cetniks had left their own battalions and were now in Tito's Partisan National Liberation Army.

Later Stane saw a young Partisan boy, a courier about thirteen years old wearing the green tunic and cap with the red star over the forehead, talking to an officer. The boy suddenly recognized another Partisan. Shouting and crying, a worn and dusty soldier ran toward him, his arms stretched toward the boy. They kissed and embraced and wept like children. Tears fell on Stane's cheeks also as he watched the two hugging and weeping. It was a father and his son. The father did not know his son was a Partisan and had not seen him in over a year. Reunions like these were the blessings and tragedies of the war. In five minutes the soldier had to leave his son and catch up with his unit.

Stric cursed and fingered his mustache. "What is to become of us? Poor wretches. Dear God, what will this war bring us to? When this war ends there will be another . . . and so it goes in this life."

Chapter Thirty

Jozeca was far from the village when the early morning sun shone on the red tile roofs and the smells of wood smoke filled the air. She knelt on her knees beneath the poplar tree, her heart pounding loudly, her hands trembling. Lying before her was a wounded Partisan soldier, his left leg sheared nearly off. Minutes earlier he had been fine; walking along, talking and chewing a plug of turkish tobacco. Then he had stepped on the mine.

"My leg! Is it gone?"

She tied a tourniquet around the leg and bandaged it as best she could. "Be brave, *Tovaris*. We will bring you to a hospital."

They would have to carry him to the *Partizanske* hospital, cut into the forest like part of the landscape.

She felt so far from home. After Stane had disappeared from his hiding place, the *Belogardisti* [1] arrived in the town. They forced their way into the homes, breaking dishes, pulling apart beds and throwing possessions around the rooms. Jozeca watched helplessly as they dragged Jakob from his bed and pulled him out of the door.

"*Zakaj*? Why? O Jesus! God! Help us!" she screamed.

Ana stayed with Jozeca after they took Jakob away. Little Josip lay in a small ball in the bed shaking the bed with his sobs. He would tremble and shake with fear even when there was no danger around.

Ana and Jozeca prayed into the night. They continued praying every night for a week. Hour after hour on their knees they prayed for the mercy of the Lord. Then a week after Jakob had been taken away and eight days after Stane's disappearance from the cave, three of the *Belogardisti* pounded on the door. Jozeca sat stunned in the kitchen listening to them heave blows against the door. At last Ana moved to open it. They had guns. The women were forced to hold their hands in the air until the flat had been searched.

Josip had hidden in the window when he heard them coming. As they were taking his mother out the door, his sobs and shaking

---

1. Clerical soldiers who led punitive expeditions on the side of the Axis. It was the Belogardisti who directed the massacre in the Jasenovac Camp where thousands of resistance fighters were beaten to death with hammers.

were so loud, he could be heard. The *Belogardisti* stopped in the steps.

"Listen!"

"*Partizani!*"

They listened, their faces set. "*Partizani!*" Then they commanded Jozeca to report to them the next day and fled quickly into the night. But the *Partizani* never came. In fact, there were no *Partizani* in the area.

"God performed a miracle, Ana!"

"They heard what no other ear could hear."

Then Josip ran in from his hiding place sobbing and frantic with fear. Jozeca swept him into her arms. "Again the Lord has used my son to save our lives. Thank you, Jesus."

Ana quickly said, "You must run into the hills and join the *Partizani* before the morning! You must leave at once! They have already taken Jakob! Next they will take you!"

Ana was right. There was no other way. Tomorrow would be too late. They would either kill her or send her to a camp or prison. She packed a few things into a basket which she strapped on her back. Ana wept as she embraced her.

"God go with you, *sestra.*"

"Take care of my son, Ana. Please. As your own."

"I shall. Perhaps you will find my Stane."

"*Nasvidenje*, Good-bye!"

"*Nasvidenje.*"

She kissed Josip, prayed, and ran into the hills.

It was several hours before she found the Partisans. They told her she was crazy to join them. "We are surrounded by the Germans and the *Belogardisti*. In fact, it is impossible that you got through! Are you alone?"

"Yes, I am alone." She could hardly define their worn and drawn faces in the darkness. "But not really alone. God is with me."

If they had known she was pregnant, they would have sent her away. One of the reasons for this strict Partisan discipline was that pregnant women were particularly vulnerable to enemy interrogation and torture. Information could be easily extracted from them.

The soldiers nick-named Jozeca their "Good Luck." One windy afternoon in late winter they were on the march in the northwestern part of Slovenia and she was ordered to take cover in an ammunition magazine. The magazine held a stock of rifles and was well hidden in the brush. She refused to take cover, explaining that she wanted to remain with the men. It was only minutes later that a low-flying Stuka dropped a bomb, a direct hit on the magazine. She and the men were safe. After that she had their respect.

She worked with every bit of energy she had. Lice was a big

problem. She washed the soldiers' clothes in cold water and hung them up to dry on branches of trees. She cut hair, cooked what there was to cook and nursed wounds. She refused to carry a gun. She prayed constantly, knowing that any minute she could lose the child she carried. Her first pregnancy had held her bound to the bed. Now she was marching through forests and mountains with the army, eating only a piece of black bread on some days and drinking only water or fiery peach brandy.

She prayed softly and quietly, thanking God for the need for prayer. "Ah, if it were a simple thing, this matter of bearing a child, then perhaps I should never pray. And, dear Lord, if I were not in the forest with this army, knowing at any minute I could be shot or blown to pieces, perhaps I would not pray as I do with every breath. Would prayer be my life?"

"O God, look down on me, your handmaiden. Forgive me! In this war I am a woman of prayer. But if it were not for the war, would I be such a woman? O God, save us all. O God, save me from myself."

As she marched, the only reality she knew was the presence of the Lord. All else was unreal, passing, of little meaning. Did it take a *war* to realize this?

The soldiers saw how she got down on her knees and prayed. Once when their detachment was surrounded on all sides by the enemy, they could hear her pleas through the crashing of the howitzers and spattering of bullets.

"O my God, if you answer my prayers, please answer today. Give us to get out of this trap. Do according to your kindness and give us to get out of this trap."

One of the officers, pulling a 20 mm Breda into position, cursed and told her to shut up.

"Do not complain," she responded. "It may look helpless but God has just told me it will be okay."

The officer was angry. "You are a fool! It is impossible to escape. If you would shoot a gun instead of wasting your time saying prayers—"

But they escaped. There was a weak spot in the enemy line and they escaped right under the noses of the Nazis. And when they passed into freedom Jozeca pointed to heaven, and commanded them to thank God for helping them.

"God delivered you from the hands of the enemy! God delivered you! Remember that!"

Now the soldier with the severed leg was being carried through the forest, his blood staining the leaves and soaking into the dust behind him.

"O God, answer this my prayer and save that man's leg. Help

him and get him to safety. Lord God, hear this my prayer."

She knew as they marched that her own time was drawing near. She had kept her pregnancy hidden from the men. She wore an army shirt and a heavy jacket with a leather belt tied around her middle. She also wore a pair of heavy artillery boots and on her head a narrow green cap with the red star sewn on the front. The men's clothes on her already round body hid her pregnancy.

That night they scouted their way through the forest with a glowing piece of wood. They were exhausted and hungry and one of the soldiers was complaining miserably.

"O for just one taste of *polenta*! Dear God, what I would not give for *polenta*!"

Jozeca heard him. "What would you give, *Tovaris*?"

"Anything, *Tovarisica*, anything."

"Would you give your heart to the Lord Jesus?"

"How can you talk of such things? I cannot put my teeth deep into this thought when all around me is death and evil."

"God works all things out so that good results even from evil. Did you not know that?"

The tired soldier lit the butt of a cigarette.

"Answer my question, *Tovaris*. If I pray to the Lord and ask Him to give you *polenta* right now, this very night, and He answers that prayer, what will you give Him?"

"Ah! Does *polenta* grow on trees? Eh? Woman, you are mad."

"Be so kind as to answer my question."

"All right, *Tovarisica*. If your God can give me *polenta* right now, this very night, I promise I will go to church every Sunday if I live through this war."

"*Tovaris*, it is your heart He wants. If you gave Him your heart, it would be more pleasing to Him than promises which are so easily broken."

The soldier was agitated. The others were listening, but nobody dared mock her. They had seen her God work too many wonders. In fact, there was talk among them that wherever Jozeca was, it was safe—because God was with her.

"Ah—all right," said the man. His tough jaw which he had stuck defiantly upward sagged agreeably downward.

That evening British planes roared overhead and suddenly the sky was filled with black dots. Packages of food, medicine and clothing fell from the planes. Villagers and special Partisan units were there to receive the supplies. They had lit torches so the pilots knew where to make the drop. The Partisans collected the supplies, loading them onto peasant carts and carrying them quickly to safety.

There were German troops in the nearby hills as well as German

Luftwaffe, so they worked quickly to get out of the open valley. The area was cleared, fires extinguished, and all traces of activity were camouflaged. The entire process took only a few hours.

Jozeca and her detachment considered the drop miraculous, as did the officers and even Tito himself. [1]

After they ate that night, for the first time in many weeks their bellies were satisfied. When the doubting soldier opened his package, he pulled out, among other things, toothpaste, chocolate, tins of fish and meat—and a package of *polenta*. That night as he ate *polenta* the tears dripped from his jaw onto his gray army coat.

Jozeca held her Bible close to her cheek, lifted her eyes to the hills and prayed. The black mountains in the distance were like sharp teeth biting the night sky. She said, "Thank you, Lord, for *polenta* and thank you for this child to which I am about to give birth."

---

1. In May 1944 Churchill said in a message to the House of Commons: "We have proclaimed ourselves the strong supporters of Marshal Tito because of his heroic and massive struggle against the German armies. We are sending, and planning to send, the largest possible supplies of weapons and to make the closest contact with him."

In August 1944 Tito conferred with Churchill and British military leaders in Italy. In the talks with Churchill, Tito repeated his earlier statements that he had no intention of communizing postwar Jugoslavia.

Chapter Thirty-one

On September 8, 1943, the Allied Supreme Middle East Command ordered the Italian Army occupying Jugoslavia to surrender to Tito's Liberation Army. Many Italian units eagerly turned themselves and their equipment over to the nearest Partisan units. Some who were not quick enough were seized by the Nazis and Cetniks.

There was a village in the farthest Julian Alps near the Italian frontier where a German general had been killed. As a reprisal, the Germans massacred the entire male population of the village. They forced the women to stand and witness the slaughter and when it was over they were lined up and herded out of the village.[1]

That same month Hitler launched the Sixth Enemy Offensive. A huge Nazi onslaught drove Partisans out of their positions in Slovenia and Dalmatia, the positions which the Italians had surrendered. It was a race to see who would capture more of the Italian equipment—the Nazis or the *Partizani*. The Partisans managed to seize most of the islands and the coastlands of Dalmatia and much of the Italian-held Slovenia, except Ljublijana, as well as Istria (then the Italian province of Venezia Guila) and most of Montenegro. The Partisans also captured great quantities of Italian arms, and they were joined by huge numbers of recruits. By the end of 1943, the Partisan army numbered 300,000.

A British military mission commanded by Brig. Fitzroy Maclean reached Tito's headquarters to organize Allied military and medical aid for the Partisan army.

The pains were closer and harder as the morning sun shone over the hills. The forest was green and sweet smelling and there was a thin layer of frost on the ground.

"*Tovarisica*," is it well with you?"

It was Georgl, the man who had eaten *polenta*. She could not disguise the pains of labor. She moaned slightly and rolled to her side in an effort to get to her feet.

---

1. But later these women were to come back and rebuild the village. And they forbade any man to ever enter it again. There they sit to this day, hollow-eyed, clad in black, a pitiful cluster of crones, living desolate, bitter lives as Slovenia's living monument to the war dead.

"*Tovaris*," she whispered, "I must draw apart from the others. Please—help. . . ."

He helped her to her feet but she doubled over with a sharp contraction.

"*Tovarisica*, are you hurt? What is it?"

"I am giving birth, Georgl."

"—You are—*what*?"

"Please, *Tovaris*, you are standing there with your mouth on your chest. Help me. Help me draw apart from the others—"

"We are not far from a village. We will find help for you there. Can you hold out for a few more kilometers?"

"I am not sure, *Tovaris*. I will try my best."

Georgl risked his life bringing her to the village where he found a midwife. She gave birth in the woman's kitchen, on a little cot by the stove. She could smell paprika and onion. During the delivery she pressed her eyes tightly closed and sighed with each breath, "Jesus! Jesus! Jesus!"

It was a girl. She was thin and red and there was a thick mass of black fur on her head. Jozeca laid her on her stomach and, thanking God, fell asleep.

She could not rejoin her detachment with a newborn child, and so after a few days she knew she would have to start walking back home. She carried the baby in her arms, and on her back she carried a few supplies which the Partisans had given her.

In the afternoon she rode about forty kilometers in a lorrie filled with soldiers and at night she slept in the forest. The baby, whom she named Julijanna, slept most of the time and cried seldom even though she received very little milk.

It was getting colder at night now and she felt the harsh air pierce through her skin to her bones. She carried Julijanna inside her coat next to her skin to keep her warm. One afternoon, lying beside a tree to rest with the baby sleeping on her belly, she heard the sound of footsteps. There were several of them advancing in her direction. They were speaking German. She pressed herself against the tree, making herself as small as she could, but she was in plain view of the soldiers. She watched them come toward her; there were four of them. They must have been separated from their detachment. She could tell by their walk that they were not scouts. Their guns were slung across their chests and tied to their belts were several hand grenades. They wore steel helmets on their blond heads.

"Dear God, do not let them see me." She lay with her breath sucked in watching them march toward her. If one of them flickered an eye just a hair to the right, she would be spotted. But they marched right past her without noticing her against the tree, just three feet from their boots.

After they were out of sight she lay holding her breath for a few more seconds, her heart beating wildly. Then suddenly behind the brush she heard a voice.

"*Halt! Halt! Oder wir werden schutzen!* Stop! Or we'll shoot!" She recoiled, "Dear God!"

But the voice was not directed at her. Through the weeds and brush she saw a youth of about sixteen wearing peasant clothes and short black boots. He stood poised like an animal about to spring behind the German soldiers. In his hand he held a long stick.

"Drop your weapons!" he ordered, jamming the stick into the back of one of the soldiers.

"Do not shoot!" the German screamed and he threw down his semi-automatic rifle.

The youth lunged for the rifle and without a pause, shot the Germans through the necks. They fell to the ground in soft thuds. Two other youths emerged from the trees and stripped the dead bodies of their clothing, weapons and mess tins. They worked quickly, not speaking. The sight was horrible, a nightmare. But it was not uncommon. Jozeca knew enough about war to know that no matter how horrible a scene, there was always something worse waiting around the corner.

The baby, awakened by the gun shots, squirmed inside her coat and emitted a high wail. Jozeca gasped. "*Ne, ne*, not now. Not now, little one!"

But it was too late. They heard her. One of them fired through the trees in her direction. Jozeca screamed, "*Jas sem Partisanska!* I am a Partisan!"

They ordered her out with her hands over her head. She carried Julijanna above her head as she stumbled into the clearing where they stood. They eyed her suspiciously. "Are you alone?"

"*Ja. Ja.* But not really alone. God is with me."

Their looks were so evil that Jozeca shuddered. A wave of nausea flooded her. "O God, help me!"

They questioned her and she told them why she had left her unit and where she was headed.

"Where is your unit now?"

"I do not know."

Then she realized, in horror, that these were not Slovenian youths at all. They were not Partisans. They were not even Jugoslav. Only one of them spoke Slovene and it was strange and broken. The others spoke Italian.

She fell to her knees weeping loudly. "Dear God! Have mercy! Have mercy on me! Have pity! Hear me, God! God in heaven, hear me! Help me! O God! Help me! Save me!"

The youths were stunned at her sudden outburst. Her body shook and she clenched her fists toward heaven screaming and shaking her fists. "Dear God! Mercy! Dear God! O Lord Jesus! Help me, Lord! Save me!"

Then the youth who spoke Slovene said to her, "We will not harm you, *Gospa*. We want only to go home. We do not wish to fight anymore."

Her face was a mass of tears. She had not heard him. "Please do not harm me! I am a mother! See, here is my child. Have mercy. You have mothers, do you not? Think of your own mothers!"

"Uh, do you have food? A gun?"

"*Ne*! I will not carry a gun. I will not kill. I beg you, do not harm me!"

They looked from one to another and forced themselves not to smile. Jozeca was on her knees holding her baby for them to see. They took her side cap with the red star sewn on it, and helping her up, the one who spoke Slovene warned, "You did not see us here. Do you understand?" She nodded her head up and down. Then they ordered her to lie face down with the baby and cover her head. She obeyed, still crying. She lay there for what seemed like hours before she lifted her head. They had disappeared into the woods and she was alone in the clearing with the bodies of the dead Germans. She winced as she looked at the face of the one nearest her. Flies were walking across his open eyes.

She could barely walk. She trembled and wept as she made her way through the woods. When she reached the river, she crossed it by scaling the rocks, and then she ran with all her strength until she reached the road. Now the baby was crying hard. She was hungry and Jozeca had no milk to give her. She would have to find a farm and beg for a few drops of milk.

Her feet were swollen and blistered when she finally made it up the hill to the little farmhouse nestled behind the grove of linden trees. It reminded her of the farm in Brice where she had grown up. By the road was a shrine to St. Cyril. Out of habit, she crossed herself.

At last she was at the door. An old man opened it cautiously. He had white hair and his eyebrows were white and the hairs in his nose were white. There were even white hairs poking out of his ears.

"Good day," Jozeca managed to say before all color and movement faded and she sank to the floor.

"*Gospa*! Wife!" shouted the old man. "Come! It is a woman with a child! I think she has died on our doorstep."

An old woman, gray haired, strong as a steel plow, hurried to help him pull Jozeca's body and the screaming baby into the house. "Lock and bolt the door! She is a *Partisanska*!"

They stretched Jozeca on the bed by the stove in the big room. It was warm in there and on the walls were many tapestries and blankets keeping out the drafts. Smells of wood burning, pine, and cooked cabbage mingled with those from the pots on the stove half-filled with cooked vegetables and apples.

"Tch, tch," clucked the old woman. "It looks very bad. She has only recently given birth. She is bleeding heavily." The old man held the baby and carefully spooned warm milk into her mouth while the old woman tended to Jozeca.

"They look like they're both starving."

They stayed with the old couple for nearly a month. Jozeca regained her strength and knitted sweaters and made quilts which would be sold in the market. The old couple were kind and loving and Jozeca told them, "God sent me to you. I know it. You have been angels. Are you sure you are not angels?"

"God forbid, child. Far from it."

"Surely you are believers."

"We attend mass when we can, always on holy days."

"But let me put to you a question."

"Please."

"Do you love the Lord Jesus with all your heart?"

Night after night they sat by the stove and exchanged words. She read to them from the Bible. It became the best time of the day. Friends and neighbors often joined them when they came to bring news of the war or to work in the old man's fields. Partisans also came and Jozeca helped boil their clothes, bathe and feed them.

The old woman told her how the Germans had been there and the Ustase and the Italians. "The Italians were the most humane. They even thanked us for the food. But the others—it is a miracle we are still alive. I believe that your God must have protected us."

"He is my God and He is your God."

"I have prayed to St. Methodius."

"*Ja. Ja.* I have also prayed to him. But I tell you, I have not prayed to St. Methodius in many years. Now I pray to the Father, Son and Holy Spirit."

"Ah, this is the Protestant way, *ne*?"

"I believe that the Lord Jesus is my Savior, *Gospa*, because the Bible says He died on the cross to save me from my sin, and the sins of others, and He gives me eternal life."

"Ah, this I can understand. Why do the priests make it so confusing? *Dominos* this and *Dominos* that. But what you say is Protestant, *ne*?"

"I do not know about Protestant, *Gospa*. I know about Christian."

"The Protestant religion is from Germany, *ne*? It is the religion of the Nazis."

"I do not know about that. I know there are many religions—Moslem, Orthodox, Catholic, Protestant—but only one God."

"Humph. I have heard of these Lutherans—'the just shall live by faith.' "

"Why, *Gospa*, that is very beautiful!"

"It is the preaching of a Protestant."

"But is it not beautiful? Is it not wonderful? Where did you learn that?"

"A preaching man came here a few years back. He told us to have faith and other things I cannot remember. In fact, he talked like you."

"Truth?"

"*Ja. Ja.* He gave us a Bible—here. I had almost forgotten. Oh, but many times I hoped he would return. He came just three times."

She held the small black Bible in her hands and carefully opened it. There on the inside cover was written "*Jakob Kovac, evangelist, 1 Cor. 2:2.*"

That night lying on the bed holding her little daughter beside her, she cried for Jakob. Just the sight of his name brought back his sounds, smells, his touch. She longed to hear his voice again, to hide in his strength, to clothe herself in his nearness. She imagined herself sitting beside him in the presence of others as he talked and gently guided the conversation. She would sit still, quiet, listening to the sound of his voice, the strength of his words, and in him, the closeness of him, she would be safe, sure, completely happy.

But the crunch of the straw beneath the blankets, the sound of the clock ticking and the biting cold air of the strange house reminded her that she was alone, without him, and she felt again unfinished, like a pot without water.

"My heavenly Father, I believe you are a loving God and I believe that you answer prayers. That is why I know that you have mercy on my son and on my husband whom I cannot see. I know you will bring us together again."

She thought of little Josip and squeezed the edge of the blanket to hold back her tears. "My Jakob, my Josip, my brave men—God have mercy. We will be together again."

Chapter Thirty-two

The Partisan army was immensely popular with the people. Their war cry, "Liberty to the People!" and their leader, Tito, whom they lovingly called their "Little Flower," won the unanimous favor of the Jugoslav people. And without the help of the peasants, villagers and farmers, the Partisans could not have known the resounding success they did by the end of the war.

Villagers sewed clothes, knitted sweaters and socks, kept arsenals beneath their rugs and hid food in holes in the fields. They helped in any way they could, concealing the soldiers, giving them food and shelter, carrying supplies in their wagons and carts to Partisan positions in the mountain and forests, and acting as couriers.

The men of the Second Group of Detachments, in fighting their way through Stajerska to Koruska, often stopped, cold and hungry, at the doorways of Slovene homesteads. Instead of banging on the doors with the butts of their rifles, they sang old Slovene songs. Maybe they recited a poem by Preseren. The people gladly received them and gave them food and shelter. This approach was a far cry from the Cetniks who rode their horses right into the houses to plunder food and supplies from the alarmed families inside.

When the enemy offensives began, whole villages often fled their homes in dread to the mountains. The songs of the Partisans were replaced by the machine guns and blazing torches of the Nazis.

Before the elections in 1944 slogans were painted on houses reading *NAZA REPUBLIKA!* Our Republic! and *HOCEMO TITO!* We Want Tito!

Hysterical crowds in the towns chanted, "*Zivio Tito! Zivio Tito!*"

Other slogans before the election in 1944 were, "Three cheers for *Naza Republika* with King Peter down the drain!"

"Tito fought but the King got married."

"*S Titom v Borbi S Titom v Republik!*" "With Tito in the struggle, with Tito in the Republic!"

"*Zivio Zivio Zivio!*"

The National Liberation Movement made wonderful promises. They announced that it was their aim not only to win the war and expel the invaders from their country but they also intended to create better living conditions for the people—in fact, to produce a new type of human being with new human relations. All of the speeches and talk were grand and strange to the peasants' ears.

The Young Communist League became particularly active in liberated territories and tried to open old schools or start new ones wherever they could, whether in barns or under trees. Except in Slovenia where literacy had a higher rate, the rest of Jugoslavia was largely illiterate. And the people wanted to learn reading and writing.

The promises sounded good. After all, anything was better than the tyranny under which the people had suffered for centuries. That is what the leaders said. And that is what the peasants told one another along the roads, in the cafes and sitting on the great stoves in their cottages.

It was spring when Jozeca finally arrived home, running through the mud of her own village road. Her face was flushed and her hair, which was now cut off because of lice, blew in wisps around her face. She was thirty-one years old. Her face was still as round as an apple and her eyes were wide and bright. She held the baby, Julijanna, in her arms.

Fifty meters away from the flat she began shouting, "Jakob! Josip!" Then a door flew open and Ana stood there like an apparition. She embraced her friend, weeping and laughing at once. Ana's body was pathetically thin. Then Jozeca saw a little boy clinging to Ana's apron—her Josip, now six years old. She held him so tightly she could have broken his ribs. They were together again.

"Praise be to God! He answered our prayers! We are together again." There was one person missing. Jozeca looked around the room and then, almost too frightened to ask, "Jakob?"

Ana nodded her head vigorously. "The *Belogardisti* released him immediately after you left. He is working in the coal mine."

It all seemed too impossible, too wonderful. Oh, certainly the Lord was good. See the mercies of the Lord. Taste and see. How good, how good, how true and how good. Praise be the name, the name of our dear and faithful Lord!

Jakob was now sixty-five years old and to Jozeca he was more beautiful than ever. His strong face and large frame seemed to hold more dignity and magnetism than ever before. And she loved him more deeply. Of that she was quite sure. They prayed on their knees until the children fell asleep with their heads on the edge of the beds. They were weak from weeping and weak from joy. They fell into bed holding one another as though for the last time.

Ana's son, Stane, was still missing, although she had received two messages from him by couriers. He was well, according to the last message, driving a wagon for the Partisans. He especially wanted her to know that he had not killed anybody and that he believed in God.

"He is eleven years old now," Ana said in a distant voice. "A man."

"A man of God," said Jakob.

Ana smiled weakly and nodded.

It was not long before Jozeca again became concerned with Josip's strange behavior. For no apparent reason he would tremble and stare oddly at nothing as though possessed by a dreadful nightmare. When this happened, she would shout at him to look at her, to stop trembling. He reacted with a blank stare.

One afternoon Josip was outside on the road when a lorrie drawn by two horses came creaking through the mud. Josip lost his balance as it passed by and fell under the rear wheel.

His limp body was brought into the house. The driver of the lorrie was deeply upset. "I am sorry! I am sorry! I have killed him!" Ana screamed when she looked at his head. It was bent oddly and the skin was blue. "My God, he is dead!"

Jozeca burst into the kitchen. "Josip! My son! Get a doctor! Get help! Please! O God, O Jesus, help me!"

There was a nurse who lived in the house upstairs. She and her husband were Germans and nobody in the town wanted to have anything to do with them. She hurried down the stairs when she heard Ana's screams.

"The boy is dead," she told Jozeca. "There is nothing I can do."

"You must! You must do something! He is not dead! God did not bring us this far to take his life away! I will not accept it! Never!" She threw her body on top of her son and began breathing into his mouth.

"That will not help, Jozeca. The injury is in his head."

She continued breathing in his mouth, refusing to believe that God would take her son away from her now. After an hour there was still no pulse, but she breathed once again in his mouth and pulled on his tongue. She thought she felt a tiny warm breath of air come from his throat.

"There is life! There is life!"

The nurse hurried out the door. "The child is dead, Jozeca. But because of you I go to fetch the doctor."

When the doctor arrived, Josip was lying on the bed breathing normally. The color was back in his skin.

But it was soon obvious that Josip was not normal. He regained consciousness but he remained in shock. He was taken to the children's hospital in Ljublijana by ambulance. After many tests, the doctors told her there was nothing they could do for him. They found no organic brain damage, but he was suffering psychological damage.

For the next five years he suffered approximately 150 breakdowns.

He was hospitalized thirty-three times in three different hospitals. But Jozeca refused to believe the situation was helpless. "God gave us this son to train for His glory. Then He raised him up when he had been proclaimed dead. I cannot believe He brought him into this world to be sick in the mind!"

Night after night she remained on her knees by his bed praying until his breathing was regular. The seizures came most often during the night. He would stiffen, scream, and slide into a state of unconsciousness. If Jozeca could get to him at the first flicker of the seizure, she could save him from it. "Josip! Josip! Wake up! It is your mother! Josip, praise the Lord! Wake up!" And if he would wake up crying, he would not slip into unconsciousness.

In a desperate attempt to do all she could for her son, she slept with him in bed at night and lined her feet up with his so the soles of their feet were touching. That way, she could feel if his nerves twitched and she would leap up and shout, "Josip! Wake up! Come, son, wake up! Praise the Lord, Josip! Wake up! Come, son, wake up! Praise the Lord, Josip! Wake up!" and the attack would be aborted.

The believers gathered to pray for Josip. Jakob held the boy in his arms as they prayed. But there was not an instantaneous healing. That very night he had another attack.

Vera, the German woman who lived upstairs, was especially kind and helpful. She was an enormous woman with arms like watermelons. She had six children of her own. In Slovene, she told Jozeca every day not to worry. "Your boy will learn to live with his troubles. Do not worry yourself so. I believe your God will help you."

Other neighbors were scornful toward Jozeca and some laughed at her. There were believers who told her that the reason for Josip's illness was her sin. They hounded Jozeca to confess her sin and make herself right with God.

The children in the village made fun of Josip. He stayed away from them, preferring to stay in the house alone rather than playing with other children.

When he was hospitalized, she was not allowed to visit him every day so she stood beneath his window and whistled "God is Love." He could hear her and he knew she was there near him and praying for him. And Jakob, who worked in the mine from sunup to sundown, often remained on his knees all night in prayer.

"Jozeca, the Bible says 'Ask and ye shall receive,' and we must believe that."

"But, Jakob, I have asked and asked and asked."

"Then ask again!"

She realized, as they stubbornly continued praying for Josip, that their biggest obstacles were unbelief and discouragement.

"Do we believe in the Bible or do we not?" Jakob asked in his loud voice. "Do we believe what God says or do we believe what our eyes tell us? Listen! Our eyes tell us our son is not normal and possibly never will be, but the Bible tells us that by the stripes of Jesus Christ we are healed. And the Bible also says that we receive not because we ask not. Ah, Jozeca, my dearest, I believe often we do not understand what the Bible means by asking."

"I shall never stop asking, Jakob. Never. I believe God gave us this son to bring glory to His name. I believe He gave us this son to raise to be a minister of the Lord. I believe he will one day serve the Lord. I will never stop praying for this son of ours. Not until either he or I is no longer on this earth."

When Josip came home from the hospital he was no better than before. The doctors could not diagnose the problem. It was not epilepsy, they said; it was a form of shock. They prescribed a bland diet and calcium tablets. "And he should never smoke or drink. This would be disastrous to his health, both mental and physical."

"That is all they had to say?" Jakob asked.

"That is all."

"Ah, so. We shall have to see what Doctor Jesus has to say."

"Yes, Jakob."

And so once again they went to their knees. But when young Josip slept that night, he suddenly bolted upright in the bed, emitted a blood-curdling scream, and frantically and pathetically trying to run from invisible enemies, fell unconscious on the floor.

It was the fourth seizure that week.

Chapter Thirty-three

Often Jakob had to leave home to find work. He would walk to Zabukovica or Zagorje to find work in the mines and he was gone for weeks at a time. Food was miserably scarce and jobs were even more scarce. Many were starving and Jakob's family was just barely eating enough to keep going.

Vera gave Jozeca milk and bread to help feed the children when Jakob was away. "But why do you do this, Vera? Why do you take food from your own mouth and the mouths of your children to feed us?"

"Maybe because I believe you are Sent Woman of God and also that *Gospod* Kovac is Sent Man of God. Besides, we have plenty to share. My husband is a doctor in the German hospital and he brings home a little extra now and then."

None of the others trusted Vera. They were certain that she was an informer. The Germans had informers everywhere. Anyone could be one. If one person in town did not happen to like another person or if someone wanted to repay an old grudge or injustice, all that was necessary to gain revenge would be to report that person to the S.S. as an enemy of the Führer. The account would be settled forever. The S.S. would come and remove the entire family from their home, either shoot them, send them to prison or to a camp, and that would be the end of the matter.

If you could not trust your own neighbors of your own blood, how then could you trust Vera, a German? Jozeca did not see her as an enemy, however. She saw her as a human being in need of a Savior. She often prayed for her aloud with the others present in their secret prayer meetings.

But then something oddly sinister happened. Vera's youngest son, four years old at the time, was playing on the road one early morning when a German jeep came roaring out of nowhere. It practically struck the child. Vera, who was watching from the window, screamed and then slumped with relief when she saw the boy was unharmed. But then the vehicle came to a stop farther down the road. A German soldier jumped out, ran back to where the boy was sitting in the dust, swooped him up and carried him to the jeep, depositing him on the seat. With a spattering of loose stones and mud, the jeep drove off and soon disappeared beyond the green and blue hills.

Vera did everything she could to find her son. She went to the German officials, wrote letters, walked to the nearby German occupied towns and villages. But she never located him. Her only witnesses were neighbors who saw what happened from their windows, as she had. None of them dared to help her in her search.

Dr. Herring, her husband, was intensely devoted to his sons. He grieved in front of Vera for his youngest son, but then he said something strange. He said, "You must understand, Vera. It is dangerous here. We must do all we can to assure our sons of a sound future."

He stood by the window skulking and opening and closing his long physician's fingers.

Ana did not sympathize with Vera. "She has five sons. I have none. For her to lose one is not so serious. For me it is everything."

Jozeca lifted everyone's spirits by reading the Bible aloud and singing. She convinced Ana that it would be all right to allow Vera to pray with them, and so the three women prayed daily together at the kitchen table. Jozeca taught them songs with which to praise the Lord.

The women felt serenely happy as they sang and prayed together. And they realized that true contentment comes from above, not from circumstances and not from material gain. They were happy in their souls, although there was not much in sight to be happy about.

Ana grew thinner but her face was the face of a heroine. She had a firm jaw and her clear, green eyes held a steady gaze. Her depressions were fewer and fewer now. She refused to believe that she might never see Stane again and she prayed for him daily.

Vera often prayed for her husband. She was deeply devoted to him and yet she was worried about his soul. He claimed to be an atheist and she longed for him to know God. Lately he seemed to be preoccupied and nervous.

The lives of the three women consisted of prayer, work and obtaining their daily bread, in that order.

Josip was attending school now. He did not have shoes of his own so he wore his mother's, which he carefully removed immediately when he came home. They wore shoes only when it was absolutely necessary so that they would last longer. When their feet grew too big for the shoes, they simply cut out the toes to make room for the growing feet. His pants were sewn out of an old pair of Jakob's trousers, and his shirt was fashioned from an apron belonging to Jozeca.

Every time they heard the roar of heavy internal-combustion

engines, they panicked and ran as fast as they could to the bomb shelter in the mine. And every day they heard salvos of a mortar or field gun in the distance.

One early morning when Jozeca was preparing a bowl of tea for Josip before walking him to school, she heard the planes.

"Let us not run to the shelter, *Mamica*. Let us remain here and pray on our knees."

"*Ne! Ne!*" Jozeca protested. "We will go to the bomb shelter!" She held the baby in her arms, took his hand and they ran with the others to the shelter. Along the way, Jozeca tripped and fell, cutting her leg badly on the rocks on the road. The baby was unhurt.

Bleeding profusely and cringing with pain, she limped to the shelter. In a few moments the planes had passed over the village and it was safe to return to their homes.

Jozeca was silent as she hobbled along beside her son. "Josip, that was the last time we will run to the mine for safety. We shall from now on remain in our house on our knees. I believe I have disobeyed the word of the Lord and I repent."

Josip shrugged and then asked brightly, "Will you play soccer with me later, Mama?"

Chapter Thirty-four

The German woman Vera slowly and steadily began making friends with many of the Slovenes in their German-occupied town. She nursed not only the German soldiers but she also helped nurse the local children and parents when they were ill. She also spoke Slovene, which helped endear her to the people. One afternoon after she had helped the midwife in the village deliver a baby, she told Jozeca, "I am thankful to the Lord for all. Do you know, Jozeca, I am thankful to be here."

"Ah, oh."

"I feel close in my heart to the people of Slovenia. You kindly, hard-working Balkan people who do not wish to be better than anyone else or take over the world—it is good to be among you."

That evening Vera was preparing a soup for their supper when her husband rushed into the flat, obviously agitated.

"Franz? What is it?"

He embraced her briefly and explained in a strained voice that arrangements had been made for them to leave Jugoslavia immediately.

"Leave? But why?"

"We must take only what is absolutely necessary," he said, ignoring her question. "There will be a car waiting for us behind the bakery at precisely 22:00 hours. Can we be ready?"

One hour from now.

"Of course, but—"

He stroked her chin fondly. "Do not be late. I must go along ahead with the children."

"Yes, yes."

"The children will accompany me now because I must first attend to some business, and the children must be with me so as not to arouse suspicion. You will meet us at exactly 22:00 hours with only what is absolutely necessary, you understand, of course?"

"Yes, yes. Of course."

She gathered the children together, wiped their faces, slicked their hair, smoothed their shirts and examined their shoes. She hardly was aware of what she gave them to carry—blankets, sweaters, a dish, a carrot from the soup.

"Now before you leave, let us pray."

Then she kissed each soft, full cheek, embraced her husband, and heard herself saying, "*Wiedersehen*."

Her husband stuck his head back inside the door. "By the way, dearest, please understand that we do what we must do—that is, for certain principles."

"*Bitte?*"

"Ah, it is nothing. I want you to know that I have changed. Something inside of me tells me that there is really a God after all."

"Franz! Do you really mean that?"

"But now there is no time to discuss these things. *Wiedersehen!*"

She quickly gathered together as much food as she could, wrapping it in a towel; some soap, a blanket and socks for the children. Then she hurried down the stairs. She stopped to knock on Jozeca's door.

There was no answer. She knocked again. Then the door burst open. She lost her breath when she looked up into the face of a German soldier.

"Ah, enter, my dear *Frau*," he said menacingly.

"What does this mean?"

She entered the room and found Jakob, Jozeca, Ana and the two young children standing with their faces against the wall.

"We are just asking a few questions."

"What do you mean, a few questions? These people have done nothing wrong."

"You will vouch for them, eh?"

"Of course I will. I am the wife of Dr. Franz Herring. I know these people. I will vouch for them."

The young soldier, brandishing a Walther 38 automatic in his hand said, "Sit down, *Frau* Herring. You may be here a long time this evening."

She had only fifteen minutes to get to the bakery. The soldiers had obviously been drinking. They didn't appear to be in any hurry to arrest anyone. They seemed to be playing some sort of game.

The minutes went by quickly. "Gentlemen. Again I give you my word that these people have done nothing wrong. I live in the building. I see what goes on."

"We are aware that you see what goes on."

"Will you kindly permit me to leave?"

"*Nein. Nein.* You must stay and tell us more about this charming family that has done nothing wrong."

"I am needed at the hospital. Will you kindly—"

"Sit, *Frau!*"

"I am a nurse and I am needed at the hospital—the *Deutsch* hospital."

The soldiers laughed. "Fix us something to eat. We are hungry. We want food."

Her heart stopped beating. They must not find the supplies she packed out in the hall. Her husband had said to tell no one.

Five minutes.

They allowed Jozeca to heat water for tea.

"Will you kindly release me? I have done nothing wrong and I am needed at the hospital."

She would leave the things in the hall, walk at a quick pace up the road so they would not suspect her of anything, then once around the corner, she would break into a run. She could still make it.

"*Please* let me go!"

"Relax, wife of the doctor. The hospital will wait for you."

"Surely you care about the lives of your own countrymen!"

Then the soldier who had not said much whirled and faced her. "Shut up! I am sick of you!"

"I beg you to release me!"

One minute left.

"Please! See how I am begging? Please let me go. I am begging you."

They could hear machine gun fire outside. One of the soldiers jerked toward the window. "Put out the light!"

In the darkness he cursed, "*Partizani!*" They both drew their guns and positioned themselves on their knees at the window. At that exact second, Vera made a lunge for the door. The soldier turned and fired, but the bullet missed her. She sprinted out the door, leaving her supplies in the dirt, and ran down the side of the road, staying close to the houses. She heard the gunfire only vaguely through the hard and heavy pounding of her heart.

She ran along the packed worn dirt path, ducked quickly behind the *kavarna* and ran across the grassy area directly behind the bakery.

The low squat building, crumbling and pocked with bullet holes, was dark, quiet. She could hear artillery fire somewhere at the edge of town, maybe at the hospital site, but here behind the bakery it was still. Then she heard the engine of a car.

She hugged the wall of the building, struggling to see in the darkness. The car was quite near. She stepped forward, listening. But the sound was going away from her instead of coming toward her. Then she saw its outline in a patch of moonlight through the trees as it sped softly away down the road into the night.

Chapter Thirty-five

On May 7, 1945, the German Commander-in-Chief signed an unconditional surrender to representatives. of America, Britain, France and Russia. Shouts of joy were heard all over the world and the happy cries of victory rang out in freedom-loving countries around the globe.

On May 8, Jugoslavia was liberated; but the joy was short-lived, because the days to come were to easily parallel the horrors of the war. There was hunger, famine and a mass campaign to arrest, execute and deport all war enemies remaining in the country. [1]

Vera sat on the chair, her face wet with perspiration. It was hot in the flat as the heat of the morning enclosed the small wood and plaster building. Her large body was bent forward and she stared at her hands, feeling the heat of a thousand furnaces.

She thought back to 1939 when the young German boys had been eager to go to war. They had been taught to believe that Germany was the rightful master of Europe. German soldiers were the heroes of the New Order. She remembered how her own mother wept at the news of another war because the sufferings of the First World War were still fresh to her. Germany did not believe they could lose this war. It was impossible to lose, they thought. Germany was invincible. The summer of 1940 had been so lovely. She had finished nurses' training and Franz had only one year left of his residency. Every German believed the British would not hold out much longer. They thought this because that is what they were told to think.

She remembered how they were not allowed to listen to foreign radio programs. Penalties for disobedience were terrible. The Gestapo had spies everywhere and those who transgressed the law could be sent to concentration camps. They could hear news only of the glory of the Third Reich and the victories of the German Army.

By winter of 1940 the British had not yet surrendered. But the

---

1. During the final stages of fighting in the Balkans and particularly after the retreat of German forces from the country, several hundred thousand people fell victim to Communist reprisals. No German responsibility is attached to these losses.—Wuscht, Johann, *Population Losses in Yugoslavia During World War II*, (Atlantic) New York, 1963.

German press and radio boasted of its ruin and devastation. She remembered, too, how the press had gloried in the bombing and fall of Jugoslavia in April of 1941.

Hitler gloated that no British bomb would ever touch a German city, but in 1942 the cities of Berlin, Hamburg and Bremen were under heavy bombing attack.

Now it was all over. The war was ended. The Führer was dead. Germany had lost. "*The meek shall inherit the earth*," it is written. Not the tyrants, not the oppressors, and not the dictators—but the meek.

The people of the village were certain that Vera would not be arrested. After all, she was one of their own. She had helped the people of the villages and had risked her life as well. After Dr. Herring and the children had fled one night four months before, leaving Vera behind, she had devoted herself completely to helping the people of the towns and villages The Partisans had gained control, expelling the Germans and she had assisted in treating their wounds and washing bandages for the National Liberation Army. Surely they would not arrest her.

And so that night in June when Jozeca went to sleep with her feet pressed against the soles of Josip's feet, she did not hear the boots of the soldiers on the steps outside. She did not hear them coming down the steps with their prisoner, dressed in only her night-clothes, a pair of soft blue slippers on her feet. In fact, it was not until morning, when the open door to Vera's flat, creaking and knocking against the wall, drew her curiosity, that Jozeca found the flat empty, Vera's unmade bed and her shoes still placed by the door as they had been the night before.

Vera was taken in a closed truck to the train where she was put with the other prisoners into a boxcar. They were told they were going to Austria, but they were taken to the border where they were divided into categories: Nazis in one group, Cetnik in another, Ustase in another. Then they were lined up and shot in rows. Vera died singing "God Is Love" in Slovene and German. By accident they put her with the Ustase prisoners, and so she died as a Jugoslav.

The villagers had a saying for the tragedies they bore. They said, "We wear the sorrow." And everyone knew what it meant, for sorrow was worn by them all. There were happy events mingled with their sadness, however, as they waited for loved ones to return from the war. Parents waited for children and children waited for parents. Ana's agony and anxiety increased by the hour as she watched the road from the window, waiting for a sign of her Stane.

She could hardly eat or sleep as she waited. "Surely he will be home any day now. Surely."

One afternoon as she sat by the window watching, she saw a tall, thin figure riding on a horse toward the house. She saw the side cap with the red star sewn on, the gray pants and black boots. She saw him riding the horse, tall, so tall, his face drawn thin and smooth and, as he rode nearer she saw his eyes, two dark holes out of which stared a stunned and weary child. Then she was jumping up and down and pounding on her thighs with her fists: "He is home! He is home! God! God! *Jezes, Marija!* Stane is home!"

Little children ran alongside him as he rode slowly on the hot dirt road. They shouted and called to him. On his narrow chest there were shining medals catching the brightness of the sun as he rode.

"Stane! Dear God! Stane!"

He dismounted and tossed the reins to one of the boys. He ran to his mother and they sobbed and clung together, crushing like flowers. The whole village watched, putting their hands over their hearts and crying. One of their own had come home.

They could not speak for a long while. Finally Stane sobbed, "I prayed every day that I would see your face again, *Mamica.* God answered prayers."

They sat at the table, weeping and laughing and looking at each other. They drank tea and ate army black bread which he had brought with him.

"If there is any one person who does not believe that there is a God, let him go to where I have been these last two years. Let him put my shoes on his feet and walk where I have walked. Then he will know."

They were all silent. Jakob held the boy's arm. The boy continued, "And if that one does not learn through those years that there is a God, then he is one without a heart and without a soul. Such a one is not human. He is a beast."

"And even beasts can learn to praise the Lord, *ne?*"

Chapter Thirty-six

They had coffee and tea but no sugar. They made herb tea from nettles and coffee from acorns. Bread was the hardest to get. The people lined up at the bakery hours before the doors were opened in the morning in an effort to buy a loaf of bread. White bread was unheard of. They ate only black bread, if they could get it. Jozeca planted a garden and they had carrots, turnips, cabbage, beans, onions and peppers to take to market to trade. Often she left for market with twenty kilos of vegetables in the rucksack on her back, to return with only two kilos of flour and a bit of sugar or salt. But one day she came home from market with a real prize—a baby pig. Julijanna and Josip were delighted. Not considering it to be a new addition to their tiny food supply, they saw it as a delightful pet and they set about to build a pen for it.

In August of 1947 Jakob brought a huge bouquet of wild flowers to Jozeca and laid them at her feet. She blushed as he kissed her hands and then prayed with his eyes pressed closed, "Thank you, gracious Lord, for the wife you have given to me. She is the joy and pride of my life. You have given to me to be the happiest husband and father in all Jugoslavia."

She was again with child.

Neighbors mocked and teased her. "Why are you giving a baby to that old man? God will punish you! It is a sin."

Jakob was sixty-eight years old, and they were as happy as soup boiling in a kettle. The mocking remarks and accusations did not annoy Jozeca. She had her husband near her. She had her children. Stane was home with Ana. Theirs was a happy home. Surely God was wonderful and faithful. Often during the night she and Jakob awoke at the same time and, in their happiness, breathed prayers of thanksgiving to God, crying and clinging together. It is one thing to be hungry, and another thing to be cold, but if you have your loved ones near you, you can withstand all.

Once again music filled the house and Jakob led in the singing of hymns at night in his deep baritone voice. Josip and Julijanna loved to sing and Jozeca began to notice that music had a calming effect on Josip. She observed that he had fewer attacks in the night if they sang hymns before going to sleep.

But then one night as the mountain breezes played in the red, yellow and white primroses, crocuses and anemones that Jakob loved to pick for Jozeca, he saw the police wagon and heard the footsteps of the new *policija*. He saw their faces, their noses and thick jaws beneath their gray caps, and he heard them call his name.

"Yes, I am Jakob Kovac."

"You are under arrest."

Jozeca could not believe her ears. "But he has done nothing wrong!" She ran to the police in town and begged them to have him released.

"He is old," she begged. "We have two small children and I am now again with child. Please, he is a good man. He has done nothing wrong."

She was informed that he was accused of having given aid to the Germans—information to German spies.

"But that is impossible. He has never had any contact with the Germans other than to be tortured by them in their prisons."

"Ah, and do you deny having secret rendezvous with a certain Dr. Herring?"

She stared at the man in front of her. Maybe she had not heard right.

"I repeat. Do you deny giving certain information of Partisan activity and whereabouts to Dr. Herring? And do you further deny holding secret meetings in your home to give information to this German spy?"

"German spy—? Vera's husband had been a German spy!"

She was placed under arrest and stayed that night in the local jail. She sat on the edge of the wooden plank which served as a bed and tried to sort things out in her mind. Dr. Herring a spy! That would explain why he did not wait for Vera that night he fled Slovenia. Vera was a Christian and would tell the truth if she were questioned. And that also explained the mysterious disappearance of his son. In order to get him back, Dr. Herring would have to accomplish certain tasks for the Nazis. "O God, have mercy. Poor Vera. God, did you create us for agony? Can we endure to your glory?"

In the morning the police released her because she was pregnant. But she was sentenced to five years in prison and given orders to return after the birth of the child.

"This is my prayer. Before you gave me this life, you gave me eternal life and you loved me. Before I called your name, you already knew mine and called me. I will put my trust in you, my every thought, because there is nothing lasting—not even these dear ones you have given me to love, and not even our deepest suffering. All will pass."

She earned daily food by working in the fields of farmers. For a day's work she would receive some milk or vegetables or maybe some eggs or cheese. Often she or Josip went to the baker's early in the morning, sometimes at three or four o'clock, to be sure to be able to buy a loaf of bread when the store opened at seven o'clock. But many times they went home empty-handed.

When she went to pick berries in the woods, she took Josip and Julijanna with her. They began picking at five in the morning and they picked until past nightfall. Then Josip would take the berries to town to sell or trade them for bread and milk.

The economic conditions were desperate in all of Jugoslavia. Food was scarce, housing totally inadequate, disease rampant, medical supplies lacking, and communications so disrupted that it was difficult to get supplies or government instructions to many parts of the country. There were severe limitations on individual liberty and strict curfews enforced.

Jozeca told everyone who had ears about the love of the Lord. "Oh, cannot you see how much the Lord loves and longs for you to turn your head upward to see Him? If you would just acknowledge Him."

A middle-aged woman, wearing a checked babushka on her head and a soiled gray apron over her worn dress, eyed her suspiciously. "Love—you speak of love with the earth you are standing on red with blood, with the bones of our people crushed into the dust which we now breathe and which clogs our noses—you speak of love?"

"Let me tell you something, dear *Gospa*, it is in crises and battle that we become acquainted with love. I am speaking of real love—the kind only God gives. Because, listen to me, without the crises and battle we can mistake anything for love—good times, peace, kisses and embraces in the dark, the lying smile of a swindler."

The woman fingered the fringe of her sleeve. Jozeca put her finger to the sky. "When the whole world is falling around your legs, you have to know God in order to know love."

She prayed for Jakob every hour, praying strength and courage into him. She knew how he must be suffering in the prison and in need of her prayers to sustain him. "We are one," she told him as she walked to the woods to pick berries. "And if you suffer, I suffer. If you are sad, I am sad." Julijanna, who could barely walk, had to be carried. She kissed her mother's face and Jozeca kissed her back.

"*Moja* Pretty one. Let us pray for your father." And they got down on their knees in the woods and prayed. Josip said, when they had finished, "Father will come home again to us, Mother. You will see. I believe it. He will not die in the prison."

She remembered how Jakob had promised her he would not die of the bullet or the knife. Now she believed he would not die in prison, either. And she remained on her knees praying for every part of his body, every thought in his mind, every word on his lips. "Ah Jakob, my beloved, feel my prayers for you. Feel the love of God there in that prison. He is with you."

But her strength was faltering. She struggled through the days slowly and painfully. She could feel the energy dropping from her. Often she felt feverish. She told no one and yet she knew that it was not well with her. She was burning in flames one moment and chattering with cold the next. She was impatient, nervous and sometimes her thoughts strayed and she lost whole sentences and paragraphs in a whirlwind of hot and cold.

She had to see Jakob. She felt desperate enough to crawl on her hands and knees all the way to Maribor to see him. "My Beloved," she murmured through tears and fever. In her sleep she could see his eyes waiting for her, like pits of dried plums, and she could see his thin hands, turned and empty, hanging at his sides. She awoke often to the sight of his face with his eyes open, staring at nothing. She remembered the bodies of the German soldiers in the woods with the flies walking across their open dead eyes, and in her mind it would be Jakob lying there. Then she heard the wails and screams of the millions of World War II wives, sisters and mothers whose men they gave to Russian, African, European, English and Asian soil.

"Love, Beloved—where are you?"

Chapter Thirty-seven

The train platform was crowded. Men, women and children, huddled together, moved and moaned in their many languages—Italian, Russian, Serbo-Croatian, Slovenian, English, French, German. She thought of the Lord who knew all languages, heard all prayers, knew every cheek sliced with tears and every mouth gathered in laughter.

"Jakob, my husband, I am coming. . . ."

The prison, a scab of a building, leaned out of the sky, its many tomb-like corners, slippery surfaces and concrete edges reeking of death and blood. She worried if her heart would split when she saw him. She planned to savour the sight of him, decided to look at him slowly; not be careless with her eyes, not waste one precious second. She would look at the top of his head first, the white thin strings of hair like spider's webs, then his forehead, bones jutting out and skin so white, white and transparent with broken blood vessels and blue thin veins—then his eyes, dear eyes wet with tears, lids drooping. Dear God! I shall die of anticipation.

Her face was bright pink when she reached the gate. Her hand had perspired and soaked the piece of paper which allowed her the fifteen minute visit once a month with her husband. She asked directions of the guard in a voice too high and loud. He glared at her, but motioned her to pass.

At last she stood before the tall window with the cold iron gates stretched across, separating good from good, love from love. She pressed her hands together and the thought came to her that if the gates were alive she might kill them. Their ugly necks reached from floor to ceiling and a hard metal wall enclosed them in a concrete block envelope. The air was sour with disinfectant and mildew and tears.

Her hands wrung the bars on the window and her knuckles were white. Suddenly a door was being unlocked. There were footsteps. The door was being opened. A man stood in the opened door. He shuffled forward on feet which barely left the floor. He moved toward the barred window, his hands hanging empty at his sides.

Her throat went dry. She felt as though dead wild flowers were caught on her tongue. Dear Lord, he was a ghost! His face had slid downward from the bones of his head, the skin sagging in gray folds. His mouth smiled pitifully, brown, slightly moist. He was crying.

"Heart. Heart of mine . . ." he croaked out in an old man's voice.

She thrust her hands through the bars reaching for his face. "Jakob!" Her fingers reached his mouth and he passionately kissed them.

"No touching!" screamed the guard. He banged on the bar with a stick.

They jumped back. "Do not lose heart," he told her. "God will bring us through all trials."

She nodded, his face dimming in her tears. "Remember there are far more strong than weak," he said.

She wanted to speak, to ask him something that would assure her that he was all right, that they were not torturing him night and day. Wrinkled and stooped, was this ghost her husband? Was he not getting even a chunk of cabbage to eat? She passed the basket of bread and cakes to the guard who inspected and crumbled each piece and morsel before handing it to Jakob.

"You must have sacrificed greatly to bring these cakes to me," Jakob said. "I will share these with my brothers. They will kiss your feet as I do."

He asked about the children. She told him they were well and they sent their love to him. He asked if they were getting enough to eat. Yes, yes, they were getting enough to eat. His tired face shone in the dim yellow light of the room. She breathed unevenly, parted her lips to tell him of her love for him. She wanted her words to caress him, hold him; she wanted to give him her words of love to kiss his gray, sliding face and wash his hidden wounds. She breathed rapidly, the fever bore through to her eyes, burning, hot, mad.

"Jakob . . ." she began. His eyes widened as he waited for her to speak.

She wanted her words to fall like dew from her lips and cover him, comfort him, nourish him. She wanted her words to do what her hands could not—stroke his broken body, caress his bones. "O my dear old soul, sweet dearest, wounded and abused, look upon me. Feel my love. O Jakob, Jakob, reach out with your eyes and your thoughts. Let me hold your thoughts. Look how I am loving you, Jakob. Drink me, drink my words. I am your warm milk. Ah, love, beloved, I can give you only words now, my only gift, words, Jakob, my soul."

Outside it had begun to rain. It fell like needles jabbing the earth's holes and sores. She pressed her face upwards and let it drill at her face.

"O God, O Lord, O heaven . . ."

She looked back at the prison, gray, swollen, ugly, and she parted her arms as in an embrace. "My prison, my sulking prison!" she cried. "You whore, you murderer, I abjure you! Ah, my misery, my heart, you have stolen my Jakob from me!"

Mumbling and stumbling back and forth in front of the prison, raging with fever, she went largely unnoticed. It was partially because she seemed harmlessly insane and also because it was raining a blinding, angry rain and few could see her.

What had she told him? Had he heard her? He had said this baby she carried would bless her greatly. Ah, the time was over so fast. It was only a second. What else had he said? He was within those foul and stinking walls, and he was polishing the wood with his bones. "Beloved body, dearest man. O dear mother of God, they have covered him with wrinkles."

She was hot and feverish. Wringing her hands she marched back and forth in front of the prison. Her boots filled with water and mud and she dropped the prison pass in the flowing mud beneath her in the ditch.

"Look down on me, Father!" she raved. "Look down on me, Holy God, Father of Jesus, Giver of life!" She held her clenched fists high over her head, punching at the rain. "My children are hungry! The earth waits for the bones of my husband! I am alone!"

She shouted and sobbed herself hoarse. "Give me bread for my children and release my husband from this prison! God of mercy! God of holiness!"

Josip waited by the window in the kitchen. The room was damp and dark and the only sound was the rain pelting against the window pane. Three-year-old Julijanna was sitting on the bed in the other room, her round eyes squinting in the darkness. She had been playing with a small ball her mother had made out of wool, but now she was starting to whimper and it made Josip more anxious than he already was. He went back into the big room and sat on the edge of the bed with her. Very softly he began to sing and pat the palms of his hands against hers. She giggled and enjoyed the little game.

He waited to give her the piece of bread so her stomach would not be empty when she slept. Mama always did it that way. Shadows filled the room and soon Julijanna's large brown eyes would dim, she would cry and he would fetch the piece of bread. After they had eaten they would climb into bed and he would lie very still until she went to sleep. She would draw her thin legs up under her and they would pray, "Dear Lord God, look down on us and on our father and mother. . . ."

He looked at her, her thick curls pressed against the pillow as she slept and he felt proud and grown up. He could fetch and carry wood, work in the garden, chop kindling, cook soup, clean and sweep the house, grind grain, go to market and best of all, mind his little sister.

But there was always lurking in the back of his mind a certain fear. He hated his "spells" and yet the thing that caused them, that certain thing—black, hideous, painful, like a drawn sabre—sometimes he could name the fear, other times he could not, but it was there. He could feel it even when he was well, just waiting to grab his throat, throttle his body and throw him into unconsciousness. Most of the time it was the fear that mother and father would be taken away and never return. The blade of the sabre was sharp as a razor, ready to slice his world into pieces and then he would be alone forever with the pounding of the rain against the windowpane and the sound of jackboots stomping closer and closer.

Julijanna slept now and he heard her short, quick breathing. He blinked, trembled slightly and then stiffened. He tried to cry out, tried to cry, "Mama!" but it was too late; the sabre whistled through the air and then it was quiet.

Chapter Thirty-eight

Jozeca climbed the hill from the train station. She was wet and still feverish. She rubbed her swollen belly and talked to it. "Do not fear, my little baby. Nobody will take you from me. You and I will be in life together, my child. I swear it. O God! O Father! O heaven!"

It was night now, very late. Jozeca did not know what time it was, nor did she care. From deep within her she heard the sound of children crying. It seemed to her it was not only her own children she heard but children from all times and all places. Hungry, desperate voices and all crying, "Mama! Mama!"

She trembled, stroked her belly, the helplessness rising up within her. Her arms ached from clenching them upward. "I will not let go of you, God, Father, Holy Jesus! I will not let go until you answer my prayers! Hear me!" And she clenched her fists and pressed her arms towards the sky.

She stalked on until daybreak, stumbling off the road and into the forest, climbing the hills and the side of the mountain. She was hoarse and ached miserably and her feet were red and bulging out of the soaked boots. The *Partizani* had hidden in these hills as had the Nazis, the Ustase, the Italians, and before them, the Austro-Hungarians, the Turks. Let them come! Let the Russians and the Bulgars come too! Let them slice off her ears. Who could prevent her from hearing the voice of God? "Lord! My children are hungry! My old husband is old and in prison! Lord God, look down on these poor hills and your children!"

The rain stopped and the sun floated in the horizon. "Dear Slovene sun," she murmured, "shining on the wicked and the good. Sun of Slovene suns, today I believe God is answering the prayers of this poor Slovene servant." She sat down on the wet grass and continued to talk to the sun.

"A beauty you are, sun, round as a tomato. Gold like heaven's streets—and hot, hot as fire!" She was determined not to budge until God answered her and gave her a sign that He had heard her from heaven and would send help.

She was hot, then immediately cold. She felt the presence of the soldiers in the trees. She was back in the army again with the same men who now imprisoned her husband and held the warrant for her own arrest. She wanted to weep for the sons of Slovenia, Serbia, Croatia, Bosnia, Montenegro, Macedonia—now all united as one Jugoslavia—broiling in their contempt for one another, never resting, always seeking one more act of revenge. . . . O dear God, speak to me, your servant. Blessed Savior, have mercy. I shall not move from this place without a sign, a sign that you have heard me from your holy place.

Then she felt the breeze, cool, sweet, gentle. But there was no sign of a breeze in the meadow between the shining green hills, calmly lying beneath in the sun. Then as she reached over to remove her boots she realized that her fever had completely lifted. O breath of God, thank you, thank you.

Hurrying on home, she saw Josip sitting on the wooden step by the door. She whooped and waved both arms. She had seen him one second before he caught sight of her and was in a full run toward him when he looked up and recognized her. His feet were peddling beneath him before he was in a semi-upright position, and he ran his very fastest, although a little crooked.

"*Mamica! Mamica!*"

He grabbed her legs and she squeezed him tightly. She did not notice him wince with pain. "O Josip, everything will be fine. God has answered our prayers. He has given me a sign. Look at your mother, Josip! I am well. I have no more fever! God has heard our prayers." She was so sure of it, as sure as the nose was in the middle of her face.

Josip did not tell her about his attack. He did not want to take away any of her happiness. But he hurt. When they were inside she noticed his odd walk and that he sat leaning to one side. She took him to the doctor the next morning where he was treated for a broken collar bone and a broken rib and given a wooden brace which he tied to his body with leather straps. He was to wear this to sleep every night in order to prevent the breaking of any more bones in his seizures.

A few days later a man came to the door. His name was Zidar. During the war and occupation he had refused to succumb to the German insistence that he change his name to a German name.

"*Ja sem Slovenec!* I am a Slovene man," he told the Germans proudly. For that retort he and his family were deported to a work camp in Croatia. Now he was back in Hrastnik and he had news for Jozeca.

"I have seen your mother and your brothers and sisters," he told her, "They are well. And also your cousins."

She cried to hear news of her mother and the others and made plans to visit them. She managed to skrimp a little more until she had the fare for a train ticket to Celje to see her mother. It had been three long years.

Trials were being held for citizens who were accused of collaborating with the Fascist reactionary elements subversive to the new Communist regime. Arrests were constantly made. Nobody trusted anyone else. Communist leaders were arrested for such things as saying that the behavior of Soviet officers in Jugoslavia had been inferior to that of British officers. [1]

Passengers on the train remained silent, keeping their eyes and voices to themselves—not unlike the passengers on the train during King Alexander's dictatorship; no one trusted another at that time either. Jozeca had read somewhere that history's moral was that war is mere butchery unless it gave rise to a more stable peace. She was sure it had been written by someone in the West where their philosophy permitted such humane thoughts.

Someone handed her a paperback pamphlet entitled, "What Is Socialism?" She read it on the way to Celje. "Eight hours of work, eight hours of rest, eight hours of self-improvement." Then she read "Aims and Ways of the World Proletariat" and she prayed.

The believers in Celje crowded around her, kissing her cheeks, patting her and embracing her sideways in order not to crush her hugely protuding belly. They covered Josip and Julijanna with kisses and embraces, and Nezka, who cried so hard the tears spiralled down her face, nearly kissed the skin off Julijanna whom she had never seen.

Not one family was untouched by the war, not one family did not mourn the loss of a loved one. A million and a half people died in World War II in Jugoslavia. In four years one out of every twelve died fighting. [2]

There must have been thirty people jammed into the tiny flat in Celje. They prayed and sang softly. Then they shared how God had moved in their lives. Everyone had a story to tell. One woman from Krajn, one whom Jakob had led to Christ during the war, told how she and her children were without food for a whole week.

"I have five children," she said quietly, "and we drank only coffee without sugar. The children were so hungry they went to the fields and ate grass. One day water was boiling on the stove but I had nothing to put in it. My three-year-old said, 'Mama, I'm hungry!' I had nothing. I was standing beside the stove crying. 'O my Lord, give me food. You have promised those who believe will

---

1. Milovan Djilas, one of Tito's three highest aides, was imprisoned for this in 1948.

2. The U.N. Bulletin *Economique pour L'Europe*, Stat. Rev. 1949 Vol. I Nr - 1S-12f. has set the wartime losses of Jugoslavia at 300,000 troops and 1.4 million civilians; in all 1.7 million dead.

never go hungry. Can you see how my child asks for bread?'

"I prayed and prayed. My husband was working in Ljublijana and we had not seen him for over a month. I was in such a misery. Finally, I prayed to the Lord, 'Please take my children and then me! I cannot watch to see my children hungry!'

"I knelt down on the floor with the children all around me. It was about 3:30 in the afternoon. Then I took the children outside. I did not know where to go or what to do. We were all very weak. My youngest one was still crying. We went to the train station. I do not know why we went there; I do not know what we expected to find. But we stood there watching a train climbing the tracks when suddenly my husband jumped off the train. On his back was a rucksack filled with vegetables. He had worked for a woman in her garden and he brought home ten kilos corn, ten kilos corn flour.

"We ran to him shouting and crying. When we entered our house, we knelt and gave praise to the Lord. I prepared the food and we had enough for a long time. This experience was so great for my faith. How the Lord answered my prayer, I will never forget. Because that very day I had planned in my heart to kill first my children and then myself, so I would not have to watch my children starve."

In low tones and in unison, the group exclaimed, "Thank you beautifully, Lord."

The children were dressed in clothes made from British parachutes. Pants were made out of army blankets and Italian and German pants. Most of them had no shoes.

Jozeca's cousin told how her husband brought home a large box of cigarettes which he had gotten on the black market. "How are we to burn these in the stove? Will they warm us in the night or feed our bellies?"

She smiled, displaying space for two missing teeth. "The next afternoon I traded the cigarettes for coal. And when I brought the coal home I counted the pieces—and, do you know, it was the exact amount as the cigarettes!"

"Thank you, Father."

Chapter Thirty-nine

In February of 1948 Jozeca gave birth to her third child. Their new boy was thin, wrinkled and red as a pimento. Jozeca held him close to her in the hospital bed in Maribor and remembered Jakob's words, "He will be of great help to you. He will be your dearest blessing."

She kissed the top of the baby's warm head, soft as lint. "Thank you, Lord," she prayed, and then her eyes closed and she realized that she was exhausted and ached from head to toe. This child had been the hardest one to deliver and the labor lasted twenty-one hours.

"His name will be Janez," she whispered, looking at his little face. "Yes, Janez Kovac—a fine name. O thank you, dear God." And she was asleep.

When she returned home with the new baby, there was not a scrap of bread in the house to eat. She boiled a litre of tea and put one teaspoon of milk into it for the baby's food for the day. Julijanna and Josip went without milk in order that the new baby could have some. They ate bread from a generous neighbor.

The only way they would survive was for Jozeca to put the straw basket on her back and go on foot into the hills, knocking on farmstead doors begging for food. The baby was only ten days old when Jozeca set out through the snow with the basket on her back to beg for some bread for her children.

She felt strong, though; not weak and not feverish. Ever since that night when the Lord had visited her and lifted her fever, she had felt strong and good. She remembered the last time she had seen Jakob at the Hoce prison when she had been delirious with fever. The Lord had answered her prayers; He had visited her and given her a sign that He was with her and that He was her help. It was this visit of the Lord that was to give her strength.

> My strength cometh from the Lord
> who made heaven and earth. . . .

She knew her strength came from the Lord. She knew that in the natural her body was not yet recovered enough from childbirth to be climbing mountains and walking the cold, snow-covered hills each day. She thought of the women in the highlands of Herzegovina, where it was the custom to keep secret the onset of labor as well as the birth of a child. A woman had to withdraw into the fields or woods alone to give birth to her baby. If she cried out in pain or received any help, she would disgrace the honor of her husband's family.

These poor women of Herzegovina gave birth alone and on their knees—it was bad luck to the child to lie down; they severed the cord with a woolen thread ready for the purpose. Afterwards the new mother then went to an outdoor spring and washed the baby, herself and her clothing. Carrying the new child in a white muslin scarf, she would walk on her own two feet back to the house with her treasure.

The Herzegovinians still celebrated over the birth of boys. If it was a boy, the husband fired three shots from his rifle, but if it was a girl no shots were fired. The new mother would be given a goatskin of grape brandy and allowed to lie down. In the excitement, someone might bring her a blanket.

"Thank you, Lord, I am a Slovene woman," she sighed and sang the Psalm:

I will lift up mine eyes unto the hills
From whence cometh my help,
My help cometh from the Lord
Which made heaven and earth.
He will not suffer thy foot to be moved:
He that keepeth thee will not slumber.
Behold, he that keepeth Israel
Shall neither slumber nor sleep.
The Lord is thy keeper:
The Lord is thy shade upon thy right hand.
The sun shall not smite thee by day,
Nor the moon by night.
The Lord shall preserve thee from all evil:
He shall preserve thy soul.
The Lord shall preserve thy going out
And thy coming in from this time forth,
And even for evermore.[1]

1. Psalm 121.

Chapter Forty

At night Jozeca and Ana knitted sweaters to sell in the market. In the little stove, Stane placed the coal he had gathered from the ground. Sometimes he would walk nine or ten hours and come home with only a few pieces of coal. But every day they got on their knees and thanked God for His goodness and His kindness toward them. They sang songs, clapping and dancing to keep warm, and they wondered how anyone could be happy in this life without knowing the great Lord.

Then something was to happen to dramatically jolt their faith upward. A Russian believer who had escaped from Stalin's Russia to Jugoslavia came to Zagorje to stay with his cousin. He was invited to speak at the prayer meeting one night and told the believers that God wanted them to fight a further spiritual battle.

"What means this? Do we not fight a spiritual battle daily even now?"

"God wants us all to fight harder, deeper." Then he saw Josip and stopped. He pointed at him and said, "My child, you have been suffering. Tonight the Lord Jesus Christ will set you free." He left the pulpit, walked right over to where Josip was sitting, placed his hands on his head and began to pray.

Then he shouted at evil spirits to leave Josip's body. The believers joined him in prayer. The man prayed on, shouting at the evil spirits to leave Josip. He told them that Josip was a child of God, that they had no right to inhabit him and cause him to be ill. He continued praying for over an hour and then he said, "Thank God! The boy is now free."

Josip pressed his eyes shut and sat utterly still. Then he told them, "I know that I shall never again have an attack. You have seen the last time I fall down to the floor. I feel clean and my body is at peace. God has touched me. Truly."

He looked at them through clear, bright eyes and smiled. He was right. From that night on he was never again to suffer another seizure.

"Prayer is battle," the man had said. Jozeca resolved to study the Scriptures to learn more about what God had to say about fighting such prayer battles. She did not have an opportunity to thank the Russian brother before he left for Austria to meet the rest of his family.

"O God! Jesus! Thank you! You sent this man to help us! You brought him here with your own hand. Praise be your name forever!"

Spring came and Jozeca walked along the creek's yellow banks listening to the quiet bubbling water and the bristle of the dried cornstalks in the surrounding fields. She walked quickly, up the bank and over the grass, its tender shoots bending beneath her feet. Birds twittered in the distance and for a second she thought she heard gunfire.

The sound of gunfire was ever rattling in the back of her mind—one of the side-effects of surviving the war. She would never forget the sound. Even years later, she would stop in her step, pause with panic, "What was that?" and then sigh with a painful relief. It was not the whistle of a falling bomb, not the volley of machine gun fire.

She was hurrying now as fast as she could. Julijanna was straddled on her back, hugging her neck with her legs hooked around her waist. She was almost there now. The letter was folded in her pocket, already worn out from reading and re-reading it. She was to report to the president of the district to receive her prison sentence.

The hard-packed dirt of the road wound through the town. Chickens jutted their heads up and down in the weeds and ahead was an old man peddling a bicycle, his hat pulled over his ears. Her only thought was *Jesus, Jesus, Jesus*!

The man behind the dark wooden desk had a voice like corn silk. "You are sentenced to four years in prison for crimes committed against the People's Republic of Jugoslavia," he said with a sigh. She was to begin her sentence immediately.

"I beg of you, *Gospod*, I am a mother. I have three children. This daughter is my middle child. My husband is in prison serving a ten-year sentence. He is old, he is almost seventy years old. I beg of you, have mercy—"

She clasped her hands; and Julijanna, frightened, began to cry. Jozeca was nearly screaming, "I beg of you. I am not an enemy of the government. I am a simple person—a mother who loves her children and a wife who loves her husband. Please—I am begging you!"

The man watched her, his face expressionless. It was a familiar scene. He sighed again and then, in that same smooth voice, told her to come back in six months, on December 24, to begin serving her sentence.

They were still crying when they left the white one-story building. Julijanna put her fingers in her mouth as they walked and Jozeca raised her eyes to the sky and lifted the palms of her hands upward thanking God. She was free for six more months.

Chapter Forty-one

They had to pray each day not only for bread to eat and shelter from the cold and heat but also for each hour of freedom. "Give us this day, Lord, we ask you, give it to us. Do not allow it to be taken from us. Please, dearest Lord, you are our Lord, you have all of the days and the nights in your hands. Give us this day, this day that we might live and not be separated."

Josip and Julijanna knelt together with little Janez. They stretched their fingers toward heaven and prayed, "Lord, please let our mother stay at home. Give her to us this day."

In June, 1948, at a meeting of the Cominform in Bucharest, the Jugoslav Communist Party was expelled from the Cominform for, among other reasons, "deviating from Marxism and Leninism" and failing to take any action against rich peasants.

In November Jozeca heard that President Tito was going to be in Trbovlje. Her heart did not race until Ana suddenly offered the idea that she should write a letter to him in Trbolvje and ask for Jakob's release from prison and a reprieve of her sentence.

She buttoned her short jacket which had belonged to Jakob, pulled on her worn artillery boots, and, taking Julijanna who was waiting by the door in her coat and babushka, said, "It is a good suggestion, but I will not write a letter to Marshall Tito."

"Why not?"

"I will go to him."

"*Go* to him?"

"Yes. I will talk to him. He will help us."

"But how will you do it?"

"The Lord will help me. Our President Tito is a kind man. He often speaks to the people. He remembers that all we people won the war together—that the *Partizani* could not have won the war without the peasants and the farmers. He knows we love him and I believe he loves us."

"But I still do not see how—"

"I believe in God, that is how."

The narrow hilly streets of Trbovlje were jammed with people. There were many policemen. "How can I reach President Tito?" she asked one of them. He looked at her, his arms crossed on his chest, white gloves holding his elbows, and laughed at her.

She passed through the first file of guards and found herself surrounded by a deep crowd of people. Julijanna was in her arms, clinging to her neck. One of the guards pushed her back, but she plowed forward with all her strength—and then she saw him. Handsome, smiling, his face was tanned and deeply lined. He was impeccably dressed with rings on his fingers and boots which shined as bright as the river Sava in the moonlight.

"President Tito!" she cried, throwing her hands up over her head and pushing past the last man who guarded the area. Julijanna straddled her mother's stomach and clung to her neck.

"President Tito!"

A guard lifted a rifle to push her away.

The president raised his arm, "*Ne, Ne.* Let her speak. What is it, woman?"

Jozeca lifted her hands as in prayer. "Please, my President, have mercy—"

He paused and faced her directly. "Dear woman, let us talk," he said, giving her permission to speak to him.

"Please, Mister Tito, may you live long and prosper. I have one plea."

He saw her clenched praying hands, "What is your plea?"

"Can you listen to me, my President? I have three children. My husband is seventy years old and in prison. I have been judged to serve four years in prison. I do not know where to put my children. Please, President Tito, forgive me if I have done wrong—please forgive me and release me from this sentence, I and my old husband. . . ."

He listened to her, the muscles of his face tense. Her knees shook, faltered and she braced herself unsteadily as she looked into his deep blue eyes which were at one moment shrewd and intense and the next gentle and compassionate. He looked at her, trembling and unkempt, her hair swept along her face, the rows of teeth showing holes here and there; hands which were hard and rough, clothes that were dark, patched, frayed; he saw her holding her daughter, begging for life.

His men seemed unaware of the drama before them. Tito walked tall and erect toward her, his steps and movements sure. The woman with the hands lifted in prayer, begging, whimpering, was wearing army boots; her daughter was thin and gaunt like most of the other children of Jugoslavia. He touched Julijanna's cheek. Jozeca saw that his hands were clean, but they were tanned, strong, and had creases of black just like everyone else's who had lived and fought in the mountains and forests.

He nodded his approval. "You will have your father back," he told Julijanna.

It was all so chaotic, so rushed and incredible. He was asking her name.

"Kovac—Jozeca. And my husband, Jakob. From Hrastnik!"

Then it was over. He was swallowed in the movement, in the gray and the leather and the voices. She swayed and the pounding of her heart drowned out all noise. Then people crowded around her. Everyone talked at once.

"What did he say?"

"Did Tito talk with you?"

"What will happen with your husband?"

She heard that it was written up in the newspaper, the wonderful thing Tito had done for her. She could hardly contain her happiness. She had talked with President Tito himself and he had given his own personal pardon. Praise be to God and all the heavenly host.

Chapter Forty-two

The people of Hrastnik and the surrounding villages shared her joy and prepared a little celebration for Jakob's homecoming.

But Jakob did not arrive.

The days wore on, and the weeks, and the enthusiasm became something of the past. Jozeca went to Hoce and pleaded with the officials of the prison. They had received no papers, nothing official. Jakob could not be released without these.

Jakob was working during the day splitting rock and building a canal. He was so shrunken and thin she had to fight back tears when she looked at him. She thought painfully of his bones polishing the wooden plank he slept on at night.

"You must be both mother and father now, Beloved," he told her. "But have faith. Trust God. We will be together again. Faith in Christ is what really matters, *ne?*"

"Yes, my beloved."

"All of these trials will pass, as well as the joys and the blessings. Heaven waits for us all. Jesus is all that matters. Have faith. Have faith."

"I will write to the highest judge in Beograd," she said abruptly. "I will not give up. The Lord will help us!"

And she did write to Beograd. In two weeks she received a letter in reply. There would be no stay of her sentence and no reprieve for her husband. In one week she had to report to begin her prison sentence.

She walked back home along the road with the letter in hand. Then she knelt down at the side of the road, spread out the letter on the ground and raised her fingers to heaven.

"Read this letter, Lord! Look down and read this letter! Lord Jesus, you see the father of three children who is in prison. You see the mother of those three children now ordered to go to prison!"

She did not care who saw her or what anyone thought. She prayed louder, waving her arms over her head. "I believe that you will not separate me from my children. I believe you can save me!"

It was December 18, six days before she was to report to begin her prison sentence. Ana watched her one morning as she was leaving with the basket on her back to gather coal. "Jozeca, you ought to go to the doctor."

"What did you say?"

"You have not seen the doctor since you had the baby. Really, you ought to go to the doctor."

She did not want to go, but she followed Ana's advice and the next morning sat in the dimly lit corridor waiting to see the doctor. When she went home that afternoon the doctor had written a letter stating she was physically unable to withstand the rigors of prison and suggesting a one-month stay of her sentence.

The following month the doctor wrote another letter stating she should have a three-month stay of sentence. When she took the letter to the government office, it was accepted and she was given May 5 as the date to report to prison.

She did not cease to barrage the heavens with her prayers and pleas. She wrote letters to Tito begging for the release of her husband. Then she received an answer in the mail. Her sentence had been changed from four years to one-and-a-half years. Jakob's sentence had been changed from ten years to seven.

Chapter Forty-three

Janez climbed the wooden rafters of the outdoor porch as Jozeca carried the wood in from the storage bin. She thought about Jakob and about how she would carry wood all day and all night for one look at his face, one touch of his hand. She was about five meters from the door when she heard the thud on the wooden steps. She dropped the wood and rushed across the dirt yard where she found Janez lying on his back rolling back and forth, his face twisted up as though trying to cry out but not making any sound. She fell to her knees at his side as he gasped and choked for breath.

"Dear God! Help him! Help him breathe! Touch him, Lord!"

In a few minutes he was breathing correctly but his eyes were dim and his skin pale. She carried him in her arms to the hospital. His head was covered with cold compresses and he remained in the hospital one week. But he could not speak. He tried to form words, but none came.

"Lord, here is your Janez! This is the second son whom you have given to my husband and me to bring into maturity for your glory! I believe he will be a preacher as his father one day. Lord, look upon him and heal him!"

The children of the neighborhood teased Janez, who no longer laughed or played in the dirt yard.

"There is the boy without speech!" they taunted.

"What a pity you cannot even ask for a piece of bread!"

"Is it true that his mother even has to say his prayers for him?"

They giggled and pointed at him and he watched them with tormented eyes which refused to release tears.

"Do you know why this suffering has been added to you?" a neighbor woman named Saraica with steely brown eyes asked Jozeca.

"*Ne*. Why?"

"It is because you must pay for your sin. You must pay for the sin of marrying so old a man. Shame, *Gospa*. God is punishing you."

"I was married in God. If God punishes me, it is not for marrying my husband whom He gave to me."

"Observe my words, *Gospa*. Your children will one day curse you."

"My children will bless me as I bless them. And they will bless the name of their father all the days of their lives, as he has blessed them!"

Jozeca rocked Janez in her arms, singing, soothing him, praying long hours into the night. She remembered the words of the Russian brother about fighting as she felt the spiritual battle taking place around her. She believed Janez was called of God to serve Him and yet she knew there was an enemy who wanted to destroy that call.

"Janez, my son, you will have to fight all the days of your life against the enemies of God. You must learn to fight, too, and you must learn to pray."

She saw from the window one day a young woman with a baby in her arms. The woman walked with a slow, sensual step, as though she were playing with the idea of where to put her foot next. Jozeca had not seen her before. She watched her step grow more languid as the men came out of the mine. She stood smiling, her hips swaying slightly, and her eyes flirting, cast downward. The men saw her, joked among themselves, and kept walking. They would find her in private.

But then Jozeca learned that the woman was Saraica's daughter. The poor woman hid herself in her house, ashamed to bring her face into the sun. The girl was her only child and she had come from Germany with her two fatherless children and her new-found occupation. Saraica's husband spent his days in his swine stall, so great was his shame.

Jozeca wept when she saw their sufferings. Saraica had hoped her daughter would marry a well-off German and have a respectable life of comfort. Jozeca prayed, "Look down upon their sufferings, Lord. Look down upon them."

Every action of Saraica's daughter seemed to add more shame and despair to her parents. She was even arrested for stealing bread from the table of a neighbor.

"O Jesus," Jozeca prayed. "Touch this family! Touch this daughter!"

In April Jozeca again reported to the doctor. She walked, carrying Julijanna in her arms. But the doctor who had written the letters for her before was no longer there. She was told to report to the hospital to another man, and so she took Julijanna's hand and began the thirty-minute walk to the hospital.

Once there, she looked through the door of the corridor and saw only a few people sitting on the benches. "I am sorry," the nurse told her. "We are not taking any more patients today."

Jozeca began to protest. She had to see the doctor in order to get a letter to give to the police. The nurse was insistent.

"I am sorry. The doctor is leaving for the day."

Jozeca saw him, wearing a dark suit and polished shoes, a sinister-looking chubby fellow with broken blood vessels in his cheeks.

"Doctor!" she called, "can you see me?"

He turned and saw her standing there, a small dusty woman probably from one of the mining villages, holding a hungry-looking child
in her arms.

"Please, Doctor! Will you not see me?"

Against his will he said, "All right. Go to the corridor and wait.
I will see you." To the nurse, he snapped, "This is the last one!"

Ceramic tiles on the walls were stained and yellowed. The ceiling
was high and a single light bulb hung from it. She sat Julijanna on
a long metal bench and waited. It was quiet.

She began to think of what would happen if she went to prison.
Many who went to prison never came home. What about the children?
What would become of them? They would die, starve to death—and
she, she could very easily face the firing squad. She shuddered as
she imagined the rifles aimed and cocked, ready to fire. She could
almost hear the clink of the police boots on the concrete, feel the
cold bricks behind her. At that moment, Julijanna stood on the bench
and, losing her balance, tipped it over. It dropped to the floor with
a loud and resounding metal-against-concrete crash.

Jozeca screamed in terror and hid her face in her hands. "*Ne!
Ne!*" she screamed. The nurse rushed into the corridor and found
her trembling and gasping for breath.

"Save me, Lord!" she cried. "In the name of Jesus, do not shoot!
My poor children! Save me!"

The nurse called for the doctor who knelt by her side. Jozeca had
her hands over her face and was doubled over on the floor screaming
and gasping. It took all their strength to get her onto her feet. She
continued to tremble and moan.

Later that evening she tried to describe to Ana and Stane what
had happened. The new doctor had written a one-year stay of sentence
letter for her. She did not understand why except that he said something about her nerves.

"Praise God! Praise the name of the Lord! He has saved me from
prison for one year!"

The following day when she brought the letter to the police, the
man at the desk said, "I do not believe my eyes!" He wagged his
head back and forth, sighed and said, "I do not know how you did
it, *Gospa* Kovac." Then with a questioning look on his face, he said,
"I believe perhaps it is that your God—helped you."

She smiled broadly.

"Now you can sleep," he said, and that was that.

She continued to write letters for Jakob's release. "I will not let
go of you, God," she cried. "I will not give up my prayers. I know
that you have helped me in this life. O Lord, do not be angry with

184

me. Please look down on my husband in that prison. You and only you can free him!"

It had been twenty weeks since Janez had lost his speech. People now were accustomed to his grunts and growls. Ana, Stane and Josip could decipher his meaning by the tone of his grunt.

Jozeca refused to accept his condition as permanent. One evening as she sat at the table writing a plea for the release of Jakob, tears dripping from her chin, she turned to her son who was making barking noises at her side. She placed her hands on his face and shouted, "In Jesus' name, speak!"

Then she opened his mouth with her fingers and held onto his tongue. "Tongue, be loosed in the name of Jesus!" To her amazement, Janez then put his hands on hers and said, "Mama, will you tell me a Bible story now?"

Chapter Forty-four

Singing and praising the Lord, they walked to the hops field to pick hops. Jozeca was happy, blessed. Her hands waved in the air over her head and she shouted, "Thank you, Lord!"

Janez smiled and held onto Josip's hand. Julijanna bounced along on Jozeca's back.

They had been picking all morning when she saw Stane running toward her from between the rows of poles.

"*Teta*! Auntie!"

"*Zdravo*, Stane!"

"*Zdravo, Teta*!"

He was out of breath. "It is well, Stane?"

"*Ja, ja. Teta*. It is well."

"—And Ana? It is well with her?"

"*Ja. Ja*. It is well with her. Listen! I have brought news! The post has delivered a notice and it is for you from Beograd!"

"And—?"

"Your sentence has been reduced to six months!"

She knelt on her knees beside the basket of hops. Josip, Julijanna and Janez knelt with her. "Get on your knees, Stane. God has just spoken!"

The sun was bright in the sky. The mountains were blue and purple and green and islands of white clouds surrounded them. "O God, my God! You have again stretched out your hand unto me! Praise be to God! Praise be to the Lord forever and ever!"

Two weeks later she received a complete pardon. She did not have to go to prison at all. Her sentence was removed and she was free.

"O Jakob, Jakob," she sobbed into her pillow. "I understand now all that you have taught me. We must never give up, never stop praying, never let go of God. For surely as we cling to Him for our help, He will come to us and He will help us. Praise be the name of the Lord forever."

The doctors in Ljublijana had advised her long ago to give Josip music lessons. She enrolled him now in the State music school where he studied violin. His hands, which had once trembled so badly he could hardly hold a pencil, seemed to know the violin bow like an old friend. Almost immediately he was playing like a third- or fourth-year student. It was soon obvious that he had promising talent of extraordinary quality. In a few months he was invited to play with the children's orchestra.

Janez was a help to Jozeca. He helped pick hops, raspberries, blueberries and apples. He could pick nearly as fast as the older children. They lived a little easier now with her sentence lifted. And with picking berries, the food from the garden, and the U.N.R.E. packages from the United States which arrived like manna from heaven, they were able to eat better and more often.

Her worries concerning Janez seemed to be over. He now had his speech back and he was behaving normally. But on a rainy afternoon when he was nearly four years old, he felt restless staying inside the house by himself. Jozeca was at work carrying bricks for a builder, Josip was at school and Julijanna was asleep.

He waited until the sun came out and he opened the door and went out into the little dirt yard. There were some boys by the trash cans and he went over to see what they were doing. One of the older boys was making a fire in one of the cans. He cursed the wet wood. But then they got a fire started with some papers and dried twigs from the wood bins. Janez watched with relish.

"What are you looking at with so big eyes? Have you never seen a fire before?"

"*Ja!* Have you never seen what a fire does?"

"Look closer! See! See how it burns!"

The bigger boy pushed him toward the smoking trash can. Janez felt afraid, but he was not sure if they were being cruel or playing with him. Then as though the pit of hell had come up through the earth to meet him, he felt his face and eyes fiery and burning. He howled with pain.

The boys fled, leaving Janez screaming in pain in the dirt yard alone. It was a neighbor woman who came to his rescue. "Dear God, it is his eyes!" She brought him into her flat and tried to wash the ash and gravel out of his eyes. He cried and wailed helplessly.

A month later he lay in the hospital in Ljublijana as the doctor told Jozeca that his right eye would have to be removed. "We can save the left one but it will only have one-third of the vision left." Jozeca could not hide her grief. "O Lord, again, I beg of you—look down upon me! See, here is my son whom you have given to my husband and me. He is your servant, Lord. He is your son. Please, Lord, be merciful unto him and give him his sight." Then she put her hands on Janez and exclaimed, "In the name of Jesus Christ, eyes be healed!"

The next day Ana brought him a little package of figs and Janez was so happy to receive them that he hid them under his mattress.

"Tomorrow I will eat them," he thought happily, but in the morning they were gone. The doctors thought he was crying because he was going to lose his eye. They decided not to tell him until right before the operation.

Janez remembered, "In the name of Jesus Christ, eyes be healed," and he repeated it over and over again.

The following day the doctors conferred again and the operation was cancelled. Janez kept his eye. In one week he was fitted for glasses. They were the thickest lenses he had ever seen but he saw through them with two eyes and they rejoiced with all their hearts.

Food was again scarce and Ana and Stane left for Krajn in order for Stane to find work. "We must follow the bread," Ana said in a low, tearful voice. There would be work in Krajn at one of the factories, or in Celje, or possibly Maribor or Ljublijana. Stane could push a wheelbarrow on a construction site for better wages than he earned picking berries and hops. Ana begged Jozeca to join them.

"I will not leave this place," she answered. "Soon my husband will come home from prison. He shall find his family waiting for him—here, where he left them."

Chapter Forty-five

It was June 1951. For supper they had eaten *polenta* and tea and now they were in their beds. Outside the window the whole village slept quietly in the hollow of the mountain's long, ragged arm. Josip awoke and peered into the darkness. He heard whispering.

Then he felt someone getting into the bed beside him. He held his breath, listening. He was not afraid.

"Mama," he whispered. "Who is in the bed beside me?"

"Hush, son. In the morning you will learn who it is."

Again Josip asked, "Mama! Who is in the bed?"

"Hush, son. In the morning."

Josip reached his hand to the head on the bed near his own. He ran his fingers across the features of the face. A man's face with deep cracks and lines, a strong prominent nose, tears at the corners of the eyes. Then he recognized him. He choked and sobbed at once.

"Papa!"

At once he was wrapped in his hard embrace crying and kissing him.

"Papa! You have come home!"

The next morning Julijanna and Janez kissed their father politely, but remained apart, staring, unsure. It had been three-and-a-half years and Janez had seen him only through bars in the prison. Julijanna did not remember him as a free man. Jakob was as thin as a piece of hemp and Jozeca fed him in the bed, holding his head in one arm and a bowl of *polenta* in the other.

"A little at a time, beloved. I heard of a man who came home from Dachow and he ate too much and died."

Jakob swallowed the *polenta* slowly, rolling it over his tongue, enjoying its taste and texture. "Potato *polenta*—it is like heaven."

He had been deloused and hosed down at the prison but she carefully washed him now, picking lice out of his ears and scalp. She washed his hair, shaved his face, cut his fingernails. His body was covered with sores and welts and she laid warm cloths on his back and legs, changing them when they cooled. Every two hours she gave him another two spoonsful of *polenta*.

"Slowly . . . slowly, my beloved. Ah, yes, that is the way to do it—slowly."

She stayed by his bed around the clock, praying, stroking, spoon-feeding, massaging, singing. He lay on the bed more dead than alive, but she saw only that it was her Jakob, that God had answered their prayers and that he was home with them again. She did not believe for one second that he would not be well again.

And she was right. One afternoon after she and the children tiptoed from the big room so he could sleep quietly, she closed the door and heard a loud thud behind her. Alarmed, she opened the door and saw that he had rolled off the bed and was on the floor.

"Jakob!"

"Nothing. It is nothing."

He was pulling himself onto his knees. "I must pray," he said. Then he was on his knees beside the bed. Looking up at her he winked.

"When I am finished I believe I can get back into the bed without help."

Jozeca nursed him back to health while working during the day digging potatoes in a farmer's field five kilometers away. Then at night she took Josip with her into the mountains and with baskets on their backs, they dug up and carried back baskets of black dirt. With this dirt, she planted sod which she was able to sell and trade.

Josip was strong and able to work like a man. He carried dirt down from the mountains, hauled sod and sold it to villagers and people in the towns for their gardens. He also tended Jozeca's garden with seven-year-old Julijanna's help. Janez stayed at home with his father while the rest of the family was at school and working. He became the joy and apple of Jakob's eye.

The daughter of Saraica by now had gained a disreputable reputation which extended from Trbovlje to Zagorje and Hrastnik. She paraded her actions in front of her parents' eyes, obviously enjoying their shame and disgrace. One afternoon as it rained and houses smelled of wet plaster and wood, Jozeca heard the slapping of feet outside her door.

"*Gospa!*" the voice called, "come quickly!" The rain sprayed into the room as she opened the door to receive the news that the husband of Saraica had sliced his throat in his pig stall and was dead.

"Ahoo! Terrible!"

Later Jozeca asked Jakob, "What can we do to help Saraica in her grief?"

Jakob scratched his chest and said, "Let us ask the Lord what He would have us to do." Two weeks later Saraica's daughter moved into the Kovac house, bringing her perfume, cigarettes, her earrings and bracelets and shiny shoes with her.

The neighbors were indignant. "Jozeca! You are a fool! How can you reach out your hand to help Saraica? She gloated in your worries, and now you take her harlot daughter into your house!"

"Why do you want to help someone who deceitfully ran daggers through your good name and the name of your husband?"

Jozeca tilted her head sideways, took in a breath and sighed. "Ah," she began, "but how much more wicked of me if I do not reach out with my hand to one who suffers even as I have also suffered in this life."

Jolanda, Saraica's daughter, remained in the Kovac house under Jozeca's watchful eye. She learned to pick berries, carry coal, gather wood, grind corn and weave baskets out of the rushes which she and Jozeca gathered along the river's edge.

Even with Jolanda's help, Jozeca worked from sunup to sundown and earned only enough to keep from starving to death. Jakob suffered to see her work so hard. "You must do all now, eh? You have much responsibility on your shoulders."

"It is not a heavy burden, my love."

"And now besides your children, you must take care of an old man!"

"It is my honor, my deepest joy to serve you, my husband. You are my sun which never sets."

During the war more than one-third of all industrial plants in Jugoslavia had been destroyed. Over 1.7 million persons, including 90,000 skilled workers, had perished. There were also those who fled the country or were able to emigrate. Jugoslavia was now like a wounded horse. The war had sapped it of its youth, strength and resources. It could stand, but not run. It could chew, but not swallow. It had been beautiful and strong, but now without flesh on its bones and lying on a swollen, starved belly, it was ugly.

Tito developed his five-year plan to build the country, to fatten the horse. Youth brigades were organized and with the combined good will of many nations, including the United States, the country went to work. Volunteer work brigades built a new university in Zagreb and workers were recruited to build roads, carry stones, mix cement, pound nails and paint walls. Nearly every young person worked on a youth brigade. They laid rail, helped build schools, houses, buildings and roads.

Jakob's strength returned to him and he was again able to go to work in the mine. He and Jozeca prayed fervently for their children and for Jolanda who was becoming a more gentle person as the days passed. She no longer protested when Jozeca prayed for her, and her smiles were less mischievous. She respected Jakob and obeyed him as a child obeys a parent.

Every night for six weeks Jozeca sat across from her at the table and exchanged words. Every night she told of the love God had for her, she read to her from the Bible and she prayed for her. Finally, Jolanda said, "I am ready now to accept Jesus Christ as my Savior. I will do all what you say to me."

It was the most talked-about event in the town when Jolanda went to her mother, Saraica, and begged her forgiveness. But Saraica, her eyes still hard and steely, had no words of apologies to Jozeca and she had no words of gratitude for what she had done for her daughter. When Jozeca met her on the street, Saraica turned her head and dug her heels into the earth behind her.

Chapter Forty-six

Josip was now twelve years old. "Mama, I would like to have shoes," he complained. Jozeca looked up from her sewing. "And the shoes you now wear? They are not good enough?"

"They are your shoes, Mama. I would like shoes of my own."

"Ah. Well, Papa is not able to walk in his shoes, so you may wear his, son."

"Mama! I would like shoes of my own. The other boys in the orchestra have shoes of their own."

She continued her sewing. "Ah, then Josip, I am certain the boys in the orchestra will be most blessed to have your father's shoes among them."

"Oh, Mama! We are so poor!"

"What did you say, son?"

"We are poor! We are without money!"

She placed her sewing on her lap and looked directly into Josip's face. "But this is untrue, Josip. We are never poor because we are without money. Surely you know that."

Josip felt ashamed. "I am sorry, Mama."

Jozeca rarely saw Josip these days. After school he went to orchestra practice. He practiced the violin and the piano whenever he had a few minutes. He came home when it was past dark and too late to help his mother with the work.

"Where is my oldest son?" Jakob would ask as the sun set over the mountains.

"He is playing in the orchestra."

"Ah, and one day he will play for the church, *ne*?"

"Yes, Jakob. I believe this."

"Then let us believe this together."

And they would get down on their knees. Many evenings when Josip came home he found his parents on their knees praying for him.

As an amateur violinist Josip found acceptance, friends, fun and the opportunity to be admired. Jozeca realized his vulnerability, and she prayed every day, "Lord, look down on my son. See how foolish he is. Look down on him, Lord. He does not know much. He runs after the useless things of the world. Ah, Lord, he is only a boy. I believe he will one day serve you. He will one day serve you with all his heart and soul. Be patient with him, Lord, have mercy. He will hear your voice one day—I believe it, because you gave this son to my husband and me. He is a gift from you. Dear Lord, look down on my son! See how he needs you!"

Josip played Schumann, Mozart and Beethoven with ease. Then came the day when he made his debut in the *Simforica Orkestar* in Ljublijana. The concert hall was grand, baroque, and Josip was not in the least bit nervous as he marched on stage prepared to play his solo in the Beethoven Concerto. In his hands the violin seemed to come alive. It did not misbehave or struggle for tone as in other less talented hands. It was mellow, controlled, and Josip could make the instrument cry, sing, laugh and whine like the wind through the mountains. His teachers were enthusiastic with his musical gifts and predicted a great future for the orchestra with Josip one day as first violinist.

As he stood in the center of the stage that night, he looked out into the audience at the faces. There they were—all directed toward him, all eyes fixed on him. A warm rush of blood came to his face. Then his eyes moved to the rear of the hall, on the right, and there sitting in the aisle seat, way in the back, he could see her plainly— Mama. Her face was tilted upward, her eyes closed, and her hands were clenched in front of her face. She was pleading with God.

In the evenings they gathered around the table in the kitchen. Jakob read from the Bible and afterwards they prayed. Janez liked to sit on his father's lap and Julijanna sat with her hands tucked under her chin listening to the deep rich tones of Jakob's voice as he read. Jolanda listened eagerly as she sewed beside Jozeca. Josip listened obediently but unhappily.

Neighbors joined them and Jakob often told stories in finest Slovenian style, holding his listeners spellbound. He talked about his years in prison. "The prisoners fought over the mice," he told them. "If a man caught a mouse he was very careful to let nobody else know about it. Then he would not have to share it with anyone.

"You would have to lunge at the mouse to catch it—mice are very quick, you know—and I have seen men weep because they allowed a mouse to get away. If you were lucky enough to catch a mouse, you then had to scheme a way to cook it. Roasting was the best. And in the winter you could do this by holding it by the tail over the flaming barrels where the guards stood warming themselves outside.

"I have done this. I held the mouse by the tail over the fire. It burned to a black crisp outside and remained raw on the inside. Believe me, it was a treasure anyhow. I rushed back with it and tore it into three parts and three of us ate it, hair, tail and all.

You will do funny things when you are hungry, do you know? We would have given anything just to have a mouse to eat."

One evening as they were gathered at the kitchen table they heard tapping at the door. Jakob opened it and there was an immediate flurry of excited embraces and raised voices as Nezka, Jozeca's mother, entered the small kitchen. With her was Franciska and one of Franciska's sons, Vanko.

They had to hear all of the news. Everyone talked at once, and loudly. First, are they well? Yes, yes, they are well. Secondly, how are the believers in Celje? Are they well? Yes, yes, they are well, and growing in number. Franciska's mother, God rest her soul, passed on to be with the Lord just recently.

"She is dead? But how old was she when she died, God rest her soul?"

"She was 103 years old. And she praised the Lord every one of those added years which the Lord gave to her."

"Praise be to the Lord."

"Praise be to the Lord."

Nezka was older, more stooped, but she shook hands like a strong man.

"Jakob, my son, many times I have dreamed of hearing you once again preach."

"You call him 'son' when he is older than you?"

"Nonsense. He married my daughter, did he not? Then he is my son. Jakob, my son, when can I hear you preach? Tell me, what is the Lord showing you these days? What are we to be admonished in?"

Jakob frowned, but then quickly smiled. "You are up to something, Nezka. Tell me, what is it? You have never asked me such questions. I suspect something."

"Jozeca, tell your husband what an honorable and trustworthy woman I am. A woman of her word, *ne?*"

"Yes, Mama. As you have said."

"Then, would you suspect a woman with such qualities to deceive?"

"*Ne. Ne.*"

"Ah, that is better. Now then, Jakob. When will you again preach?"

"Immediately."

"Good. I shall listen with my full heart and also I shall listen for the poor believers in Celje who are without a preacher."

"Ah, oh."

"Yes, imagine, Jakob. A flock with no shepherd. It is pathetic. They are all crying and praying."

"A pity."

"Yes. Yes. Shall I tell you what they are praying for?"

"Please."

"They are praying that Jakob Kovac will come and be their pastor."

"Ah, Nezka. So that is what you are up to."

"Surely you have a heart like gold, Jakob. You will not say no to these poor lambs who need you."

"I shall pray to the Lord. He will show me what to do about the poor lambs in Celje."

"He will surely tell you to come to them because I believe that is why I am here today."

"I shall pray to the Lord."

"Do not take too long at it, Jakob,"

"Pardon?"

"You see, we are praying that you will have your answer by morning."

"Ah, now Nezka, this is improper. I have many things to consider."

"We are prepared to help you all we can. We have men who will help load the wagon, women who will help pack everything and—"

"Nezka, I shall pray to the Lord."

"And then, Jakob—?"

"Enough, Nezka. There have been enough words. I shall pray to the Lord."

He was frowning again and he excused himself politely, blessing them all, and retired to the big room.

Chapter Forty-seven

In one week they were settled into two tiny rooms in Celje. The rooms were upstairs in a private house, the kitchen was in the back hallway and the toilet was outside in the backyard near the road.

Jakob was made pastor of a small growing Baptist church and he worked in the Celje coal mine. He worked with renewed energies and dedication and sought every opportunity to preach and tell someone about the Lord Jesus.

He received boxes of tracts from Germany and Austria printed in the Slovene language. These he gave out by the thousands. The members of the church also distributed them, children and adults alike.

"I believe we must preach as much as possible," he told his congregation. "And we must pray always. We are the first in Slovenia. In countries where for generations they have prayed and prayed, there is not the war to wage as we have. I tell you, my beloved ones, we must prepare the way for the generations of Jugoslav Christians to follow us. We do not know what the days will bring when we are finished here. We must pray for those who will follow us. We must bring many generations into being. O God! O Jesus!"

The believers held hands and lifted them upward. They sat in the small room with the wind blowing gently against the trees and the sun stepping across the mountains.

"Help us be an example, Lord! Help us pray! God! Holy Spirit!" They knew God in heaven would answer them and that He was with them forever.

Jozeca's mother was ecstatic that Jakob had brought his family to Celje. "Jakob is Sent Man from God, I know it," she proclaimed to the members of the church. "Look what a fresh breath of life he has brought to us! Look what new strength we have! Praise God! Thank you, *Jezes!*"

She walked the muddy road toward her daughter's house, carrying a wicker basket of wool and yarn. A group of teenagers by a sagging wooden fence were standing in a little knot talking. Their faces were placid, there were no quick, darting movements of the hunted; they were laughing and slapping each others' arms and singing current popular Slovene songs being sung on the radio.

Nezka remembered World War I when the Italians pointed their barettas into the noses of Slovene patriots and fired. She remembered the burning homes and screaming women of that war as well as those of World War II. She remembered how, in 1923 and 1924, everything in Slovenia became Italian. Even their Slovene language was forbidden. Libraries were burned and Fascist soldiers searched homes in villages and towns for Slovene books and newspapers to destroy.

All this they had suffered and endured and fought against for the sake of these youth—so they could stand in a little knot and sing and laugh and live.

"God, save them," she prayed.

Jozeca examined the pieces of wool for the quilt they were making. Her mother squeezed her neck. "Ah, Jozeca, my daughter, now that you are here among us the bread is not so hard."

"My beloved little *Mamica*."

"You know, I have one regret," Nezka told Jozeca as she licked the end of the thread to go through the needle.

"What?"

"I have never heard of the whereabouts of Lojze."

Jozeca examined her mother's lined face, her small round eyes and drooping lips. "Mama, do you mean that now, after thirteen years of being free of that man, you have thoughts for him? Is it possible?"

"From time to time I pray for Lojze's soul and I believe he is still alive."

"Impossible. He was sent to Dachow. In addition, his behavior was quarrelsome, nasty—"

"We shall speak no more of it."

Nezka's health was failing and soon she was unable to move from her bed. In July of 1953 she died. Jozeca mourned her loss, feeling suddenly very small and alone.

Nezka had been dead only three months when an old man, stooped and scowling, a stubble of a beard on his face and gold teeth gleaming in his mouth, appeared at the door.

"*You*? But we thought—"

"Thought I was dead, no doubt."

"But *menda ja,* of course, we are happy that you are not."

Lojze had travelled from Germany by train. His clothes smelled of perspiration and cigar smoke. He sighed when Jozeca told him Nezka was dead.

"Three months ago she was alive, Lojze. If you had come earlier, my mother may have gone to her grave with peace in her mind regarding you."

"Ah, but once I was freed from the prison camp, I could not get out of Germany."

"Thirteen years is a long time to keep your fingers from holding the pen, Lojze. You are as a dead man returning from the grave."

He lived in the house with Jozeca and Jakob until Franciska agreed to take him into her house. He lived as though haunted, crying and sleepless, complaining of imaginary and real pains, consumed with guilt. His memories were like mad dogs snapping at his heels. He despised everyone who crossed his path and especially tormented those who helped him most.

Chapter Forty-eight

Jakob rode the train from Celje to Trbovlje to preach each week and with him he brought tracts. The tracts told about the love of Jesus and gave Bible verses explaining the way to salvation in Christ. On a trip to Kocevje, he was arrested.

"Are you the perpetrator of this religion's literature?"

"I am."

"Did you know it is against the law to perpetrate such religious propaganda upon the people?"

"I am aware."

"Then do you acknowledge your guilt?"

"I am not guilty before God."

He was taken to Stari Piskar jail in Celje. The sight of the familiar dreary and hateful walls made him recoil, a rush of nausea swept over him, causing him to reel slightly, stumble off balance.

He prayed on his knees three nights and three days, refusing food and sleep.

"Lord, have you brought me this far to end my days in prison? I will not sleep until I receive a sign from you! Lord, look down upon me and answer my prayer. My only desire is to serve you! Give unto me more years that I might serve you and that I might see my sons serve you! Lord!"

He was released in three days with no trial and no explanation.

"Surely God is faithful!" Jakob shouted. "Look upon me! I am a free man! Is not God wonderful?"

Jakob had not arrived home yet from Stari Piskar when Josip rushed into the house out of breath and upset. "*Mamica!*" he called. Jozeca was pulling the bedclothes in from the window where they were having their daily airing.

"Branko, one of the boys in the orchestra, has sliced his wrists."

"Josip, how terrible!"

"They are saying he is mentally ill."

"But he is alive?"

"*Ja.* They have taken him to the hospital."

Jozeca plumped a pillow and brought it into the room.

"*Mamcia*, will you go and visit him?"

"Certainly, Josip."

She hurried along the road, with Josip two steps ahead of her until they arrived at the hospital. They walked through the gate and up the long walk along the green lawn to the main door. There were few places in town where the grass was so green and well kept.

Inside, Branko lay in his bed staring at the ceiling.

"Branko! Branko! Do you recognize me?"

The boy looked at Josip with glazed eyes and nodded his head.

"Branko, why did you do it? Why?"

No answer. He was not able to speak.

Jozeca touched his shoulder. "Do you know who I am, Branko?"

He nodded again. Everybody in the orchestra knew who she was. They saw her during the performances praying in the back row with her hands knotted in front of her face. They teased Josip about her.

"Branko, do you know what I am going to do?"

He stared at her.

"Branko, I am going to pray for you. Are you agreed I pray for you?"

He only stared.

Jozeca clasped his bandaged hands together on his chest and placed hers over them. "Lord Jesus!" she called in a loud voice. "Look down on this Branko! Look what he has done! Look down on him and have mercy!"

When she had finished praying she asked him, "Branko, would you like to leave this hospital and come to our home?"

He nodded slowly.

He stayed three weeks with the Kovac family. Every day Jozeca prayed and urged him to speak again. She started helping him form words as she had once done with Janez, syllable by syllable. "Do - bor - dan, good day," and then she would read from the Bible. Nobody else in the family had the patience she had with him. He was often rude and insulting, but she paid no attention and continued to show him love, understanding and patience. She remembered how God had touched Jolanda and given her a new life of hope and love. He could do the same for Branko.

One evening during supper, he threw his soup on the floor. Jozeca rose up from the table and shouted in a loud voice, "In the name of Jesus Christ, all demonic powers leave this man! I command you in Jesus' name, Branko, be free!"

The stunned family sat with spoons poised and mouths dropped wide. Jakob instantly began to pray quietly and Jozeca shouted, "Unclean spirits, you leave this boy now in the mighty name of Jesus Christ!"

Then abruptly and horribly there was the sound of an angry wind.

It screamed across the room and disappeared out of the window. When it had gone, the room was silent. Janez began to whimper. The noise had frightened him. Julijanna cowered beside her father.

Then Jakob and Jozeca got on their knees and began to pray. "Lord Jesus! By the power of your Holy Spirit, enter this boy! Come to him now, Lord!"

Branko got on his knees beside them and prayed. "For - forgive me, Lord Je - Jesus. Ma - make me clean. I want to belong to you - I am through - I am through belonging to the devil."

After that there was a very dramatic change in Branko. He began to speak better every day. He loved church and was soon normal and became involved as a regular member of the church. At the end of the year when he graduated from music school he moved to Izola on the Adriatic coast where he met a lovely Christian girl and was married. He thanked Jozeca and Jakob before he left.

"You saved my life," he told them.

"No, Branko. Jesus saved your life. Remember that."

Branko was one of many who came to the Kovac home for help. The doors were always open to anyone and everyone who needed help. Jozeca and Jakob were called *Teta* and *Stric*, Auntie and Uncle to everyone who knew them.

But there were those who did not share this love for them. Lojze, who lived with Franciska's family in the low white house with a drooping red roof, became more sour as the days passed. He would sit outside his door on a small wooden stool and shout abuses at the people as they passed by. He had special diatribes for Jozeca and would call to her in a high, shrill voice, "Are you not ashamed? Shame! How can you show your face in the town and on the roads?"

"Pardon?"

"Do you not know that everyone knows about you—about your sin? God will make you pay!"

"Does my stepfather speak to me?"

"That husband of yours! He is an old man! And that son of yours! Running around town like a drunken Turk."

Jozeca was startled at Lojze's berating remarks. She told no one about it; she only prayed. She did not answer him back because she was afraid her tongue would deceive her and she would say unkind things.

Jakob was cutting wood with Janez one morning, and Jozeca went to Celje to look for a larger flat to live in. She negotiated with a man named Macek who managed a block of flats, and he told her if she agreed to clean his house and cook for him she could have the next available apartment. This additional work for no money was a hard bargain but she agreed to do it. Her family needed a larger place to live. On the way home that day she passed Lojze who sat on his stool outside his door.

"Ah ha! You must work night and day to support your family—and to support that old man. Are you not ashamed?"

Jozeca interrupted him. "Lojze, you are an unfortunate man," she said. "You know little in this life. Do you think it matters to me how old my husband is? If he were 110 years old, I would love him. And do you think I love my son any less because he behaves foolishly now? He is still my son and he will always be my son!"

Lojze grunted and spit on the dirt. "Married to an old grandpa."

Jozeca ignored the gesture. "My husband is mine and I am his. Lojze. Is that not wonderful? We are one."

Then praying quietly to herself as she continued along the road, she asked the Lord to forgive her anger. "I know you died for Lojze, too. I pray you will have mercy on him, Lord Jesus. You see, he does not know much."

Chapter Forty-nine

Josip organized a small band to play in nightclubs and bars on the weekends. Jozeca was grieved at his decision. "Ah, Jakob, what shall I do? Our son who is so near heaven chooses to walk in hell."

Jakob took her hands fiercely. "What shall we do? I will tell you! We shall pray? Pray!" and he raised his finger toward the ceiling. "Where is your faith? We shall pray!"

Often during the night Josip would be awakened by some movement at his side. He would stretch out his hand and his fingers would find the top of his father's head as he knelt beside him praying for him.

"Papa! Is that you?"

"Yes."

"Go to sleep, Papa."

And Jakob would continue praying.

Josip's little band played the Hotel Europa in Celje, at school dances in Slovenia, at the Dom Zelezricarjev, the Union Hotel and in other towns such as Zalec and Krajn. After they had finished the last set one night and were leaving the bar in Celje, Josip noticed someone waiting outside by the door in the shadows. He recognized the short round shape.

"Mama!"

Jozeca stood in the late night light, her eyes wide and ready to plead with her son.

"Go home!" he screamed. "Go home!"

Then she prayed with her hands clenched in front of her face.

These visits so enraged Josip that even his friends found him difficult to get along with. He became a bear; he wanted nothing to do with anyone.

Every day Jozeca prayed as she walked along the road to her cooking and cleaning jobs, her hands clenched upward and calling, as though she were heaven's alarm clock, "Touch him, Lord! Touch my son! Touch him!"

Macek, her employer, was a fat little man with thick-lensed spectacles who smoked short turkish cigarettes. He had a small upturned mouth which opened to crooked stained teeth. Macek was not married but he had a girlfriend named Minka who dyed her hair red and was shaped something like a milk can.

Minka's one virtue was that she loved to laugh. Whenever Jozeca saw her she was giggling away, her large body bouncing happily up and down like bubbles in a washpot. She worked in the glass factory and spent the rest of the time with her "puppy," Macek, who generously rewarded her for her attention. Minka wore stockings with black seams running up the backs of her legs. The other women in the block wore cotton stockings or went bare-legged. Minka had a change of dress for nearly every day and she had her hair curled by the *frizer*.

Jozeca was always kind to her and she prayed for her. "Such a shameful waste of life," she would think as she scrubbed Macek's floors and boiled his shirts. Macek promised her that the next available flat would be hers, but Jozeca worked for him for seven years before that promise was fulfilled.

She cleaned Macek's flat and several others' as well, and also found a job cooking and cleaning and helping with the children in the neighborhood kindergarten. This meant hurrying from one job to the next on her bicycle from one end of the town to the other.

One afternoon Josip was just coming out of the shoe store with a pair of new shoes tucked under his arm when one of his friends pointed across the narrow cobblestone street, "Look, Josip, is that not your mother?"

Josip looked at the round figure in the dark coat wearing worn men's shoes with wisps of uncombed hair poking out of her babushka. She was riding her bicycle along the cobblestones, carrying a load of laundry on the back of it.

"No, that is not my mother."

Jozeca fought tears and quietly kept on pushing the pedals of the bicycle so she would not embarrass her important son.

But she refused to allow her son to leave her life. She went to the bars and she sat at the tables to hear him play. She drank *turska kava*, and she prayed.

"Lord, touch him! Touch him!"

Josip ignored her, refusing to acknowledge the little round lady who sat praying at the table to the right.

In his last year at Mechanical School[1], Josip discovered soccer. He graduated from school and found a job as a mechanic where he was paid $2.00 every hour. He worked from 6:00 a.m. until 2:00 in the afternoon. Then he went home to eat and immediately after he ate he went to play soccer. He played every day, including Saturdays and Sundays.

Young Janez was fascinated by the game and begged Josip to

---

1. Vocational High School.

take him along so he could watch him play. Jakob watched from his bed as his eldest son marched down the road to the soccer field and his youngest son ran along behind him, calling, "Please, Josip! Wait for me!" Josip never waited.

Jakob now was often too ill to get up from the bed. Julijanna worked during the summer at a rubber factory. She gave her earnings to Jakob. She had grown into a strikingly beautiful girl. She had a firm jaw, piercing black eyes and her thick, black hair hung to her shoulders in waves.

"Father, I respect you," she told Jakob. "You have done so much for me. It is my honor to now do something for you."

Her brother Josip had grown large-boned, tall, muscular and robust. The money he earned as a mechanic went into his own pocket. He did not give one para[2] to his mother and father. He liked to go to the cinema, to buy clothes for himself along with candies and sweets. On pay day he bought *cremsnite*, rich cream-filled pastries, and brought them home in a paper bag. Janez and Julijanna saw the bag and looked at it hungrily. Josip changed his clothes and brought the *cremsnite* to some girl friends who lived on the other side of town. Janez and Julijanna watched him leave, then ate bread and lard for their dinner that night.

Josip was becoming more nervous in spite of the money jingling in his pocket, friends, job and music. He had frequent temper tantrums. Although he did not have seizures as he did when he was a child, he would fly into wild and frenzied rages, screaming until his face turned red and then a pale blue.

Neighbors and friends told Jozeca, "If that son of yours ever repents, it will be a miracle."

Lojze shouted across the fence that her son was a vandal's son, doomed forever because of his mother's sin.

Jozeca walked three to four kilometers to town every day to work. As she walked, she prayed. People became accustomed to seeing her with her face turned toward the sky, her hands clenched in front of her. She was the Praying Lady and the only one of her kind, they said.

She was able, from time to time, to bring home food for the family as special treats. Sometimes it would be *sir kajmak*, cheese and cream, or *sne nokle*, an egg pudding. She never touched one bite for herself, but presented it to her family as a surprise.

In 1958 Josip was asked to play soccer on the Adriatic coast. He had built a reputation for himself as a soccer player, and the well-

---

2. There are 100 para in the dinar as there are 100 cents to the dollar.

known teams were now asking him to join them. When Jozeca heard he had the offer to go to the Adriatic coast, she forbade him to take it. She knew about the parties and immoral behavior that accompanied such trips.

"Do not give me orders!" Josip shouted. "I am my own boss! And stop praying for me! I do not want your prayers!"

Jozeca folded her arms across her chest. "All right, Josip. Look at me here. Here is your mother speaking to you. If you go to the Adriatic coast with that soccer team, I will from this day on pray for you no more."

The words startled Josip. He did not think his mother would ever speak such words. She who had slept for five years with her feet pressed against his so she could wake him up if he started a seizure. "Ah, the devil," he muttered and walked out of the house with such heavy feet that she thought he might go through the floor.

He went to the Adriatic coast. And eleven days later he returned, his face puffed and red, his body wet with perspiration, and his mind nearly delirious with fever. Jozeca took him to the hospital immediately.

The doctors examined him; later in the gray light of the corridor, they explained he had a tumor on the brain but it was inoperable. They were sorry, but it was too late to help him.

She took him home and stood by the edge of the bed. He writhed in pain, gasping and moaning. His temperature read 40° and 41° C.[3] He tried to focus his eyes on her face, unable to control his rolling eyes.

"Mama—you promised me you would not pray!"

"Josip, I did not pray."

"Why—why then—this?"

"I prayed many years for you, Josip. In eleven days God has answered."

"I am dying, Mama."

"Look at me, Josip. Here is your mother speaking to you. When you were a child you loved Jesus. I want to put to you a question—"

"Ahh . . . I am dying."

"Listen!"

There was no compassion in her voice. Not like when she nursed Branko back to health and not when she spoke to so many others who lay on sick beds—years and years of gentle preaching. Why was she not gentle now?

"Josip! Do you love Jesus now?"

"O God, help me, I am sick. Mama—help me."

---

3. 40° and 41° C is equivalent to 104° and 105.8° F.

"Answer me this one question, Josip. Do you love Jesus now?"

"I have been far away from Him."

"Josip, I love you very much, but I would rather see you receive Jesus Christ and die than to go on living without Him."

Josip turned his face to the wall. With that gesture, Jozeca turned and left the room. She was gone. Always she had been there when he needed her. Always at any time he could call her. Her hand was always outstretched. Why? Why did she leave him now? He could not shout. He could not move even the tiniest part of his body without feeling as though he would explode into a million pieces. He felt as though every hair on his body was ignited in flames.

"Lord Jesus, I know you are real," he prayed, as the room twirled off in the distance. "I know that it is true what is written in the Bible. Lord Jesus, if you will heal me, I will serve you with my whole heart. Forgive me for the shame I have brought to you and to my family. I know I am dying, but Lord, my God, let me live a little longer so that I may serve you."

One year later Jozeca stood in the kitchen chopping cabbage for soup and her mind went back to the day her son Josip lay dying. She remembered his prayer and his promise. Now the letter from the Baptist seminary at Novi Sad lay on the table near her. She had read it over and over again this afternoon.

Dearest Beloved Mama and Papa:
    I have met a wonderful girl. Her name is Brigita. I will be so happy for you to meet her because I want to marry her. . . .

Everyone who had known Josip marvelled at the change that took place in him. They called it a *cudez*, a miracle.

"He lived in hell. And now just look at him! He is an angel! Ah, *ja ja*, only God could do such a *cudez*!"

Jozeca kissed Jakob and tickled his chin with her fingers. "Ah, Jakob, Jakob, my beloved, see how our prayers have been answered! Our son has been restored to us. Ah, the life has much to rejoice in, eh, my Jakob!"

Chapter Fifty

Jozeca took on extra jobs in order to send money to Josip at the seminary. Her work began at 5 a.m., when she went to the neighborhood kindergarten and cleaned two stairways and entrances. From 6 a.m. to 7 a.m. she walked the children from their homes to the kindergarten. At 7 a.m. she hurried home by bicycle to prepare coffee and see Janez and Julijanna off to school and to make sure Jakob ate breakfast. Then she hung the bedding out to air, cleaned, and at 8 a.m. began her day cleaning houses. She cooked the meals for the kindergarten children and had to rush by bicycle from the homes she cleaned to the kindergarten to prepare the food for the children and help with serving and feeding. She cleaned windows, dishes, and clothes also at the kindergarten. The children enjoyed her and laughed with delight at her antics. Their favorite was watching her wash floors with her feet while doing a little dance and singing songs.

On most days her work was not finished until 8 p.m. or 9 p.m. And then she bicycled home and washed her own family's clothes by hand and cleaned her own flat. Julijanna had her studies and was able to help only a little. Jozeca believed it was more important for her to do well in her studies than to scrub the clothes until her knuckles were red and her back aching.

Janez was now her biggest help. He carried coal, wood, helped her scrub and clean. He was by her side every minute when he was not in school. Jozeca remembered Jakob's words before Janez was born, "You will be most blessed by this child. He will be of most help to you."

At the end of the day when she was finished with her work, Jozeca played soccer with him. He had no friends and so she became his friend. She was never too tired to play with him, to kick and to catch the ball.

She prayed every day that Macek would fulfill his promise to rent her a larger flat. Even with Josip away at school they were uncomfortably crowded. The rooms were too small for a family to live in and it was difficult for Jakob to get to the toilet outside. Then, one day, after seven years of cooking and cleaning for him, Macek finally told her she could move into the large block of flats which he managed. But she must agree to caretake the block and continue to work for him without pay.

Macek watched her carrying furniture and boxes into the block. The flat was on the sixth floor and it was splendid. The bathroom was inside the flat, there was a tiny kitchen and two small bedrooms connected to a living room. Jozeca wept with happiness when she saw it. "Thank you, Jesus! Thank you, Jesus!"

Macek held his cigarette between his stained teeth and reminded her of her duties as caretaker. She was so happy that the thought of additional work did not worry her. Janez stood beside her, able to do the work of two men.

"God has made you strong," she told him, smiling.

"Ah, *Ja*," he laughed. "God knew I would have to be strong to keep up with you!"

She carried the last of the boxes up the stairs and was coming back down when she met Minka in the hallway, eyeing her with a strange expression on her face.

"*Gospa* Kovac, what do you have from life, eh?"

Jozeca stared at her, surprised at the question. Minka continued, "Look at your life. Hardship, hard work, an old husband who cannot help you. You and I are the same age. You could be a pretty woman, but look at how old and worn you are."

Jozeca wiped her cheek with the palm of her hand. "Ah, but Minka, I am the most happy woman."

The woman with the curled red hair looked at her oddly. "Happy? How can you be happy? Look at you. You have only a life of work and work and more work. I have never seen you at leisure. Never have I seen you on holiday. Have you ever been to the seaside, eh? Tell me that."

"*Ne.*"

"Work and work and work! You have no husband to comfort you or make love to you."

Jozeca shook her head. "Minka, do you know that my husband calls me 'God's gift' for him? Can you imagine that? He calls me 'God's gift'! Tell me, does Macek call you God's gift? Eh?"

Minka shifted her weight and did not answer.

"Listen to me, Minka. I am the most happy woman. I live for my husband—for him and my three children whom God gave to me through my husband. For whom, Minka, do you live?"

There was no extra money to spend on such things as pencils, exercise books or other school supplies. In order to buy these things, Janez and Julijanna awoke at three o'clock in the morning during picking season and walked with Jozeca six kilometers to the mountainside to pick berries. All day long they would pick until they had from twenty to fifty kilos. Then they walked the six kilometers back to town where Janez sold the berries.

In the autumn they picked hops. At three o'clock in the morning they were out of bed and after a breakfast of hot coffee and bread they hiked to the fields and picked all day. Sometimes it would be raining and sometimes it was cold enough to see their breath on the air. But they trudged up the mountain to the fields.

Jozeca told her children, "If you have two hands and two feet, you will always find a way to get what you need. If you cannot, then you must ask the Lord if you really need it."

Besides caring for the family at home, Jozeca sent money every month to Josip, her son who was studying for the ministry.

Chapter Fifty-one

It was a warm Sunday morning in October and the town which lay in the crease of the hills was quiet. They walked slowly down the dirt path to the road where the car was waiting. Two men held Jakob's arm and helped him inside. He sat in the front seat by the driver. Jozeca sat in the back with Julijanna and Janez. The talk was light. Jakob did not speak. He was praying.

The people were already in their seats when they arrived at the white red-roofed house, one room of which was their church. When Jakob entered, they stood up. He walked to the wooden pulpit which he had built himself and said, "Let us pray."

They prayed and they sang just like every Sunday. But this Sunday was not like every Sunday. It was Jakob's last sermon. He had announced it last week. He knew he could no longer stand in the pulpit. For the last month he had been suffering severe pains in his stomach and groin and he was becoming incontinent. It was time to preach his last sermon.

He read from the Psalms: "The meek shall eat and be satisfied: they shall praise the Lord that seek him: your heart shall live forever" (Ps. 22:26).

Then he closed the book.

"There was once a Baptist preacher named Soba," he said, "and during the war he was a Partisan. But he refused to take the gun. The war took him to Croatia, although he was a Slovene. The soldiers tried to persuade him to take the gun but he always refused. One day the leader decided he should be shot because he was a bad example to the others, who were, quite frankly, a nervous and hungry lot to begin with. So the captain asked the Baptist preacher, 'Are you ready to take the gun? If you are, then we shall give you your life. If you are not, then we shall now shoot you.'

"The Baptist preacher refused the gun, saying, 'What is my life? —but a vapor. Far more important is my reward in heaven for obeying my Lord who said that He loves all men.'

"What do you suppose happened? There were over three hundred soldiers in the division, and they all rose up against the captain and requested the life of this Baptist preacher be saved. So a decision was made and the man was not shot."

"Praise be to the Lord."

"But that is not all. After the war I preached in a little church in Kocevje. I was there three days and I visited one family. There was an atheist in the family. Oh, this man hated God, I tell you. He hated even the name of God. I talked to him about the love of God and about how great God is. I told him about the power to become children of God when we believe in Jesus Christ.

"Then this man said to me, 'I was a Partisan. I was the captain of my division. And I remember a man who refused to take the gun and we decided to kill him. He was not afraid to die—'

" 'Did you kill him?' I asked.

" 'No,' he said.

" 'What was this man's name?'

" 'I forgot his name.'

" 'Was it Soba?'

" '*Da! Da!* Yes! That was his name.' All the soldiers wanted to be in his presence because they said that where Soba is, there is God. 'Where there is Soba,' they said, 'there is safety.' "

Jakob paused, then continued.

"That man Soba was in prison with me at Hoce. And I saw him night after night on his knees praying. One morning the guard came and told him he was being released. We were all rejoicing. Then the next afternoon all of the men in his cell, about five of them, were taken out and shot as enemies of the Republic. But Soba was not among them. He was released just in time.

"Soba refused to kill. And God, in turn, refused to allow him to be killed. 'Blessed are the merciful, for they shall obtain mercy.'

"O beloved, remember, we cannot alter God's order of things. You shall always reap what you sow."

Chapter Fifty-two

Julijanna walked slowly home from school, taking the longest way possible. She held the report card behind her back and she felt as though the world had sunk from beneath her feet. She had failed her last year in Economical School and she would have to repeat the whole year.

How could she look into her mother's eyes? "Dear Lord, *Mamica* will have to wait another year before I can help her by working at a job. I must again go to school to repeat what I have failed." Tears slid down her cheeks.

But when Jozeca found her wandering along the road, she called to her, "Julijanna, it is not well with you! Julijanna! Look at your mother. What is it that worries you?"

Julijanna averted her eyes. "Mama, it is nothing."

"Speak up! Tell me."

"Mama . . ."

Then Jozeca saw the report card in her hand. "Ah, I believe I understand."

Julijanna burst into tears. "*Mamica*, I am sorry. I must repeat the year! I will not graduate and I will not be able to go to work to help you!"

"You were my beloved daughter when you were receiving good grades in school, and you are my beloved daughter when you have failed. I will help you. We will work together and you will do much better. You shall see. Come now, come, let us go home. I have a surprise for you."

Julijanna walked along with her mother, her arm tucked under Jozeca's strong, warm embrace. When she was beside her there was always a feeling of being safe, of being secure. It was because Jozeca, although weak and emotional, walked in a supernatural strength. Everyone could feel it. All they had to do was to tuck their hand under her strong arm and feel the power of a greater presence. Even now with the knowledge that another year was added to her suffering, she remained strong.

At home Julijanna found her father sitting up at the table. Jozeca had prepared her favorite food, *pasulj*, a Serbian bean stew in which cabbage and meat floated. On the table were raw onions and black bread to be eaten along with it.

"O dear Papa, how wonderful to see you sitting up at the table! You are looking well!" and she kissed her mother for the *pasulj*.

Julijanna had no girl friends in school because there were no other Christian girls her age. In the church there were no girls her age either and so her only friend was her mother. Many afternoons after school as she walked along the road listening to the cluck of chickens and the barking of dogs, she longed for just one girl to talk to, to walk with. She wondered what feelings other girls had, what they dreamed about, and what they hoped for. Julijanna hoped for three things: a girl friend, a loving Christian husband one day and a good home for her mama and papa.

"*Mamica*," she told Jozeca one evening as they sat bent over Julijanna's schoolwork, "I love you very much."

Jozeca squeezed and kissed her daughter's hands.

"And, *Mamica*, I want you to know that just as you work and serve your husband, so will I one day do for you."

When the youth brigades were calling for volunteers, Julijanna asked if she could join them. Jozeca flatly refused. "Lord, help me. I must watch over my daughter, Lord, a girl. Help me. I was pure when I went to my husband. Lord, help me to teach her to be pure for the day when she goes to her own husband. Help me, Lord, for the days are wicked."

But one of the young girls in her class tried to persuade her to join the youth brigade, "Ah, Julijanna, tell your mother you must go! We will have such fun! We will go to Serbia to build the roads. Do not you care about your country?"

"Of course, I care."

"Then you must serve."

Then Julijanna looked at her friend and said, "Tatjana, why are you wasting your youth?"

"What?"

"Why are you wasting your youth? Look at you, attending dances, parties, going out with boys! Now on the brigade you will look only for good times. Do you not know these things mean nothing without God? I mean that only when you enjoy life through God, through His love, do you really learn what fun is! Oh, Tatjana, have you given your life to Him?"

Tatjana, a tall, heavy-set girl with short dark hair and high round cheeks, shrugged her shoulders. "I am sorry you will not go with the brigade. Maybe we can talk another time."

When Tatjana returned from the brigade in Serbia, she told Julijanna how they went into the graveyards and ate the food set on the graves for the dead. "I tell you, Julijanna, the dead eat better than the living!"

Tatjana liked Julijanna and was drawn to her, even though she did not want to hear about Jesus Christ and about giving up her way of living.

But one day Tatjana's father was taken to the hospital after suffering a stroke. He was only fifty-three years old and Tatjana and her mother were frantic. They hurried without delay to the house of Kovac.

"Julijanna, please ask your family to pray. Our father is very ill. He is in the hospital!"

Jozeca rushed with Julijanna and Tatjana to the hospital to see the stricken man. He was lying on the bed as cold and stiff as an old bone. Softly Jozeca began to pray and she prayed for over an hour. Nothing happened.

The next day Janez went to the hospital and prayed for the man. He washed him and combed his hair and sang songs to him. Finally the man opened his eyes; he saw Janez looking at him through his thick-lensed glasses. Tatjana's mother celebrated with tears of joy.

"God will heal you, *Gospod*," Janez told the man. "But He will heal you only if you give Him the glory. Do you understand?" The man nodded. "I will give God the glory."

They organized round-the-clock prayer. Jozeca came and prayed. When she left, Julijanna came and prayed. The next day Janez came again and prayed. This time he shaved the sick man and talked to him about the love of the Lord. Tatjana's mother was deeply moved by the concern of a family of complete strangers. Even her own family had not shown this much concern.

In one week he was discharged from the hospital. But his story has not a happy ending. He did not keep his promise to God. "Huh!" he snarled one evening at his wife's suggestion that it was God who had healed him. "God did not heal me. The medicine did! Besides that, I am not yet an old man. My body is strong. It mends easily."

"But you were a dying man—"

"Ah, the devil. You are too quick to give credit to something that you are not even sure exists."

"But I am sure. And so is your daughter—"

"Huh!"

Two weeks later he was back in the hospital and four days after that he was dead of a cerebral hemorrhage. Nobody cried harder than Julijanna and Janez. "I am so sorry, Tatjana," Janez told the new friends. "I would have died in his place if I could have."

Tatjana and her mother gave their hearts to Christ, and Julijanna had a girl friend.

Chapter Fifty-three

At night Jozeca sat on the edge of Jakob's bed and read the Bible to him. His strength was leaving him and slowly his strong, large frame began to shrink and his prominent proud features became hollow, cadaverous. His eyes which were once intense and filled with fire and passion now wandered loosely about in his face, faded and disinterested.

Julijanna arranged to stay home in the mornings to take care of him and she went to her classes in the afternoon. She shaved him, washed him and then showed him his reflection in the mirror. "Look, Father, how beautiful!"

Jakob looked at his daughter's bright eyes, and he could not contain his tears. "O my daughter," he wept. "Look what you must do with me. You must clean me and care for me as a child." Julijanna held his hands and kissed them.

"Father, I would do this all my life. Only please live. Live, Father."

By Jakob's eighty-third birthday he had suffered two strokes and had been in the hospital seven times. Back in his own bed, with Julijanna taking care of him, he lay quivering with the thought, "I shall rise up out of this bed. I shall walk. I shall walk to the toilet alone, unassisted, and, praise be to God, I shall be at once strong." He sat up, lifted his feet over the edge of the bed, stood to his feet, and walked to the door.

When Julijanna saw him, he was leaning against the door frame crying. He was without control of himself. Julijanna covered him, washed him, and brought him back to the bed, and then cleaned up the floor.

He could not explain the tears. He could not tell himself in words. His life, his own dearest ones now were beyond his reach. He could no longer extend his fingers to them, give them hope and strength, hold their lives.

"O my dear Lord, look down on my family. See my Jozeca. See how she has been my heart all these years. See how she has loved me as though I were you, dearest Lord! O God! Can I leave my heart? And my sons, Lord—my sons. My Janez, the apple of my eye, who never had a father to help him or to play with him. And see my Josip who shall walk in my shoes. And, Savior, look upon the dearest flower of all Jugoslavia, my Julijanna, a picture of her mother. O Lord, Lord, how can I leave them? These are your dearest gifts to me, unworthy man that I am. But how can I remain here in this condition? How can I stay to see them cry for me? Lord, I am an old man. . . ."

"Father, Father, I would wash you and clean you all of my life. Father, live—only live!"

He had one more stroke and this one partially paralyzed him. He could barely move a few muscles of his body. Janez sat by his side weeping.

"Papa, do not leave us!"

"My son, be brave. . . ."

"Papa, look upon me."

"My son, my son . . . Janez, I know I have not been the best father to you. I could not play with you and do many things with you. But I have prayed for you. I love you very much, my son. But now your mother is your father. Listen to her, my son. Obey her."

"Papa!"

They were alone in the room. Tears fell from Jakob's eyes and slid down over his ears onto the pillow. "Your mother is God's gift to us. Remember that. There is none in the world like her."

"Papa, promise me that you will be in heaven and that you will wait for me there."

"If I promise you, son, will you promise to follow me?"

"Yes, my Papa. I will follow you. I promise."

There was a soft glow in his smile as he closed his eyes.

A few moments later when Janez had gone to the kitchen, he heard a loud reverberating thump coming from the sleeping room.

"What was that?" he asked, startled.

Jozeca, her face taut, said, "Go and look, Janez. You will learn something."

Janez rushed into the room. Jakob was lying face down on the floor.

"Papa!"

He had pushed himself out of the bed onto the floor and was struggling to get to his knees.

"Papa! What are you doing?"

"I am going to pray, son."

"But, Papa, must you get on your knees? Can you not pray in the bed?"

Jakob looked at him through green eyes which saw only shadows and forms now. "Janez, I have prayed all my life on my knees.

I shall pray on my knees to the end. Come now and help me."

Janez propped him up at the edge of the bed on his knees.

"Thank you. Now please return to me in one hour and help me back into the bed."

"Yes, Papa."

It was March 7, 1962, and Janez was leaving his chemistry class with the other students when he saw Julijanna beneath the oak archway in the hall. His heart stopped. He did not want to know she was there. And the Lord knew he did not want to hear what she had to tell him. He walked toward her. He saw her eyes. "Do not say it," he wanted to tell her. "Do not say the words." But he did not say it and she did say the words.

"Papa is dead," she said.

They walked home in silence. Julijanna was crying. Jozeca was alone in the room with him. She was sitting on the bed looking at his face. The windows were closed and the room was cold. Cold and quiet.

In the kitchen there was a little flat pan on the burner of the stove with three pieces of coal glowing gray and pink to give extra heat. Janez stood beside his mother and then leaned down and kissed Jakob's cheeks.

"Thank you, Papa," he whispered to the dead man. "Thank you for everything." Then he turned and left the room.

Later they came with the coffin and Josip was there with Julijanna and some relatives whom Janez barely knew. Jozeca's eyes were wide and frightened and she was talking louder than usual with a voice an octave higher than normal. The door of the bedroom opened and they saw the coffin, half in and half out of the door. The men were trying to figure out a way to get it through the door and around the corner without tipping it on its side. As Janez watched them, something left his heart. Something cut deep into him and took a certain something else out; and then the discussion was over, the coffin jostled out, and the door closed behind them.

The following day at the graveside Jozeca looked down at her feet. Out of the corner of her eye she could see the stiff body in the open wooden coffin. It was lying hard and cold in the box in the wagon, piled high with wreaths and ribbons, his chalk-white face, shrunken, and his dear strong hands clasped forever on his ribs. Shovels were jabbed into the piles of freshly turned black dirt around the grave. The people gathered awkwardly and gazed downward.

"Ah, Jakob, my Most Beloved, just look at what is left of you. Please try to understand that it is difficult for me to see you this way."

There were so many people, with their dark coats, their caps and their bowed and bent heads. She looked at Janez, brave, young, his thick-lensed glasses strapped around his bowed head, fatherless forever. "Our sons, they will both miss you, Jakob. Ah, Jakob—"

A chink of dirt fell and caused a rumble of falling dirt and stones. Jozeca shivered, leaned over the black box holding its prize, kissed once more his cold and totally unyielding face, and then she sang slowly and triumphantly for the whole countryside to hear:

> God is love, God is love,
> He dwells in love
> forever,
> His hand reaches out with love,
> Only love,
> He gives and He takes in love. . . .

When she finished singing there were tears in every man's and woman's eye who stood there beside the grave. Julijanna held Janez' hand tightly and the tears burned behind their eyelids. But they would not cry here, not in front of everyone. At home, at home they would cry. Josip stood behind his mother, his tall, strong frame above the heads of the others. Then they whispered, "*Na svidenje*, Good-bye, Papa," and it was over.

Chapter Fifty-four

A new preacher came from Germany to pastor the church and the people liked him immediately. He had a commanding presence; and Jozeca thought as she listened to him speak that he could tell the people anything he wanted to and they would believe him. This worried her because she had felt uneasy about him right from the beginning. He always had plenty of marks in his pocket and he owned two German cars. Besides, he had a too-ready smile.

It was only six months after Jakob's death that this new preacher was telling the congregation strange things—things Jozeca could not understand. He said, "God was not really a God of salvation—that is, He did not really want to save men's souls. He just wanted to be God; and Jesus Christ, His supposed son, was really only a man—"

Jozeca could not listen to this strange preaching and told him one day she did not think he was preaching the truth. "If you are here to preach the word of the Lord, then you should preach what it tells us in the Bible. The Holy Spirit is in God's Word—preach the Word."

The preacher, a man with intense eyes and a voice like chocolate pudding, put on his quick smile. Jozeca was puzzled by his expression. "You do not think I preach from the Bible, eh, Sister?"

"*Ne*, I do not."

"Then let me ask you this. Do you personally read the Bible?"

"Yes, I personally do."

"Can you read it in the original German?"

"Pardon?"

"Can you read it in the original German? That is, the way the apostles wrote it?"

"I can read a little German. I learned it in a German prison."

"Ah, then you should not worry about your minister's preaching." There was that peculiar expression and his voice was slightly more chocolate. "You should just leave the preaching to me. I read German as well as Russian and Hebrew."

"Ah, oh."

"As for you, uh, there are certain ways I believe you can serve the Lord."

"I try to serve the Lord as best I can."

"Now, I know how lonely it must be for you being without a

husband and all. I think I could help you out a little."

"But I am not lonely. I have my children and I have Jesus."

"But you cannot hold Jesus in the night, now, can you, *Gospa*? And your children do not touch you and tell you how beautiful you are."

She now understood the odd expression. His hand was on her shoulder and his face was very close to hers. She could feel his breath and his youth. His hands were not knotted and arthritic; they were smooth and strong. His face was handsome, and his voice smooth.

She whacked his hand with hers and pushed him away from her. He lost his balance and nearly fell over.

She received a message during the week that she was not welcome in the church. She was told not to return because she was barred. She stood outside the small white frame house shaking and praying. This was the church her husband had founded. He brought in every one of the converts by preaching in the hills and villages, loving and caring for his Slovene people. Now he was gone and she was excommunicated. Her name was sent to the Baptist convention in Zagreb and put on a "black list" which the denomination kept for such people as false teachers, blasphemers and heretics.

While the congregation sat inside singing "God Is Love," Jozeca inched painfully around the church on her knees praying for the pastor and the people inside. Her knees were torn and bleeding, but she continued praying and continued marching on her knees.

"Lord, look upon me! You see the comely qualities of this preacher! Forgive his ways, Lord! Forgive him! He does not know much, Lord. He is caught in the ways of the flesh. O God, O Jesus! Give me a sign that you have heard my prayer! Give me a sign!"

On and on she prayed. When the people came out of the church, they met Jozeca on her knees, tear-stained and disheveled. They fell on her neck and embraced her. The next week there were only half of the people in the little white frame house. The rest of the people were jammed into Jozeca's flat, praying and praising God. They would start a new church and they would pray for a new pastor.

"This time, Lord, send us one of your pastors," they prayed. "Like our Jakob Kovac who was Sent Man of God."

Chapter Fifty-five

Josip was married in 1960 to a beautiful girl named Brigita who was two years older than he. She was tall and slim with large brooding brown eyes and dark hair, resembling a Modigliani painting. She was a teacher and taught at the University in Novi Sad. It was unusual for a Christian to teach at the University. Most of the teachers were Communists.

"But my Brigita works the hardest, the longest, the best. That is why they hired her. She is actually more dedicated than the Communist teachers who also work hard and long," Josip told his family.

A year after they were married Brigita became pregnant, but due to an error on the part of the doctors the baby died a few minutes after it was born. Brigita did not regain her health. She lay soaked in fever in the hospital. Josip called home frantically, "Pray, *Mamica*! Pray for my Brigita!"

She lay precariously on the edge of life and Josip knelt by her side praying around the clock. "I will not let you die, my soul. The Lord has taken my son, but He will not take my wife also."

And Brigita did recover. But she was never quite the same. She had frequent relapses, and one day Josip took her to the military hospital in Beograd for tests. He received a deadly diagnosis: an incurable blood disease, Lupus. Josip remembered how his mother and father refused to let go of God for his own soul—how they prayed night and day for him, as well as many others, until God answered and this is how he would keep his wife alive—by prayer. He would not give up.

Brigita continued teaching. She taught at the University and led the demanding life of a pastor's wife. Josip had the energy of ten men, she always said. He pastored three churches in Croatia and seventeen mission stations. Each week they walked together on foot to the villages to pray for the sick, to visit families and encourage the believers. He was indefatigable. Brigita struggled to keep on her feet. "Josip, my darling, you are making up for the time lost when you had turned your face from God."

"Yes," he answered. "I shall never forget how I brought shame to my father and deep pain to my mother. I rejected my family and caused them much sorrow. The Lord saved me. I shall never forget what He did for me. I promised Him that the same energy

I used to serve the devil, I will double to serve Him."

But Brigita grew more weak. "*Mamica*," Josip sobbed in Jozeca's arms on a visit to Celje. "I know all that you have taught me in this life. Pray, pray and pray some more! I know that there are strong forces against us and that we are called to break through these strong forces. Oh, but, *Mamica*, I cannot stand to see my beautiful Brigita wither away before my eyes . . . my beautiful wife . . . O *Mamica*, help me."

He was again her little boy needing her feet pressed against the soles of his feet. "Feel my strength, son," she said. "Touch my hand and listen to me. You are tired, weak. I shall be strong for you. I shall believe and pray for our Brigita—rest now."

And hour after hour Jozeca knelt in prayer for Brigita. She prayed daily for her as for her own daughter, faithfully and without faltering or accepting less than all she asked of God.

Brigita could feel the prayers. She knew they were her breath. Now she was tired and walked slowly through the small. hilly park, listening to the sounds of her footsteps along the path. The air was bitterly chilling and an unfriendly wind blew, pushing her hair upwards from her neck and across her face. She trembled, stopped and started again. The faces of her students were before her in her mind. All eyes were upon her, waiting. They were like little birds with open beaks waiting for food. She had a fever that day and she was perspiring heavily. It was hard to focus on their faces.

Someone seemed to call her name; "Yes, is that you, Vaslj?"

"Please, Professor Kovac, could I speak with you a few words?"

"Of course, Vaslj. Sit down here by me."

He was young. His broad face held a pair of black brooding eyes. He pulled his chair closer to her desk. His voice was low, his words slowly spoken. The fever dimmed her eyes. She was hot. So hot.

There was Sonja, Slavko, Ivo, Thomez, Marijana . . . so many others. They crowded in at the desk. "Please. . . ."

All during the years of teaching she had listened to the cries of their hearts. They wanted to know God. "Is it not true that we are created to know our Creator?" Vaslj asked.

"Yes, I believe," she answered.

Sonja said, "I have seen God because I have seen you, Professor Kovac."

It was hot, so hot.

"Sonja, God loves you."

The voices pressed closer, all speaking at once.

"Please, Professor, how can I believe in God?"

"Professor, is God as wonderful as you?"

"We are not worthy to kiss your feet, dear Professor."

How many of them had there been? So many, so many. In the beginning she had been healthy. Only during the last five years had she struggled against the "sickness." Her students did not know. For thirteen years she had taught them at the University and the students as well as the teachers had loved her. She would not let sickness deprive her nor them of the love God had placed between them.

She had always obeyed the rules and did not proselytize. She never made her faith in God known publicly, but they streamed to her to ask questions about God and how to have faith. "I want to be as you," she heard again and again. Without a single word of open witnessing she had won more people to the Lord than she was able to count.

She was always careful about speaking of the Lord. She prayed for the right words. Sometimes she would be reluctant to speak and this enticed the students further. They were drawn to their tall linguistics teacher like moths to light.

"What is there so different about you?"

"I am not sure what you mean, Marija."

"Tell us, Professor, what is it you have? We want it too!"

"Tell me what you see, Ladislav."

"You *have* something. What is it?"

"What kind of something, Nadja?"

Then she would smile, "All right, my children. I shall tell you all that you ask of me."

The air was cold and she was perspiring. The wind blew her thin coat open and she tucked her arms across her chest, folding it closed. The years of training and schooling which had prepared her for a teaching position seemed so far in the past, almost as though they had never happened.

"It is God's will for me" she had told herself, "and I will do my best for Him."

There were no teaching positions for anyone not belonging to the Communist party. She was a believer in Christ and it was impossible for her to teach in a university. But by a miracle, she received a post at the University because she had been top in her class and top in her school and her record had been spotless. They were in need of a teacher and she came with the highest qualifications. This would have marked her thirteenth anniversary at the University.

"Professor mine, you are as a bright light in this place."

They were all looking up at her, the room was filled with students. She saw their faces all shining, their eyes solemn, waiting. "Feed us," they were saying. "We love you. The bread you give us is good bread. It fills us."

Suddenly their faces vanished. She looked before her at the wooden park bench which nobody ever sat on. She stopped and looked at the small patch of earth which would be a flower bed in spring. The air was cold and she was tired. It was all over now. She had emptied her desk of her things, she had shaken hands with her students and the other teachers. They had kissed her face, and it was over.

There were clouds moving slowly in the sky like ships lost at sea, and the wind blew hard and cold. Soon she would be home and she would lie down, yes, lie down on the bed; put her head on the large cushion with the white lace slipcover. She had been the only Christian teacher in the University. All the others were Communist. They had put her away like an old glove. She was forced to retire but not only for medical reasons. She was not a Communist and that was the school board's deciding factor.

Josip was waiting for her at home. He held her in his arms and kissed the top of her head. She was wet and hot with fever and there was a butterfly-shaped rash on her face.

"I refuse this fever!" he shouted, startling Brigita. "In the name of Jesus Christ, I command this fever to leave!"

She stood leaning upon him and he held her face in his hands, "My darling, I do not care what the doctors say. You will be well! I will never stop believing that. God will heal you completely and we will rejoice together in your good health."

He helped her to bed and she lay down, so thin she barely made a crease on the lace covering quilt. "Josip, who will tell them? Who will tell my students about God?"

Chapter Fifty-six

Janez graduated from secondary school with offers from three Jugoslav soccer teams in his hand. The coaches came to the flat to talk terms with him. Jozeca confronted him one afternoon, "Janez, my son, what shall it be? Shall you play soccer or shall you serve God?"

"Can I not do both, *Mamica*?"

"Look at our Jugoslavia, Janez. Can you, Janez, play soccer until the Lord comes with your conscience satisfied that you have done all you were called to do for His kingdom?"

Jozeca's cheeks were flushed, the blood rushed to her eyes. The early sunlight shone through the window on her head. She held knitting needles in her hands, characteristic of her refusal to allow herself to be idle.

"I will consider all the words that you have said to me, *Mamica*," and he bowed slightly as he left the room.

Janez was young, strong. His body had no pouches of fat, no tight unstretched muscles. His vision was weak but his eyes were clear, his gaze direct, confident. He walked straight with a steady, strong stride. His movements were sure, his hands left no confusing trails on the air when he talked.

Now the world lay before him. He could be a soccer star. He was already the best in Celje. He imagined himself as one day the best soccer player in Jugoslavia. Money, girls, friends; ah, yes, and he could be of great help to his mama. He had lived through too much despair to turn his back on the call of success. If he signed with a team, his mama could drink sugar in her coffee, wear silk dresses and nice lady's shoes. "O Jesus! O God! If I am famous, I will have opportunity to tell many people about you. Think of that, Lord, my God. May I speak of these things to you? Think of how my fame could help to spread the Gospel! And think of the money I could give to further your work!"

The following afternoon when he came home from soccer practice Jozeca was waiting for him in the same place by the window. "Janez, some men were here. They asked if you would be pleased to go to Beograd to be on one team. I did not answer for you, my son. I told them the answer would come from my son."

Janez smiled, kissed his mother's cheeks and said, "My *Mamica*, there is none like you in all the world. I shall not play soccer, *Mamica*. I shall go to Novi Sad to the Baptist seminary. There I shall study to become a minister of the Lord Jesus Christ as my father was."

"Janez . . . this is your decision?"

Tears welled in her eyes and, blinking them away, she threw her hands in the air, "Dear God! Thank you! Thank you!"

She shouted and praised the Lord, dropping her knitting to the floor, "Thank you, Lord! *Hallelujah! Ljubim te Jezuz*, I love you, Jesus!"

Janez pushed the bridge of his glasses with his finger, slid his feet into a pair of slippers by the door and went into the kitchen. He could hear Jozeca shouting, "Praise be to God! You are faithful! Praise be your name! Hallelujah!"

He looked to see what was cooking in the pot on the stove. "Ah, *petrsil*, potato soup," he said and he sat down at the table to eat.

Jozeca's voice could be heard singing and praising the Lord as she carried coal from the road to the basement in the mornings. "O my Jesus! I love you, my Jesus!"

She chopped wood into small pieces in the dampness of the dark basement singing as though she were in heaven.

> Hallelujah every day.
> And when troubles come your way,
> Lift up your head and say,
> Hallelujah every day

Julijanna was graduating from Economical School, wearing her mother's dress, which Jozeca had altered to fit her somewhat thinner figure. She looked beautiful. As a special surprise, Jozeca presented her with the news that she had arranged for her to go to a Christian camp for one week on the Adriatic coast. Julijanna wept with gratitude when she learned of this. She knew how hard her mother had worked to earn the extra money for a week at camp. She must have sat up nights knitting sweaters for six months.

Janez secretly envied his sister's good fortune of going to a real Christian camp, something he had never dared dream of. Jozeca ruffled his hair, grabbed his arm and held it behind his back. "And you, my son! What would you give to go to such a camp, eh?"

"I am not jealous, *Mamica*. I am happy Julijanna can go. I speak the truth!"

"Ah, ha! And what will you do if I tell you that you are also going to this camp on the Adriatic?"

Janez held his face with his free hand. He realized the sacrifice and long hours of extra work she must have endured to send both of her children to camp. He wanted to cry but he did not.

"*Mamica*, I want to be like you one day. I pray to God that I can love others and do all for others as you do. Our father was right. There is none in the world like you."

Janez and Julijanna went to Christian camp; and it was there they made commitments to God that would last their lives. Never had they dreamed of such wonderful things as a group of Christians around a campfire singing songs and praising the Lord. They saw other young people who loved God and who gathered together in the name of the Lord. It was too wonderful. Janez, who never had a Christian friend, was now sitting in the presence of more than twenty people who loved God. It was like a dream, a miracle. How could he ever repay his mama for such a wonderful experience. He would never forget it, never.

It was at this camp that Julijanna met a young medical student from Bosnia named Filip. He was tall, thin with deeply brooding eyes, a straight, narrow nose, and the kindest smile she had ever seen. Her prayers for a good Christian husband were answered. In three years they were married.

Her friend Tatjana said, "Julijanna did not follow the ways of sin in her youth. She chose to remain alone rather than accompany the rest of us to the dances and parties where there was wickedness and immorality. Look at Julijanna. She has a wonderful life and a beautiful man who loves her deeply. She is happy down to her soul. Now Julijanna is eating the fruit of her obedient youth."

More of Jozeca's prayers were answered again, for Filip trained at the Baptist Seminary at Novi Sad and, although he was now interning at the medical center in Ljublijana, he became the part-time pastor of their little church. He brought sweetness and love to the church, and Jozeca wept as she thanked God for him. Julijanna and Filip moved in with Jozeca into her flat on the sixth floor.

Julijanna told her mother one evening, removing her shoes and massaging her toes, "*Mamica*, my dear mama, do you remember long ago when I promised you that as you served my father, so will I serve you?"

"Ah."

"I keep my promise. I shall work at the factory and we shall move into a flat where Filip and I pay the rent. You will not have to work hauling wood and coal and cleaning halls and other people's homes any longer in order to have a flat to live in. I have already informed Macek."

Jozeca sat quite still. Not haul wood and coal? Not clean and work? "Ah, daughter."

"It is all settled and taken care of, *Mamica*. You shall work no more."

Chapter Fifty-seven

They were able to eat better now. The usual diet of coarse bread, fruits and vegetables and an occasional pottage of haricot beans, potatoes and dumplings, now had some meat added to it and they even had pastries made of spinach, curds, honey and nuts.

But Jozeca refused to consider a life without work. To Julijanna and Filip's shrill protests, she only scoffed. Then she prayed quietly, "Forgive them, Lord. They do not know much."

She cooked, cleaned, scrubbed, washed, ironed and shopped for her daughter and her husband. She rose early in the morning to pray on her knees while it was still quiet, and after her work was finished she went out to the streets to preach the Gospel. She took trains to villages and towns in Slovenia and Croatia, visiting the homes and churches where Jakob had preached. She prayed for nearly every face her eye looked upon. Never in her life had her hours been so full.

One October morning when the wind plucked at the bedclothes hanging out the windows, Josip came for a visit. He had driven up from Croatia in the blaze of autumn colors, the browns, the golds, the reds, and he had driven up in the new car which the Lord had given him.

"Imagine, Mama. After all these years of walking and riding our bicycles the Lord saw fit to give us a car. Praise be the name of the Lord!"

"Praise be the name of the Lord."

But Josip's heart was heavy, and he had no sooner gotten his shoes off and pushed his feet into the waiting slippers than he began to unravel his heart to his mother.

"I do not understand," he said; "please help me to understand."

"Please?"

"Mama, the people come to me from many places. They ask me to pray for them. A woman, a Communist woman who was a teacher at the same school Brigita taught, was unable to have children. She and her husband came to me secretly and they asked me to pray. I told them how Brigita and I cannot have children but we are happy. They did not want to hear this. They wanted me to pray for them. So I did, and, Mama, six months later the woman returned to our house and told us, 'I have good news. I am with child.' Now they have two sons and they both know that the Lord has given them their sons."

"Ah, oh. Praise be the name of the Lord."

"Praise be the name of the Lord. And then another woman came to me and she told me her husband had decided to divorce her because she can give him no son or daughter. I told her that, really, I could not help her but I knew of One who could. She asked me, 'Who is that one? Please, I must know!'

"And so I told her about our dear Lord. 'His name is Jesus,' I told her. Then she was crying. I said to her, 'Are you agreed I pray for you?' Never in her life had she heard such prayer. Six months later she came back and the tears were upon her face. She said to me, 'I just came to tell you the good news!'

"'What good news?'

"'I am with child.' "

"And one brother one year ago had a son who died. I buried him. I said to him, 'Dear brother, I shall pray that the Lord shall give you another son very soon.' Do you know what he said to me? He said, 'Pray for yourself! Pray for yourself, Preacher! Pray that the Lord will give you a son!' "

She heard the pain in his heart.

"After one year the Lord gave that man another son!" His voice was loud, punctuated with the pounding of his fists against the table. "And, Mama, the sick people! I pray for many sick people to be healed and they are healed! But look at my Brigita. She is every month ill, then well. She has an incurable disease. I pray, I fast, I pound the floor, I hound the heavens. I refuse to let her die. I do all, Mama, do I not?

"Sometimes, Mama, I want to ask God, 'Why do you heal this stranger and not my wife? Why do you give this man and this woman sons and daughters and not Brigita and me?' ".

Her head moved slowly up and down.

"Mama. Pray for me."

And then Jozeca prayed. She lifted her head and her arms in a gesture that seemed to lift the glory of God in her hands. She began slowly as though listening for the right way to pray. Then she was singing. And finally she stood to her feet and shouted, "You self-pitying spirit, I forbid your presence in this, my son's body and mind!"

On and on she raged. Sometimes weeping, sometimes laughing. There was no interrupting her. This was her tirade with unseen forces and with God. She was interceding for her son. Where her son was concerned she would accept nothing less than God's finest, God's best. He was the son of Jakob Kovac.

"My son," she said at last, "my son, God is giving you His very finest."

"What means this?"

"He is giving you strength. Keep fighting in His name. Keep praying. The devil wants to discourage you. He wants to defeat you. Do not allow him to! The apostle Paul said he *fought the good fight*. So must we!"

Josip returned to Croatia to find Brigita throbbing with fever. "O my Lord," he prayed. "Please give me a sign that you are with us, that you hear our prayers, and that you will make my Brigita well. I will not leave you until you answer me."

He stayed all night on his knees beside Brigita's bed. She awoke several times in the night to the sound of his voice droning in the stillness and the heat. So hot it was, the air so heavy, fervid. "Josip, my soul, are you not tired? Will you not rest? Ah, dear, it is hot, so hot."

In the morning she rested peacefully. Her brow was dry. He prepared her breakfast of fresh yogurt and bread and sat at the edge of the bed praising God with a loud voice.

"Soul, are you not weak?" he asked. "Are you not hot?"

"*Ne*, my only one. I am rested and I feel as though I have been to the seaside."

He touched her ear, held her face. "Thank God, Mama was praying," he said.

As he sat beside his wife, wiping crumbs from her chin and stirring sugar into her *kava*, a man on the other side of town was twisting his bedclothes in terror. He had awakened from a frightening nightmare which directly involved Josip.

Josip had never met the man. His name was Cudic. He was a Communist who had served the last four years as the local Party secretary. During the night he awakened screaming, alarming his wife. In his nightmare he saw a deep dark hole in which he saw nothing but black emptiness. Then he looked up and saw brilliant light around him as bright as a sunny day at the Adriatic coast. Then he fell into the hole and could not get out of it. The harder he tried to get out, the farther he fell from the light. A voice came to him then and said, "Look to your right."

Cudic looked to his right and saw a road that led to the light. Then the voice again spoke to him and said, "Follow this road and see what you will find at the end of it."

Cudic did what he was told. He followed the road and at the end of it was a church. He panicked. As an atheist and a Communist, he was proud of the fact that he had never entered a church in his life. Christians, to him, were despicable characters, and he considered himself noble to even shake the hand of one of them.

But then he saw a man standing in front of the church. He was a big man with a wide face, intense green eyes and straight brown hair slicked to the side.

The voice again spoke, "Do you wish to remain in the darkness?"

"*Ne! Ne!*" Cudic responded without pondering for an answer.

"Look upon this man," the voice told him. "Through this man you will come into the light and there you will remain."

Cudic looked at the man. Behind him was the darkness licking at his heels. He saw sickness, sorrow, pain—all packed into the black pit which waited for him. He screamed for help and tore at his pillow. And then it was morning.

Later that day Cudic was sitting at his desk in the municipal office and a man entered and stood at his desk. He had a wide Slav face, intense green eyes and his hair was brown and slicked to the side. It was the man he had seen in his dream. He even wore the same brown coat.

"Pardon, I should like some information regarding hospitalization."

Cudic stared in disbelief. "Who—who are you?" His voice was choked, distant.

"My name is Kovac, sir, Josip."

"Kovac? And are you a Christian minister?"

"Yes, sir, I am."

That evening Cudic began a series of visits to Josip's house. When Josip heard of his dream, he got to his knees, raised his hands to the ceiling and shouted, "Thank you, Lord, for you have looked upon us and given us a sign as I have requested of you! Thank you, Jesus!"

After several more dreams in which the Lord spoke to him about darkness and light, Cudic resigned from the Communist party. Josip led him to Jesus gently and lovingly. The tears streamed down Cudic's face and onto his starched and pressed collar. "Just two weeks ago I would walk on the other side of the street if I approached a Christian. Just two weeks ago I boasted that my hands had never held the Christian Bible. O God, O Jesus, forgive me!"

Cudic became the most energetic Christian in the church.

Chapter Fifty-eight

The year 1963 was a historical year. In Macedonia it was the year of the devastating earthquake which destroyed eighty percent of Skopje's buildings and took more than a thousand lives. It was also the year a new constitution was established for Jugoslavia using the title "Socialist Federal Republic of Jugoslavia" without using the word "People's." The principles were, "All power comes from the people and belongs to the people." Tito was president for life.

For freedom-loving countries it was a tragic year. That year America's President Kennedy was assassinated. Tito made a moving tribute to the late president over Radio Belgrade and then went to the American Embassy in person to pay his respects. All Jugoslav flags were flown at halfmast and the nation's school teachers were ordered to devote an hour in class to discussing the western leader's achievements.

Janez graduated from seminary that year. He was filled with hope and enthusiasm, eager to pastor his first church. But most churches expected their pastor to be married, so when he met a girl who told him that she believed it was the will of the Lord that they be married, he complied and married her.

Her name was Darinka, a Serbian girl with long, bony fingers, unsmiling eyes and thin lips. She gave the impression that she disapproved of almost everything and everyone. She was unfriendly to Jozeca and clung to Janez, whispering and whining in his ear. Jozeca watched with dismay but held them both up to God. A woman who is truly loved and cherished by her husband has no need to jealously cling to him or demand his attention. She discerned Janez had acted impetuously outside of the will of God by marrying her so soon.

"My son has chosen to eat bitter bread," she told the Lord, "but I pray that you will bring him closer to you because of it."

One afternoon only a week after the wedding, Franciska sent the news that Lojze had gone to his final reward after suffering a heart attack during breakfast. He was complaining about the dampness of the weather when he suddenly clutched his heart and slumped over the table, dead.

Janez preached at the graveside. It was his first burial as a newly ordained Baptist minister.

Janez and his new wife, Darinka, moved to Holland that first year.

Jozeca watched them go with a lump in her chest. "I believe that you have called my sons to bring Jugoslavia to you, Lord, and now my young one runs to Holland like Jonah running from Nineveh. Touch him, Lord, touch him!"

Janez was not happy, although Holland is a beautiful country and the people friendly. During the day he walked from building to building looking for Jugoslav names on the mailboxes. He found Jugoslav workers and he talked to them; he told them about the love of the Lord and sang Jugoslav songs and played his guitar for them.

He saw his people from the Balkans with their broad faces, sturdy bodies and homely dress placed in the midst of western European fashion and finesse; saw them in the streets with their loud voices and giant-sized gestures, the women in thick dark stockings, babushkas, aprons and babies in their arms and the men with their mustaches and large rough hands which poked out of too-short shirt sleeves. "Like lost calves," he thought. They lived together in tiny flats—sometimes seven and eight people crammed into one room. The children wore ill-fitting clothes and always had a hungry look around their eyes; and the men drank too much.

It was here his first son was born. Darinka became a proud and doting mother, demanding even more of Janez' time and attention. One evening she confessed that she had been warned not to marry him.

"But why?"

"I was warned about your mother."

"Mama?"

"*Ja. Ja.* She is a known woman all over Jugoslavia. They say she can see right into the heart of a person. And that she has special powers."

"My mother is a woman of prayer. The power is God's."

"I am afraid of her and I am happy we are here in Holland and she is there in Slovenia."

Janez held meetings regularly for the Jugoslav workers and their families. They were supported by a European mission, but Janez was restless. One night as his wife and son slept, Janez heard loud thumps and scratching noises in the kitchen. He turned on the light to discover three large rats running across the floor. Before the morning sun shone through the window, he had moved his little family out and they were preparing to go home to Slovenia.

Back in Croatia, Janez' older brother, Josip, was enjoying a growing ministry. He received several invitations to speak in other countries. He asked Janez to accompany him to Germany where they would preach, sing and minister as brothers to Jugoslav workers there. Jozeca rejoiced that her sons would minister together. "Thank you, Lord!"

At one of their meetings in the town of Düsseldorf an Italian man with black, thick eyebrows joined at the bridge of his nose and stretched across to his temples begged Janez and Josip to come and pray for his son. "Please, please!" he begged.

Jozip told Janez to go and pray for him and he would remain with the group of people there at the church.

Janez agreed reluctantly. When he arrived at the hospital, he discovered the young man was dying of leukemia. Janez wished with all his heart he had not agreed to come. "O God! O Jesus! I cannot pray. I cannot look upon this young man. O dear God!"

His knees buckled and his stomach churned. The sight of the young man lying there in the bed, his skin the color of rotting bananas, thin and emaciated with tubes and I.V.'s running into his veins, was more than Janez was prepared to handle.

He prayed a short prayer. The room smelled of death and human waste. "O God! *Jezes, Marija!* Lord, if it is your will to take this young man—what is his name?"

"Giovanni."

"—if it is your will to take Giovanni from this world, then let him understand the Gospel which I will tell him right now."

The young man opened his eyes.

"Giovanni, you must prepare yourself, for you will go to heaven if you believe in Jesus Christ. Do you understand?"

His father translated. The boy nodded.

"The Lord is preparing a place for you. Whosoever believeth on Him shall not perish but shall have eternal life."

The young man nodded again. His mouth was dry and blue.

Janez blinked and pushed his glasses with his forefinger. "Uh, then, Lord Jesus, if it is your will to take him, then take him, but if your will is to help him and keep him alive, we want to thank you."

"*Grazia.*"

"*Grazia.*"

Then Janez cleared his throat, feeling himself getting dizzy at the sight of the bottle of blood hanging from an aluminum stand and dripping into Giovanni's body.

He got on his knees, touched the boy's hard, cold hand and said, "Lord God, have mercy! Look upon this young man and heal him for your glory—if it is your will. In Jesus' name! Amen."

He left the hospital quickly. Giovanni's father kissed his cheeks and wept gratitude. "God has answered your prayer. I am certain of it!" he said. "Praise be the name of the Lord!"

"Praise be the name of the Lord," Janez answered without enthusiasm.

236

Three months later Janez and Josip were back in Düsseldorf on
a preaching tour which included Munich, Hamburg, Wuppertal,
Frankfort and Köln. After the service one evening a man approached
Janez and said, "I bring you greetings from one young man named
Giovanni."

"Thank you, and who is Giovanni?"

"He is a young man who was dying of leukemia and you prayed
for him some months ago."

"Ah. He is still alive?"

"Ah, ja, ja. Alive and well. He is at home now growing stronger
every day. He and his father will never forget what you did for them."

Janez was amazed. "Lord Jesus! Heavenly Father! Look what
you have done by your Holy Spirit who heals and loves! Ah, Lord!"

Jozeca prayed for her children night and day. She set her schedule
according to theirs so she could be with them on their journeys, praying and supporting them in the power of the Holy Spirit as they went.
She was well aware of the battle that needed to be fought to see
the Lord's will on earth accomplished, and she knew the number
of the Lord's enemies was great.

"My Holy Father! My Jesus! I will fight in your name. Lord Jesus!
Father! Look down on my sons! See my youngest son whose time
is not yet mature. O Jesus! O Lord!"

She saw the hoards of spiritual enemies raging and ferociously
clamoring to destroy the work God had begun. She saw how God's
own people kept themselves in walled gardens ignoring the spiritual
war, praying only when it was convenient. She saw them amidst
their sweet-smelling flowers, far away from the battle front where
the enemy was busy destroying their own lives and the lives of their
loved ones. O God! O Jesus! In the language of the heart, the Spirit;
in Slovene, heavenly, known and unknown, she prayed. She stormed,
she raged, she wept, she praised, she insisted.

And then she listened.

"My little ones, you come to Me with many requests. You cry
to Me and beat your breasts. You ask Me for the world. And now
I ask you . . ."

"Speak, Lord! Your servants are listening!"

"You require Me to move mountains, to bring forth the glory of
My Son, Jesus. I am pleased with the desires of your hearts. But
what price are you willing to pay that I might bring to pass all that
you ask of Me? What are you willing to give to see My will fulfilled?"

"Anything, Lord! Anything! As you say, we will do!"

"And do you know what I shall ask of you?"

"O Lord, we will go without food, without a place to lay our heads;

we will travel to any corner of the world in your name; we will give all our goods to the poor; we will give all our energies to you to spread the Gospel of peace. We will suffer persecution, cold, wind and rain—"

"But My little ones, I ask you . . ."

"Speak, Lord! Your servants are listening!"

"Will you pray?"

Chapter Fifty-nine

In 1970 Janez moved to Macedonia to pastor a small church in a dusty little mountain village near Skopje. It was here Darinka gave birth to their second child, a daughter. The peasant people of the village welcomed them and came to visit the baby. Leaning over the cradle, they drew their heads back and spit lightly at her. Darinka was horrified. Several times during the day she wanted to cry out, "Stop!" but she held her tongue. At the end of the day the little cradle, the blanket, the tiny cotton smock and the baby were wet with the villagers' saliva. Janez explained to his frantic wife that it was the custom to spit at a newborn baby so that it would be assured of a long life and good luck.

The people of the village arose early in the morning to work in the tobacco fields. Janez awoke to the sound of horses clopping along the road and footsteps and voices of the people below his window. He quickly dressed and hurried to the dairy where there was already a queue waiting for milk. He waited sometimes two and three hours to be told there was no more milk to be bought. Many times their new baby went without milk all day.

He loved the Macedonian people and they loved him. Under his youthful enthusiasm the church grew and the believers felt happy, a rare sentiment. The District Communist President did not appreciate his efforts, however.

"Who gave you permission to hold these public meetings?"

"Nobody except my God."

"You must stop."

"I will. As soon as the meetings are finished."

"You must stop this evangelism."

"According to what law?"

"The new law."

"I want to go to Beograd and see President Tito."

"What means this?"

"President Tito set my father free from prison several years ago. Do not play with me. I am an unusual man."

"If you continue to hold these meetings, you will be put under arrest!"

He continued the meetings, and one evening he saw the crowded church surrounded by police. He asked one of the men to open the windows wide, not telling him why. Then he hurried to the pulpit, and, omitting the singing which usually began each meeting, he began to preach. He preached as loudly as he could, causing his voice to ring against the walls of the little plaster and wood church and echo outside to the dirt street. Each of the policemen heard the message of God's love loud and clear. Night after night they heard it. To his surprise, he was not arrested.

At the end of a special week of evangelistic meetings, a handsome black-haired young man approached him whom he had not seen at any of the other meetings.

"*Capisco 'Taliano?* Do you speak Italian?"

"*Poco. Poco.* A little, a little."

They decided to speak in German.

"I came to thank you for what you did for me. *Vielen Dank.* Thank you very much."

"But what have I done for you? You are a stranger to me."

"Ah, then you do not recognize me?"

"No. I am afraid I do not."

"One year ago you came to my hospital room in Düsseldorf where I lay dying."

Janez peered at him through his glasses. "*Nein!* No! It cannot be!"

"Yes," said the young man, smiling broadly. "I am Giovanni."

Janez kissed him and could not control his tears. That night as Giovanni stood before the people telling them what God had done for him, Darinka began to weep. She asked the Lord to save her, really save her, and in the little white-washed room smelling of wood smoke and woolen wraps, she gave her heart to Jesus. She was one of the nearly one hundred Macedonian people who gave their hearts to the Lord during those nights of meetings. When Janez thanked God and exclaimed, "I do not understand why we were not arrested," his wife answered, "I know why."

"Ah so? Tell us the reason."

"Your mother was praying," she smiled, "that is why."

Near the church lived a Communist school teacher and his family. The wife was very ill. Janez visited the bedridden woman to pray for her and read the Bible to her. The house was lined with colorful hand-woven rugs. Goat skins decorated the walls. The main room, filled with over-sized furniture, had, amid the crystal lamps and porcelain vases, a hanging mobile of Mickey Mouse with an inner tube around his belly and blue wrinkled water at his feet. Hanging over the door by the enormous television set hung a picture framed in red paper—of Pluto eating a hamburger.

"God is love," he told her. "God loves His people and loves His children to call upon Him. It is His will to heal His children and to give them life. God has a heart for His people. He has a heart which beats for His children and for His life to be in their hearts. Never despair! For the Lord God will lift up the downtrodden, He will make well the sick and make live that which was dormant. Believe in Him and you shall be saved."

The woman was fascinated by the Christian message of love and hope. She forced herself to get up from the sickbed as Janez instructed her to do. She attended the services in the church. This was a serious offense to her husband. He objected, but at the same time he saw his wife was well. Marx, Lenin and Engels had not made her well—Jesus had.

Janez sensed he would not be in Macedonia for long and so he preached with new fervor. He spoke to anyone who would listen to him about the love of the Lord. He stopped little children on the streets, carrying loaves of bread under their arms on their way home from school, telling them, "The Lord Jesus loves you!" Then he played with them until they went home.

He also went into the shops—old, tiny closet-like enclosures with walls of crumbling plaster and falling paint, lights which were turned off and the shopkeeper sitting in the dark until a customer came in. "*Dobor Dan!* Good Day! The Lord sent me to you today to tell you that He cares about you!"

He was popular with the young people. Everywhere he went, the young people gathered around him to hear him play his guitar, sing, to play soccer with them, wrestle or just to talk. His own childhood had slipped out of his fingers like clear soup in a sieve, but now the Lord was giving him the youth of hundreds of young people.

It was only one month after Brigita, Josip's wife, had prayed the Lord would send other Christians to the universities and to the youth of the nation that Janez was telling university students throughout the country about the love of God.

A Moslem priest came to visit Janez one morning. He climbed the wet cement steps leading to the flat above the church. It was Moslem Christmas, December 22, and he came to invite Janez to speak to his young people. Janez was thrilled. He removed his shoes at the door of the mosque and preached for fifteen minutes. There was not enough room inside the building for all the people who came to hear him. Many sat outside on the steps to listen. Janez invited them later to his home where a group of young people stayed to pray and sing until the sun rose over the rooftops.

Three weeks later Janez received an unsigned letter:

> You came into Macedonia like a snake into the garden of Eden. Leave Macedonia. You are a Slovene. You are not welcome here.

A Methodist pastor pounded on his door one late evening and, refusing to enter, told him in the yellow light of the hallway, "You are not welcome in our town. I am praying you will leave here. You come to our churches and steal our youth!"

"It is not my intention to steal. I want only to preach the Gospel of Jesus Christ."

"You are like a carpet of mud!"

"*Ja*, but only on muddy, rainy days. Not when the sun shines."

Darinka worried about these threats. Her arms grew thinner and her face was pale and tear-stained. She refused to eat, drawing the curtains every day and sitting in the middle room of the flat, dreading the sound of footsteps in the hallway. She reminded him of the British missionary who had been martyred right in their own village. "What if they kill us, Janez? What will become of the children?"

"Ah, Darinka, to die would be a simple thing." He opened the curtains and the window. "But to die daily—this is another thing."

Chapter Sixty

The letter came from the United States and Jozeca held it in her hands examining the postmark and the writing. It was addressed to Rev. Josip Kovac and Rev. Janez Kovac.

"*Iz Amerika!*" she shouted to Josip over the telephone.

"Open it, Mama, and read it to me," he called back to her.

"I cannot read it, Josip. It is written in English. It looks very nice, though."

"Ah, oh. *Mamica*, I will come up tomorrow. Give Julijanna and Filip my love. *Addio.*"

"*Addio!*"

They sat around the living room staring at the letter. The light from the lamp was bright. Janez fingered the stem of his glasses and exclaimed for the fourth time, "Ah! So!"

Jozeca, round as a cantelope, her gray hair pulled back from her face with her cheeks flushed, sighed again. "Can it be? My sons invited to preach in America? Imagine!"

"Will we really go there?"

The smell of plum brandy and cigarette smoke permeated the train car. Jozeca sat between her sons on the seat listening to the group of men in the front of the car talking.

A Croatian man with a thick mustache and black flashing eyes waved a plastic cup filled with brandy in the air and called loudly to the men with him, "Our history is a struggle for liberty and unity!"

"And the Serbs!" A thick-necked Slovene interrupted, "what about the Serbs? Think of the Austrians, the Turks, the Maygars—all blistering the soil of Serbia!"

"Ah, from the mouth of a Slovene—you! You, who have been under German influence for a thousand years."

"Until 1918. In 1918 we were freed."

The Croat growled, weaved and leaned with the jostling of the train. "Ah, you Slovenes. What have you given the world that is of value?"

A Slovene suddenly reared his head indignantly, dramatically. "Slovenia! My magnificence! Producer of the greatest poets and artists in the world!"

"Namely Preseren—who else I ask you? Died a miserable alchoholic."

"We are all poets. Show me a Slovene and I will show you a poet."

"And Croatia has Ivan Mestrovic! Have you a sculptor better than Mestrovic?"

Jozeca looked at her sons. "We are such ordinary, simple people. What will you say to the Americans?"

The men's discussion at the front of the car rolled and tumbled as though it were orchestrated. Their voices crescendoed. Sometimes they were passionate and pleading, then harsh, brittle, or soft, velvety. That was the beauty of the language of the Balkans. Musical, rolling, each word with a different musical intonation. She felt herself being serenaded in the sound of their voice. Josip sat quietly beside her, his face turned toward the window.

Outside the fields, green and silver in a white spray of rain, lay rumpled and wrinkled like the sleeve of a shirt. Swarms of clouds hid the peaks of the mountains, and a rolling white fog moved across the woods and fields.

A narrow dirt road ran along the tracks and a woman carrying a basket on her head walked with smooth strides taking no notice of the train. Men with heavy jackets and pants stuffed into their boots pedaled bicycles with cigarettes dripping from their mouths.

The men at the front of the car were getting louder and more drunk. Now they burst into song, laughing and trying to stand up in the aisles.

"Ha! Ha! That crazy Serb will be dancing the *kolo* in the aisle of the train if he drinks any more of that poisonous brandy!"

They entered the dusty depot at Zidani Most and opened the wooden door to the *restavracija*. The room was dark, lit only by dim light bulbs hanging from the high ceiling from wires. The floor was made of concrete, cold and hard as the faces of the people sitting at the tables. It was a dark, damp barn of a room filled with smoke which nipped their eyes and nostrils. But on each table was a white table cloth with little vases of fresh flowers on top.

Josip ordered three cups of tea and some *klobasa* sausage with hard crusty bread. Behind them on the wall hung greasy portraits of President Tito taken when he was younger and leaner. Jozeca folded her hands on her lap and smiled at her sons, showing two rows of tiny teeth, some of which were now gold-capped.

"I shall pray every hour for you, my sons, until your return. The Americans are very wise, you know. I shall pray that you do not make fools of yourselves."

"I am worried, Mama. What can we possibly bring to them? We are a simple people."

"Janez, Josip—listen to me. Tell them in America and all over the world that we love God. Tell them about us in the Balkans. Tell them about our great God who loves all men. Tell them about Him, my sons. He will help you."

She looked at the faces of her sons, strong, unafraid to suffer, unafraid to sacrifice, with hearts as gentle as lambs, yet brave as bulls. "Because of these sons of mine whom the Lord gave to Jakob Kovac and me," she thought, "and to thousands of believers all over the world from America to Australia, there is hope. Hope for Jugoslavia, hope for the whole world."

And she believed that.